PREACHING
THE
NEW COMMON
LECTIONARY

PREACHING
THE
NEW COMMON
LECTIONARY

Year C

After Pentecost

Commentary by:

Fred B. Craddock
John H. Hayes
Carl R. Holladay
Gene M. Tucker

ABINGDON PRESS
Nashville

Preaching the New Common Lectionary

Year C   After Pentecost

Copyright © 1986 by Abingdon Press

This book is printed on acid-free paper.

Library of Congress Cataloging in Publication Data
Main entry under title:
  Preaching the new common lectionary. Year C,
After Pentecost
  Includes index.
  1. Bible—Homiletical use. 2. Bible—Liturgical
lessons, English. I. Craddock, Fred B.
  BS511.2.P73   1986   251   85-28792
          (pbk.: alk. paper)
        ISBN 0-687-33850-6

Scripture quotations unless otherwise noted are from the Revised
Standard Version of the Bible, copyrighted 1946, 1952, 1971, © 1973, by the
Division of Christian Education of the National Council of the Churches of
Christ in the U.S.A., and used by permission.

Those noted NJPSV are from *The Writings,* a new translation of the Holy
Scriptures according to the Masoretic text, Third Section. Copyright ©
1982 by the Jewish Publication Society of America.

Quotations noted NEB are from The New English Bible. © the Delegates of
the Oxford University Press and the Syndics of the Cambridge University
Press 1961, 1970. Reprinted by permission.

Those noted JB are from The Jerusalem Bible, copyright © 1966 by Darton,
Longman & Todd, Ltd. and Doubleday & Company, Inc. Used by
permission of the publisher.

Those marked NIV are from the Holy Bible, New International Version.
Copyright © 1973, 1978, International Bible Society. Used by permission of
Zondervan Bible Publishers.

MANUFACTURED BY THE PARTHENON PRESS AT
NASHVILLE, TENNESSEE, UNITED STATES OF AMERICA

Contents

*Propers 1, 2, and 3 are part of Epiphany

Christ the King

Special Days

Introduction

It might be helpful to the reader if we make a few remarks about our understanding of our task and what we have sought to accomplish in this volume. The following comments will touch on four topics.

The Scripture in Preaching

There is no substitute for direct exposure to the biblical text, both for the preacher in preparation and for the listener in worship. The Scriptures are therefore not only studied privately but read aloud as an act of worship in and of itself and not solely as prelude to a sermon. The sermon is an interpretation of Scripture in the sense that the preacher seeks to bring the text forward into the present in order to effect a new hearing of the Word. In this sense the text has its future and its fulfillment in preaching. In fact, the Bible itself is the record of the continual rehearing and reinterpreting of its own traditions in new settings and for new generations of believers. New settings and new circumstances are properly as well as inescapably integral to a hearing of God's Word in and through the text. Whatever else may be said to characterize God's Word, it is always appropriate to the hearers. But the desire to be immediately relevant should not abbreviate study of the text or divorce the sermon from the biblical tradition. Such sermons are orphaned, released without memory into the world. It is the task of the preacher and teacher to see that the principle of fidelity to Scripture is

sermon
bring text forward.
new hearing.
Bible

not abandoned in the life and worship of the church. The endeavor to understand a text in its historical, literary, and theological contexts does create, to be sure, a sense of distance between the Bible and the congregation. The preacher may grow impatient during this period of feeling a long way from a sermon. But this time of study can be most fruitful. By holding text and parishioners apart for a while, the preacher can hear each more clearly and exegete each more honestly. Then, when the two intersect in the sermon, neither the text nor the congregation is consumed by the other. Because the Bible is an ancient book, it invites the preacher back into its world in order to understand; because the Bible is the church's Scripture, it moves forward into our world and addresses us here and now.

The Lectionary and Preaching

Ever-increasing numbers of preachers are using a lectionary as a guide for preaching and worship. The intent of lectionaries is to provide for the church over a given period of time (usually three years) large units of Scripture arranged according to the seasons of the Christian year and selected because they carry the central message of the Bible. Lectionaries are not designed to limit one's message or restrict the freedom of the pulpit. On the contrary, churches that use a lectionary usually hear more Scripture in worship than those that do not. And ministers who preach from the lectionary find themselves stretched into areas of the canon into which they would not have gone had they kept to the path of personal preference. Other values of the lectionary are well known: the readings provide a common ground for discussions in ministerial peer groups; family worship can more easily join public worship through shared readings; ministers and worship committees can work with common biblical texts to prepare services that have movement and integrity; and the lectionary encourages more disciplined study and advance preparation. All these and other values are increased if the different churches share a common lectionary. A common lectionary could conceivably generate a community-wide Christian conversation.

This Book and Preaching

This volume is not designed as a substitute for work with the biblical text; on the contrary, its intent is to encourage such work. Neither is it our desire to relieve the preacher of regular visits to concordances, lexicons, and commentaries, rather it is our hope that the comments on the texts here will be sufficiently germinal to give direction and purpose to those visits to major reference works. Our commentaries are efforts to be faithful to the text and to begin moving the text toward the pulpit. There are no sermons as such here, nor could there be. No one can preach long distance. Only the one who preaches can do an exegesis of the listeners and mix into sermon preparation enough local soil so as to effect an indigenous hearing of the Word. But we hope we have contributed to that end. The reader will also notice that, while each of us has been aware of the other readings for each service, there has been no attempt to offer a collaborated commentary on all texts or a homogenized interpretation as though there were not four texts but one. We have tried to respect the integrity of each biblical passage and remain within the limits of our own areas of knowledge. It is assumed that the season of the year, the needs of the listeners, the preacher's own abilities, as well as the overall unity of the message of the Scriptures will prompt the preacher to find among the four readings the word for the day. Sometimes the four texts will join arm in arm, sometimes they will debate with one another, sometimes one will lead while the others follow, albeit at times reluctantly. Such is the wealth of the biblical witness.

A final word about our comments. The lections from the Psalter have been treated in the same manner as the other readings even though some Protestant churches often omit the reading of the psalm or replace it with a hymn. We have chosen to regard the psalm as an equal among the texts, primarily for three reasons: First, there is growing interest in the use of Psalms in public worship and comments on them may help make that use more informed. Second, the Psalms were a major source for worship and preaching in the early church and continue to inspire and inform Christian witness today. And third, comments on the Psalms may make this volume helpful to Roman Catholic preachers who have maintained the long tradition of using the Psalms in Christian services.

This Season and Preaching

Pentecost completed the liturgical year which began with Advent, the coming of the Christ into the world, and concludes with Pentecost, the coming of the Holy Spirit to the church.

The Season After Pentecost begins with Trinity Sunday, important for two reasons. First, it reminds the church to set the emphasis on the Holy Spirit at Pentecost within the inclusive doctrine of the Trinity. Second, the proclamation of the Trinity announces the tradition of faith within which the texts of this season will be explicated and heard. This season concludes with the celebration of Christ the King on the Sunday preceding the beginning of Advent.

In some traditions these Sundays between Pentecost and Advent are called "Ordinary Time." During this period there is no concerted movement toward a day of high significance or the clustering of texts with a governing focus as is the case in the seasons from Advent to Pentecost. What this means for the preacher is the opportunity to work with texts that do not possess the thematic unity that characterizes the lections for the remainder of the year. Although the readings for each Sunday are not unhappily joined, an effort has been made to provide continuity of readings from books of both Old and New Testaments. The benefits of this opportunity to develop sustained themes and to deepen one's understanding and appreciation of texts that continue for several weeks are not inconsiderable, both for the preacher and the hearer.

> *Fred B. Craddock* (Gospels)
> *John H. Hayes* (Psalms)
> *Carl R. Holladay* (Epistles and Acts)
> *Gene M. Tucker* (Old Testament)

Trinity Sunday

Proverbs 8:22-31; Psalm 8; Romans 5:1-5; John 16:12-15

In the early church, this Sunday was observed as the Octave of Whitsun, that is, as the eighth day of Pentecost. The day assumed its character as a celebration in honor of the Trinity in the later Middle Ages. As such, it concludes the commemorations of the life of Christ in the liturgy and the descent of the Spirit and thus brings together the three persons of the Godhead.

All four of today's texts are classical biblical pericopes utilized in expounding trinitarian doctrine. In the passage from Proverbs, playful wisdom delights in the self-proclamation of herself as the first product of God's actions, as one who reveled in the presence of the Maker at creation. The psalm praises God who created the world for the sake of humanity and assigned humans a place of dominance in that creation. The Gospel reading announces the coming of the Spirit while the Epistle speaks in trinitarian terms of God—Jesus Christ—Holy Spirit.

Proverbs 8:22-31

Trinity Sunday is a time for theological reflection, and that is what the Old Testament reading presents for us. It contains serious and sophisticated reflection on issues closely related to the questions that finally led to the doctrine of the Trinity. The text does not contain doctrine in anything like the formal sense, but its affirmations respond to the questions of the relationship of a transcendent God to the world and the means of divine revelation.

13

The passage is part of a larger literary context, the collection of poems in Proverbs 1–9. These chapters contain some twelve units, most of them wisdom instructions generally regarded as examples of late Israelite wisdom thought. They are quite different from the remainder of the book of Proverbs, which is mainly a series of short proverbial sayings, admonitions, and exhortations. Most of the poems in Proverbs 1–9 begin with the address, "My son," reflecting the situation of a teacher addressing students.

The distinct poem (8:1-31) of which our lectionary text is a part is a wisdom speech. Following a brief introduction characterizing her appearance in public places (verses 1-3), wisdom herself speaks, mainly to give the reasons why people should listen to her voice and attend to her ways. Wisdom recommends herself because her words are true and valuable (verses 6-11), she has qualities to be desired (verses 12-16), and she can be trusted to reward those who follow her (verses 17-21). In this context, verses 22-31 give the final reason for attending to wisdom: she was the first of God's creations.

Throughout the passage wisdom is personified as an attractive woman. In the light of the parallels with the other instructions in Proverbs 1–9, it appears that Lady Wisdom assumes the role of the teacher. She stands in sharp contrast to the other women of these chapters, variously described as the "loose woman" (5:3, 20), the "evil woman , . . . the adventuress" (6:24), the woman "dressed as a harlot" (7:10), or "a foolish woman" (9:13). The last of these is the personification of folly, the antithesis of Lady Wisdom. On the surface, most of the others seem to involve practical moral advice to young men, to avoid certain kinds of women. In the context, however, they reflect another dimension as well, suggesting that same personification of folly one sees in 9:13.

Unifying our passage is wisdom's assertion that she was the first of God's creations and present with God during the creation and ordering of the cosmos. This theme is developed in three distinct movements. First (verses 22-23), wisdom proclaims that she was the first of all creation. Second (verses 24-29), wisdom describes the stages of God's creative

14

activity. Each sentence begins with a temporal clause ("when . . . ;" "before . . . ;"), and most include the reaffirmation that wisdom was present when God was creating all things. Third (verses 30-31), wisdom reports the manner of her presence with God at the beginning.

In pointing out that wisdom was created first and stressing the creative power of God, the poem dwells at length, and with genuine joy, on the wonders of the created world. These include the earth itself (verse 23), the waters of both oceans and springs (verse 24), mountains and hills (verse 25), land (verse 26), the heavens and their circular limits (verse 27), the heavenly vault and the primeval waters (28), and the boundaries for the waters and the earth's foundations (verse 29). Though the cosmos thus described includes facets visible to the human eye, the description also includes those features (such as the heavenly vault, primeval waters, foundations of the earth) only assumed to exist in the ancient Near Eastern world view. In a skillful and subtle way the poet both marvels at the wonders of the world and reminds the hearers that it is, after all, created by God, and thus has its limits.

Remarkably, human beings are not mentioned until the very end (verse 31), probably for emphasis. As wisdom is the first of God's creations, human beings are the last.

In the concluding verses (30-31), wisdom describes her presence with God during creation. There is no explicit sense that God created the world through or by means of wisdom, as one sees in Proverbs 3:19-20. Verse 19 states:

"The Lord by wisdom founded the earth;
    by understanding he established the heavens."

Instead, these lines stress wisdom's playful presence: "playing in his presence continually" (verse 30, NEB), "playing on the earth" and "delighting in mankind" (verse 31 NEB). We are reminded that Israelite wisdom literature has its playful side, using even riddles to discover and communicate truth. Moreover, if wisdom is in any sense a characteristic of God, according to our poet, it must be also God's playful and joyful side.

Although such reflections as this one stand behind the Prologue to John, wisdom here, while personified, is not in any sense an incarnation or extension of God's person. Other wisdom literature goes further. Wisdom of Solomon 7:24-25 sees wisdom as a virtual hypostasis of God ("a pure emanation of the glory of the Almighty").

Nevertheless, this passage—like the doctrine of the Trinity—is a way of coming to terms with the deep awareness of God as both almighty and transcendent on the one hand, and present in and with creation on the other. If God is distinct from the world—it is an act of divine creation—then how is God active and how is God known? According to the historical and prophetic literature of the Old Testament, this God is known through acts of revelation and intervention in history. The wisdom teachers take another direction that leads to poems such as the one before us. God's will and ways are known in the created order and through wisdom. Wisdom—both as that one who was created first and as a characteristic of human thought and behavior—is the link between God and all who inhabit the earth.

Psalm 8

This hymn was composed in praise of God the creator whose name and handiwork pervade all the earth. This is made evident in the prologue and epilogue verses (1a, 9). The second person speech—direct address to God—which appears throughout the psalm is unusual in hymns which are normally human speech to a human audience intent on instilling and enriching faith. Psalm 104 supplies another example of such a second-person hymn. The hymn could have been spoken in worship by the Judean king who, it appears, may have referred to himself circumlocutionarily as "son of man" (verse 4b; see also Pss. 80:17; 144:3).

Two aspects of human existence are highlighted in this psalm. There is, first of all, the human sense of insignificance when confronted with the awesome reality of the created order. Whoever penned verses 3-4 must have viewed the heavens on some clear, crystal Palestinian night and wondered, like many of us who have beheld the earth as televised from some silent sailing spaceship, where humans—invisible from such heights—fit into the scheme of things. This is the feeling in the psalm that viewed matters from the human side looking upward.

A second set of anthropological affirmations center on humankind's high status in the created order—"a little less than God" with "dominion over." Humans are thus the intermediates between the heavenly and the non-human world. The positions in this psalm should be compared with Genesis 1, the priestly account of creation. In the latter, man is made, unlike any other part of the earthly order, in the image of God (1:26) and is granted dominion over the other orders of creation—fish, fowl, and land animals (1:28). As a little lower than God, humans are thus affirmed as related and akin to the divine order. The other side of this affirmation is seen in the role of humans as supreme in the world of creation. Domesticated animals, wild beasts of the field, fowl of the air, and fish in the sea are all seen as subservient and subordinate to the human world. Such a claim and understanding allowed the Israelites, with a sad conscience nonetheless, to slaughter and consume animal and fish flesh only returning the blood (symbolizing life) in sacrifice or burial to God as an apology for killing (see Lev. 17:1-13).

In this psalm there is only a tinge of that anthropological ambivalence which has occupied the thought of philosophers, that concern with humanity's double quality of greatness and depravity. (For the Yahwist, the first human was viewed as a divinely animated clod—Genesis 3—which preserves the twofold quality of human existence.) There is little of that ambivalence one sees, for example, in the description of mankind by the French philosopher-mathematician Blaise Pascal (1623-62): "What a chimera then is man! What a novelty! What a monster, what a chaos, what a contradiction, what a prodigy! Judge of all things, feeble earthworm, depository of truth, a sink of uncertainty and error, the glory and the shame of the universe."

The elevated, exalted state of man in this psalm and its employment of the phrase "son of man" made it possible for the early church to use this text in expounding an undertaking of Jesus, who as "Son of man" reigns over God's order (see Matt. 21:16; I Cor. 15:27; Heb. 2:6-9).

Romans 5:1-5

This is one of those passages that is Trinitarian in the sense that God, Christ, and the Holy Spirit are mentioned, but not in the sense that it presents a fully developed picture of the Triune God (cf. II Cor. 13:13; also Matt. 28:19). Even so, read within the context of Trinity Sunday the passage will echo Trinitarian themes as it speaks (1) of the God who bestows peace on those who are justified by faith (verse 1), who lavishes us with love (verse 5), and invites us to share in the eschatological glory (verse 2); (2) of the Lord Jesus Christ as the one through whom God's *shalom* becomes a reality and continues to remain a reality because of his mediating role in granting us access to the divine grace (verses 1-2); and (3) of the Holy Spirit given to us as the means of experiencing the love of God (verse 5).

We should notice that the central focus of the passage is what results for those who are justified by faith (cf. 4:5; Gal. 3:8, 24; Eph. 2:8-9; Phil. 3:9). That we are "rightwised" before God by faith, and not by religious works, provides the premise of the passage (cf. Gal. 2:16; 3:2; Rom. 3:28) and is the point toward which the argument of the letter has moved through chapters 1-4. Given this, certain things follow, the first of which is peace, or a state of reconciliation with God (cf. Isa. 32:17; John 16:33; I John 3:21). This emphatic affirmation is based on the reading "we have peace" as opposed to the alternative reading "let us have peace." The former is indicative and implies a present possession while the latter is a hortatory subjunctive and suggests the goal toward which justification directs us.

It is Christ through whom peace is accomplished (Eph. 2:14; Col. 1:22). But he does not merely initiate peace, he sustains it through his role as mediator who grants us access to God's grace (cf. Eph. 2:18; 3:12; I Pet. 3:18; Matt. 11:27; John 14:6). Here, as elsewhere, divine grace is presented as that realm in which we position ourselves and find our place to stand (cf. I Pet. 5:12).

From this point of existential definition, we already begin to experience eschatological joy—that is, rejoicing anchored in our future hope of participating in God's glory (cf. 8:18, 30; Col. 1:27; Tit. 2:13). But not only is the rejoicing future-oriented, it is also directed to the present where there occurs the rhythm of suffering giving way to patience, patience giving way to perseverance, and perseverance giving way to hope (cf. James 1:2-4; I Pet. 1:6-7; Heb. 6:18-19).

Nor is this a futile quest in which we chase a fragile hope. It was already an axiom of Old Testament thought that Yahweh could be trusted, and that those who place their trust in Yahweh would not be disappointed (Ps. 22:5; 25:20). Further assurance of this is provided because the Holy Spirit, the earmark of the eschatological age, has already been unleashed, ushered into our lives as a gift providing tangible evidence of God's love (cf. Acts 2:18, 33; 5:32; 10:45; Tit. 3:5; I John 4:13).

In reflecting homiletically on this epistolary reading for Trinity Sunday, we note the way in which the work of God brackets salvation history: it is the love of God that stands at the beginning and the glory of God toward which all things move, with the reconciling peace of God serving as the ongoing relationship in which we are able to deal with God. The role of Christ throughout the passage is one of active agent, the one through whom we are able to experience God's salvation. This reminds us of the early Christian confession of the "one Lord, Jesus Christ, through whom are all things and through whom we exist" (I Cor. 8:6). Finally, the Holy Spirit is envisioned here as the one through whom and in whom we actually experience the love of God. It is the Spirit who gives concrete form to divine love and does so within us where God's self converges with our own selves.

John 16:12-15

We linger one more Sunday in the Gospel of John which nourished and informed Pentecost as well as the Sundays immediately preceding that festival. We do so because one further word needs to be said about the Holy Spirit.

John 16:12-15 is the fifth and final Holy Spirit saying in

Jesus' farewell discourses to his disciples (14:1–16:33). A careful reading of these discourses reveals that they are both the parting words of Jesus to his followers and the present word of the risen Christ to his church in the world. Therefore the promises, warnings, and instructions are in the future tense because they are spoken prior to Jesus' death and resurrection, but for the readers of John's Gospel (and for us), they are in the present tense because the message of the now risen and exalted Lord is addressed to them. The reader of this Gospel is not to make distinctions between pre- and post-resurrection words of Jesus.

Central among the promises of Jesus to his followers is the Holy Spirit, the Spirit of God, the Spirit of truth, the Comforter or Counselor. Before attending to the text for today, the preacher would be helped by a review of the first four Holy Spirit sayings (14:16-17; 14:25-26; 15:26; 16:7-11). Briefly stated those passages make the following promises and affirmations: Jesus will ask God to send the Spirit of truth as another Counselor to be with the disciples forever; the Holy Spirit will be sent from God in Jesus' name to teach and to remind the disciples of Jesus' words; the Spirit, sent by Jesus but proceeding from God, will bear witness to Jesus; and finally, upon his departure Jesus will send the Counselor to convict the world of sin, righteousness, and judgment.

The fifth saying, John 16:12-15, continues in the same vein, making three important statements about the Holy Spirit, the third bearing directly on the meaning of Trinity Sunday. First, the words of the historical Jesus did not touch every human condition or question that might arise. In fact, had Jesus so spoken, his followers would not have been able to comprehend his message (verse 12). For example, Jesus left no instruction covering the case of a Christian convert whose spouse remained an unbeliever. Paul faced such a problem at Corinth and had to interpret the will of God (I Cor. 7:12-16). He concluded his comments on marriage, divorce, and remarriage with the words, "And I think that I have the Spirit of God" (I Cor. 7:40). This leads to the second statement in our text concerning the Holy Spirit: the Spirit "will guide you into all the truth" and "will declare to you the things that are to come" (verse 13). This is in some ways a frightening promise, for it can be quoted to bless every new notion and footnote with authority all manner of behavior as well as prophesies as to the fate of the world, the time of the eschaton, and the certain will of God in every crisis. But that danger notwithstanding, that the Spirit continues to guide and enlighten the church is a conviction not to abandon. To do so would be to deny that the present is as surely God's time as was the first or any other century. The preacher is a proclaimer of God's word to each gathered community, not a curator of ancient records of once glorious days. Were this not so, the Gospel of John itself, an interpretation of the meaning of Jesus Christ, could make no claim on us as Word of God because it could not claim the guidance and enlightenment of the Holy Spirit.

The third and final statement of our text brings us directly to the significance of Trinity Sunday. The Holy Spirit will not speak or act independently, but rather will glorify Christ and will reveal only that which comes from Christ and from God (verses 14-15). Here is offered a canon by which to test if the spirit by which any person or group acts and speaks is really the Holy Spirit: Are the actions and words in accordance with what we know of God and of Jesus Christ? To be sure, this is no simple test to apply but it does provide the church a measure of defense against spirits not of God and a measure of confidence in affirming the leading of the Holy Spirit in new and changing circumstances. The Holy Spirit is the hallmark of Christianity, but the church affirms the Holy Spirit as from God and from Christ and as witness to that which God has revealed in Jesus of Nazareth. For example, notice how Paul introduced the Trinity to address excesses and confusion related to the Holy Spirit at Corinth (I Cor. 12:4-6).

A doctrine of the Trinity has seemed to many to be remote, ancient, and irrelevant, but such is far from the truth. The affirmation of God, Christ, and Holy Spirit has been and is essential for the health of the Christian faith.

Proper 4

Sunday Between May 29 and June 4 Inclusive
(If after Trinity Sunday)

I Kings 8:22-23, 41-43; Psalm 100; Galatians 1:1-10; Luke 7:1-10

Beginning with today's lectionary readings, the Old Testament begins a season focusing on selections from the books of Kings. The first of these is a few verses from Solomon's prayer at the dedication of the temple in Jerusalem. For the following nine Sundays, the Elijah-Elisha narratives make up the Old Testament readings. Following Trinity Sunday, the Gospel for the remainder of the year is Luke (except for Christ the King Sunday) while the Epistle readings, for this and the next five Sundays, are drawn from Galatians.

The texts from Solomon's prayer emphasize the incomparability of Israel's God, and they petition God to hear the prayer of the foreigner who offers up requests in the temple. Psalm 100 like Solomon's prayer highlights the theme of universalism, calling on all to bless God. The Epistle reading concerns Paul's affirmation of the distinctiveness of the gospel which he preached, a gospel singular in its meaning yet universal in its appeal. The Gospel reading contributes its perspectives to the theme of universalism in the report of the healing of the centurion's slave and in the celebration of the foreigner's faith.

I Kings 8:22-23, 41-43

With the reading for today we begin a series of ten semicontinuous readings from the books of Kings. The text for today, selections from the account of Solomon's dedication of the temple, stands out from the rest, all of which concern the prophets Elijah and Elisha. Those texts are followed by a series of fifteen readings from the prophets Jeremiah, Ezekiel, and the Minor Prophets, leading up to the festival of Christ the King, which concludes the season. The assigned text for that day concerns the beginning of David's reign. Thus the Old Testament lections for the season are readings concerning or from the prophets, framed by accounts of events concerning kings and temple.

First Kings 8, as the account of Solomon's dedication of the temple in Jerusalem, lies near the heart of what later generations considered most important about Solomon. Foremost among his many building projects was the magnificent temple. The verses assigned for reading on this day come from the king's dedicatory prayer. The prayer had been preceded by the account of the assembly and the installation of the ark of the covenant in the new building (verses 1-13), and Solomon's address to the assembly (verses 14-21). After the prayer (verses 22-53), the king addresses the people again with a sermon (verses 54-61), and then concludes the ceremony with sacrifices and a feast (verses 62-66).

Virtually all the chapter bears the marks of the theology and style of the book of Deuteronomy, and thus stems from the Deuteronomistic historian or historians who were responsible for collecting and editing the account of Israel's history from the time of Moses to the Babylonian Exile (Deuteronomy through Second Kings). While there are numerous older written and oral sources in the work, and there likely was a preexilic edition of it, the work as a whole was completed shortly after the last event it reports (II Kings 25:27-30), during the Babylonian Exile (ca. 560 B.C.). Consequently, the report of the dedication of the temple was composed for a people who had lost their land and holy city, and who knew that the temple lay in ruins.

Solomon's prayer of dedication is a series of four prayers of petition. The first (verses 23-26) is a prayer that God confirm the promise to David that one of his sons would always sit on the throne in Jerusalem. The second (verses 27-30) and fourth (verses 52-53) are general requests that God hear and respond, while the third (verses 31-51) contains a series of petitions concerning seven possible future situations.

Our assigned verses contain the beginning and the initial lines of the first prayer in the narrative (verses 22-23), and the fifth of the petitions concerning future circumstances (verses 41-43), the one that expects "foreigners" to come to the temple.

The first verse (22) of the reading, as well as its larger context, invites reflection on prayer, particularly public prayer. Some of the liturgical features are obvious here, and others are not. It is assumed that Israel's kings performed important priestly functions as a special link between Yahweh and the people. As the temple is dedicated, Solomon is said to be before the altar and in the presence of the assembled people, but the precise location is difficult to identify. (The parallel account in II Chron. 6:13 has him in the courtyard of the temple on an elevated platform.) The posture of prayer is standing with hands outstretched "toward heaven" (cf. Exod. 9:29; Isa. 1:15). In view of the fact that gods, like kings, in the ancient Near East generally are pictured as sitting on thrones, the posture of supplication is to stand with outstretched arms. Note, however, that when the prayers are concluded, Solomon is said to have been kneeling before the altar (8:54).

The initial lines of the prayer (verse 23) invite reflection on several matters central to the biblical faith. First, Yahweh, God of Israel, is addressed as incomparable ("no God like thee"). This is not an assertion of monotheism, although it comes close. Rather, it parallels the view of the first commandment: "You shall have no other gods before me" (Exod. 20:3). Devotion to their God, rather than the abstract question of the number of gods, is the central concern for ancient Israel. Second, Israel's God is trustworthy and loyal, "keeping covenant" and "showing steadfast love" to those who are faithful. These two expressions are virtually synonymous, emphasizing the stability of God's relationship with the covenant people.

The petition in verses 41-43 indicates that ancient Israel's concerns reached beyond boundaries of nation and culture. It is an intercessory prayer on behalf of any "foreigner" who comes to pray in the temple. If Yahweh is incomparable, other peoples will hear and come to worship him. Solomon

24

asks that their prayers be heard. While stressing the importance of the temple, the petition acknowledges that God's true dwelling place is "in heaven" (verse 43). The goal is that the Lord's "name"—who he is and what he has done—be known to all peoples (verse 43). The Lord does not actually dwell in the temple, but it is called by his name and is the place where he chooses to "put his name" (Deut. 12:5).

Psalm 100

This psalm is one of only a few in which its use is noted in the superscription (see Pss. 30; 102). The occasion for its usage is said to be the presentation of a "thank offering," a sacrifice offered when an individual or the community wished to express its appreciation to the divine (see Lev. 7:11-18). Such sacrifices were consumed—that is, the entire slaughtered animal except for gift portions paid to the priests was cooked and eaten—by the worshipers in a great "religious barbecue" in the temple courtyard. According to the law in Leviticus, the thanksgiving sacrifice had to be consumed completely on the day it was presented (7:15). This meant that extravagance, even gluttony, for the day was a requirement. Thanksgiving was a joyful celebration.

Psalm 100 is a communal psalm. All the imperative verbs are in the plural in the Hebrew, a fact that is not apparent in English translation. The psalm does not contain the full features of a thanksgiving psalm; in fact, it is an extended summons or call to praise and to thank God. Those called upon to make a joyful noise to God were probably only the Israelites in the psalm's ancient usage. Note that the phrase translated "all the lands" in the RSV is actually "all the land" (although "all the earth" = everybody is possible; see RSV marginal notes).

The elements in thanksgiving are noted as "joyful noise," "gladness," "singing," "thanksgiving," "praise." When we think of thanksgiving only as verbal expressions or as cognitive communication, we restrict too greatly its range of meaning and its forms of expression.

Two motivations are given for the praise and thanksgiving. The first stresses God as creator and preserver of human life (verse 3). Thus thanksgiving flows from the dependent humans to the divine. Here thanksgiving is anchored in a theology of creation, although the creation spoken of may refer to the creation of Israel, its origination in the past (see Isa. 29:23; 41:1, 21). The second, although not as clearly drawn, offers as the reason, God's fidelity in history (verse 5). Here the idea is the continuing, recurring love and fidelity of God. Thanksgiving throughout the psalm is associated with public worship, in the temple "come into his presence," "enter his gates . . . and his courts."

Galatians 1:1-10

Since today's epistolary reading begins the semicontinuous reading of the Epistle to the Galatians over the next six weeks, a few introductory remarks are in order.

At least two sets of issues emerge in Galatians—one theological, the other personal. As we shall see, they are closely related. Theologically, the fundamental question is soteriological. On what basis are we accepted by God—by faithfully keeping the law or by faithfully hearing the gospel (3:2)? The practical issue had to do with the terms on which Gentiles could be admitted into the membership as people of God—generally, whether they had to live "under the law" (4:21; cf. 2:16-21; 3:2–4:7), and specifically, whether they had to undergo circumcision as the required initiation rite (5:2-12; 6:12-15; cf. 2:3, 12). For Paul, it was a question of freedom versus slavery (4:1-11; 21-32; 5:1).

The personal issue centered on the legitimacy of Paul's apostleship. He had been seriously challenged by those who opposed his theological position and argued for salvation *through* Torah as opposed to salvation *apart from* Torah. For them, Paul's gospel had unduly relaxed the requirements of God. They saw his message of freedom from the law as mere concession to human weakness. In their eyes, Paul's gospel offered an easy solution to the pain of circumcision by simply doing away with it. Construed one way, this was a "men-pleasing" approach calculated to gain popular appeal (1:10). The decisive question, then, was where and how Paul received the authority to preach a message so radically challenging to a well-established interpretation of Torah and an equally well-established way of being religious based on this interpretation.

The fusion of these two issues within the churches of Galatia prompted one of the most severely polemical letters from the hand of Paul. Not only his gospel but his personal integrity as well was on the line, and at every turn we can see the blood vessels in Paul's enraged eyes. The tone of the letter is bombastic (1:6; 3:1, 3), sarcastic (2:2, 6, 9; 5:12, 15), even desperate (4:11, 19-20). Even in those rare moments when he seeks to be pastoral and conciliatory, his encouragement gives way to stern words of warning and rebuke (5:13-15; 6:11-16). It is a letter written in white-hot heat.

In today's epistolary lection we have the opening words of this letter. The text easily divides in two sections, the opening greeting (verses 1-5) and a solemn warning (verses 6-10).

The Greeting (verses 1-5). Compared with other Pauline greetings, this one is colder and more abrupt. Nothing commendable is said of the Galatians. There is, however, the traditional prayer of grace and peace in their behalf (cf. Rom. 1:7; I Cor. 1:3; II Cor. 1:2; Eph. 1:2; Phil. 1:2; Col. 1:2).

Even in these opening words, the two central issues of the letter emerge: the source of Paul's apostolic authority (verse 1) and the work of Christ as the sole basis of our deliverance (verses 3-4). Paul insists that his apostleship is neither humanly initiated nor humanly validated—it is not "by human appointment or human commission" (verse 1, NEB). On this note, his defense begins (1:11). What he preached "came through a revelation of Jesus Christ" (1:12), and his prophetic call to preach resulted from the divine intervention of God who had raised Christ from the dead (verse 1).

The essence of his gospel is stated in the form of a kerygmatic summary (verse 4), which aligns him with well-established orthodox Christianity. It is a move reminiscent of Romans 1:1-6, where he commends himself to an unknown audience by introducing his theological position in thoroughly acceptable terms. Three important elements should be noted: (1) the vicarious death of Christ "who gave himself for our sins" (cf. 2:20; II Cor. 5:15; Eph. 5:2, 25; Tit. 2:14; I Tim. 2:6; also Matt. 20:28); (2) our deliverance "from

27

the present evil age," elsewhere seen to be under the dominion of satanic forces (II Cor. 4:4; Acts 26:18; also 4:8-9) and a competing threat against Christian existence (Rom. 12:2; Eph. 5:16; I John 5:19); and (3) God as the approving agent of the gospel (cf. Heb. 10:10) to whom all glory is due (Rom. 11:36; Eph. 3:21; Phil. 4:20; I Tim. 1:17; II Tim. 4:18; Heb. 13:21; I Pet. 4:11; II Pet. 3:18; Jude 25; Rev. 1:6; 4:11).

The Warning (verses 6-10). Instead of the usual prayer of thanksgiving offered on behalf of his readers (cf. Rom. 1:8-17; I Cor. 1:4-9; Phil. 1:3-11), the opening greeting is followed by this stern warning. By the absence of this opening pastoral prayer, we already sense the severely strained relations between Paul and the Galatians. To dispense with prayer marks the extreme urgency of the situation.

The source of Paul's astonishment is not only the Galatians' fickleness in changing loyalties but the speed with which they have deserted the ranks. He can only attribute it to a combination of their stupidity and the beguiling tactics of the competition (3:1-3). He stresses that it is a desertion of their divine vocation—a "deserting him who called you in the grace of Christ" (verse 6; cf. 5:8). It is God whom they have abandoned.

What had seduced them was "a different gospel" (verse 6), which suggests that the competing message was also Christian (cf. II Cor. 11:4; cf. I Tim. 6:3). On second thought, Paul is only willing to concede that there is one saving gospel which his opponents are distorting (cf. 5:10; II Cor. 11:4; Acts 15:1, 24). So convinced is he that his gospel stands in direct continuity with the apostolic tradition, he issues an anathema on his opponents (cf. I Cor. 16:22; also 12:3; Acts 23:14; Rom. 9:3). Indeed, it is a double anathema, repeated for emphasis (cf. 5:3, 21; II Cor. 13:2; I Thess. 3:4; 4:6). The Galatians are in sharp contrast to other Pauline churches who sought steadfastly to adhere to the apostolic tradition (I Cor. 11:2; 15:1-3; I Thess. 2:13; 4:1-2; II Thess. 2:15; Eph. 5:23).

This second section concludes on the note on which the opening greeting began—whether Paul's gospel was merely a ploy for human acceptance. Here, as elsewhere, he insists that his motivation is not to curry human favor (I Thess. 2:4). Had he wished to play the game of gaining acceptance from his peers and living according to human standards, he would never have forsaken the race for religious one-upmanship to become a slave of Christ (cf. Phil. 3:4-11). Paul stoutly denies having preached with one eye always on the opinion polls and one finger on the popular pulse.

Luke 7:1-10

During the liturgical year (Advent to Pentecost) biblical texts cluster thematically around the great festivals and observances, but following Pentecost the church enters what is sometimes called "ordinary time." This extended period offers the preacher opportunity to follow the texts in continuity, achieving an immersion in the biblical narrative over a period of time. Such series of sermons provide both preacher and listener a refreshing variation from messages governed by theme or season. There is nothing on the calendar to interrupt our attending at length to Luke.

Luke 7:1-10 opens a section in the Gospel (7:1–8:3) sometimes referred to as "the little insertion" which consists of six units inserted into the Markan framework. Today and the next two Sundays we will consider four of the six units. Some of this material is found also in Matthew. This is true of 7:1-10, the healing of the centurion's slave, which appears not only in Matthew (8:5-13) but also in John 4: 46-53. Both Matthew and Luke place the story after Jesus' great sermon (on the mount in Matthew, on the plain in Luke), and John joins the two of them in locating the incident in Capernaum. The Matthean and Lukan accounts contain more than sixty identical words, but even so, differences are noticeable and significant. The two most important are Luke's use of intermediaries in the centurion's appeal to Jesus, and Matthew's insertion of a saying of Jesus (verses 11-12) which Luke places elsewhere (13:28-30). The preacher may wish to read Matthew's and John's accounts in order to set in sharper focus the accents peculiar to Luke.

The centurion, a Roman military officer, represents the believing Gentile living within Jewish territory. Luke's practice of relating parallel events from the life of Jesus and the life of the church is continued here. Luke 7:1-10 has its parallel in Acts 10: "At Caesarea there was a man named Cornelius, a centurion of what was known as the Italian Cohort, a devout man who feared God with all his household, gave alms liberally to the people, and prayed constantly to God" (verses 1-2). The story in Luke 7:1-10, therefore, not only foreshadows the mission to the Gentiles which unfolds in Acts but also gives authoritative precedent for that mission from the ministry of Jesus himself.

Luke paints a most favorable portrait of the centurion. He is deeply concerned for an ailing slave (verse 2) and believes Jesus can heal him (verses 3, 7, 10). However, rather than approach Jesus directly, the centurion sends two sets of intermediaries. The first, Jewish elders, appeal to Jesus on the ground that the centurion is worthy, loving the Jews and building a synagogue for them (verses 3-5). The officer might have been a proselyte-at-the gate, a Gentile who believed in and worshiped Israel's God but who had not submitted to the rites whereby a Gentile became a Jew. The second set of intermediaries, friends of the centurion, brought word to Jesus that the man felt himself unworthy to receive Jesus in his home (verses 6-7a). Regarded worthy by others, regarded unworthy by himself; not a bad combination of credentials. Joined to this quality was the man's confidence that a word from Jesus had performative power. As a member of the Roman army, he knew the authority of a command given and received (verses 7b-8). Jesus praises his faith (verse 9) and the slave is healed (verse 10).

Matthew inserts into the story a saying of Jesus which prophesies a mass influx of Gentiles and the rejection of many in Israel (8:11-12). Luke does not. Even though Jesus says the centurion's faith is not matched in Israel (verse 9), still it is important that Jewish elders interceded for a Gentile. Although history forced Luke to recognize the shift from a Jewish to a Gentile majority in the church, his two volumes make it abundantly clear that he understands God to be a "both-and" and not an "either-or" God.

And so begins the story of faith among those afar off, not only geographically or racially but also generationally, those who have not seen Jesus but who have believed his word (Luke 7:7; John 20:29).

30

Proper 5

Sunday Between June 5 and 11 Inclusive
(If after Trinity Sunday)

I Kings 17:17-24; Psalm 113; Galatians 1:11-24; Luke 7:11-17

Verse 7 of the psalm for today provides one perspective for looking at the other readings: "He raises the poor from the dust, and lifts the needy from the ash heap." That is, God is the one whose intervention changes the fortune and reverses the fate of those in need, as in the Kings and Luke passages, or changes the status and orientation of life as with Paul in Galatians.

I Kings 17:17-24

Today we begin a series of five Old Testament lessons concerning the prophet Elijah. All the readings come from the collection of stories of the prophet, found in I Kings 17:1–19:21 and II Kings 1–2. The historical and geographical setting of the stories is the Northern Kingdom (Israel) during the reign of Ahab (874-852 B.C.) of the dynasty of Omri. While these stories, like all the other material in the books of Kings, have been edited and incorporated into the Deuteronomistic history which was completed during the Babylonian Exile (ca. 560 B.C.), they are part of an old collection of traditions that is much older and must have been handed down in prophetic circles. Prophetic traditions are particularly important to the Deuteronomistic editors because of their conviction that history was set on its course by the word of God through prophets. Moreover, Elijah would have been a particularly appealing figure because he, like the Book of Deuteronomy and the Deuteronomistic history, vigorously opposed the corruption of Israel through Canaanite religion.

The immediate context of our story is the account of

31

Elijah's abrupt appearance on the scene, announcing to King Ahab that there would be "neither dew nor rain these years, except by my word" (I Kings 17:1). The Elijah story as a whole will move toward conflict between prophet and king, but for the moment that is in the background while the incidents of I Kings 17 establish Elijah's credentials as a powerful "man of God." So the word of the Lord led the prophet to a brook east of the Jordan to be fed by ravens (I Kings 17:2-7), and then to the town of Zarephath (beyond the boundaries of Israel) to be fed by a poor widow. Elijah, as well as the widow and her son, are fed from the jar of meal and the cruse of oil that do not fail. Our lectionary text concerns the same characters and a similar theme. A miracle of feeding is followed by a miracle of healing.

As the account begins, it assumes the setting of the previous story, Elijah in the house of the widow of Zarephath. The initial verse moves directly to set out the crisis that provides the narrative tension—the woman's son became so ill that "there was no breath left in him" (verse 17). Although the text never states explicitly that the boy died, one should not use that fact to rationalize the miracle that follows. He was as good as dead. In the Old Testament view, "breath" is the essence of life (Gen. 2:7). (The word translated by RSV "soul" in verse 21, *nephesh*, is better read as either "breath" or "life.") If the narrator has intentionally omitted at the outset a direct reference to death, it is to increase the tension by leaving open the possibility that the boy may be revived. As the story moves on, it becomes clear that the child is dead, for Elijah accuses Yahweh of "slaying" him (verse 20).

The primary movement of the plot is in the direction of resolving the crisis of life and death. Elijah takes the widow's son to the "upper chamber" (verse 19) of the house and puts him in his own bed, prays to Yahweh, stretches himself three times on the boy, who then revives (verse 22). He then carries the child down to his mother.

Virtually every element in this plot is pregnant with meaning in the ancient context. Both the act of putting the child in the prophet's bed and Elijah's stretching himself on the boy strongly suggest sympathetic magic. Here, however, the actions put the widow's son within the realm of Yahweh's power through the prophet. Elijah's prayer (verse 20) is a complaint or lament, like many in the book of Psalms. Note the strong tone of accusation against the Lord. Ancient Israelites were not timid about expressing their anger to God. The full prayer on such an occasion would have included a direct petition for help.

The narrative is by no means simple. In addition to the main movement from death to life, there is the thread of the conflict between the widow and the prophet. She responds to the boy's illness by accusing Elijah (verse 18). Behind the accusation are the assumptions that the prophet has potentially dangerous powers and that the mother's sin can cause the death of the son. Once the child is revived, the widow affirms that the prophet's powers are for good, that it is God's power at work through him, and that he speaks Yahweh's "truth" (verse 24).

Both these themes, then, lead to the same conclusion. Elijah is a true prophet of the Lord, one in whom divine power is not only active but visible to others as such. The story, as a legend, is told not to glorify Elijah, but to show how the power of God and the word of God are active through him. As readers we are expected to see ourselves in the role of the widow, first angry, fearful, and doubtful, and then finally joyful as we affirm the power of God and the authority of God's servant.

Psalm 113

Three general considerations about this psalm should be noted initially. (1) It, along with Psalms 114–118, was employed in both temple services (at the time of the slaughter of the lambs) and home celebrations (as part of the meal ritual) during the Passover festival. Thus the imagery of the psalm came to be associated with the events of the Exodus which was commemorated in the Passover ritual. (2) The psalm has many similarities to the Song of Hannah in I Samuel 2:1-10 with which it may be profitably compared. The similarity of both of these to Mary's Magnificat in Luke 1:46-55 has led to their connection with Visitation celebrated on May 31. (3) The psalm shares in a common biblical motif, which might be called the "reversal of fate" or the "from rags to riches" sentiment.

The genre and structure of the psalm are clear. It is a hymn utilized to express and instill faith and particular beliefs by and in the congregation. The initial verses (1-4) are a summons to praise God, temporally in all times and forever (verse 2), and geographically in all places and everywhere (verse 3). Verses 5-9 provide the motivations, the reasons why God should be praised. These are presented in the form of a question (verses 5-6) and an answer (verses 7-9).

The psalm develops a dialectic in the divine and thus speaks about God in contrasting ways. In the question (verses 5-6), God is the highly exalted who, sitting above looks far down upon earth and even far down upon the heavens. If such a transcendent God must squint to see the earth, then surely the course of events and the status of individual persons must be beyond divine purview. The answer given to, "Who is like Yahweh?" comes, however, as unexpected in its content. Yahweh is the one who reverses the fate of the unfortunate, who transforms the status of those whom society judges as failures. Yahweh is not an unconcerned transcendent Deity but the caretaker of the dispossessed and the unpossessing.

Verses 7-8 concern the reversal of status of the male. The poor and the needy would have been those condemned by fate and fortune to marginal participation in the life of the community. These would have been those forced to live in poverty at the peripheries of society. Perhaps they had gotten in that condition by misfortune, poor harvests, illness, or debt. The dust and the ash heap refer to the city garbage dump where the dispossessed and unpossessing as well as the sick and leprous (see Lam. 4:5; Job 2:8; Lev. 13:45-46) made their domicile, grubbed for survival, begged for a handout, were left food and clothing by family and friends if they had any. Such places of last resort are similar to modern workhouses, old folks' homes, and public shelters as well as dump hovels where the world's refugees congregate. A male living under such conditions in ancient times would have been without social standing and without self-respect and

34

confidence. So much for verse 7, the *before* in the psalmic commercial.

The *after* we find in verse 8. The ones suffering deprivation and ostracism are made to sit with the nobles/princes, that is, with the rich and the powerful. To "sit with" implies acceptance by others and self-assurance by the new participant. (Remember the difference between standing integration and sitting integration in the South. "Sit-ins" marked a new state in the civil rights movement because to "sit with" is to share.) For the ideal of one who sits with the nobles, see Job 29:1-25.

The transformation of the unfortunate female is noted in verse 9. The mother was not really "at home" in the extended family of her husband, that is, she had no real security or sense of fully belonging and participating, until she and her children created their own space and place in the family. The wife, always brought into the husband's family, was an outsider to her in-laws until children transformed her into an insider and made her "at home." It must have been lonely in such a situation for the barren wife, so much so, that barrenness could be understood as a disgrace if not a curse from God (see Gen. 16:2; 20:18; I Sam. 1:5; Luke 1:25). Many of the matriarchs of Israel, however, were barren (Sarah, Rachel, Hannah) for a long time before they produced a child viewed as the result of divine intervention.

The minister, in preaching on this psalm, can see it as expressive of Israel's confidence that Yahweh was a God of transformation and liberation. The Hebrews did not believe in a world where the rich lived in a castle, the poor at the gate, each had a place, and a proper estate. And all lived uncomplaining forever. Israel recited its past that began when the impoverished slaves in Egypt cried out, complained to God about their condition, and got things changed.

Galatians 1:11-24

It is rare for Paul to engage in detailed discussion of his personal circumstances, as he does here. Given a choice, he would have preferred preaching Christ over explaining himself. But his back was against the wall. His personal integrity as an apostolic witness was being seriously challenged, and what emerges is an extended account of the circumstances that led to his becoming an apostle of Christ. Clearly, he rehearses these events as a personal apologia. He determines that the best defense is to let his own record speak for itself.

Today's epistolary lection comprises the first part of this rather extended personal defense (1:11–2:21). It serves as a rich resource for reconstructuring the historical Paul. Its special value lies in its autobiographical character. Unlike the lengthy and detailed account of Paul found in Acts 13–28, these are his own words told under oath (verse 20). With its careful attention to chronological sequence (note verse 18; 2:1), this passage is one of the most useful resources for constructing Pauline chronology. The sequence of events differs substantially from the account in Acts, and one should consult the commentaries for detailed discussion.

The overall effect of Paul's rehearsal of his former life is to underscore his independence of the Jerusalem tradition, or what might be called Judaean Christianity. His apostolic commission was not validated by consulting with others, much less the Jerusalem authorities (verses 16-17). Even when he did visit Jerusalem, it was a short, fifteen-day visit where he conferred only with Peter and James (verses 18-19). Consequently, he was virtually unknown to Palestinian churches, and then only by reputation (verses 22-23). Even when he went up to Jerusalem fourteen years later (2:1), he came away with his independent apostolic mission validated (2:7-10). In the crunch, he finally resisted the conservative position of Peter and Barnabas (2:11-14), both of whom caved in under pressure from the Christian rigorists, the "circum-cision party" (2:12).

Two themes emerge from this defense. First, the radical reversal in Paul's life occurred through divine intervention. Paul's gospel "came through a revelation of Jesus Christ" (verse 12), which is doubtless a reference to the encounter in which the risen Lord appeared to him (cf. I Cor. 9:1; 15:8; Acts 9:17; 22:14; 26:16). It was in this event, insists Paul, that God "was pleased to reveal his Son to me" (verse 16). Prior to this, he was bent on destroying the church (I Cor. 15:9; Phil 3:6; cf. Acts 8: 3; 9:1-2; 22:14; I Tim. 1:13), motivated by undiluted zeal for "the traditions of my fathers" (verse 14; cf. Mark 7:2; Acts 22:3; 26:4-5; also Rom. 10:2). Paul could hardly account for this radical reversal in his life on natural grounds. It was not the result of his own intuition, and could in no sense be explained as humanly predicated. His own experience attested that the source of his gospel lay with God who raised Christ from the dead (1:1).

Second, in his encounter with the risen Christ he experienced a prophetic call. In words reminiscent of Old Testament prophetic calls, Paul insists that he had been especially delegated by God even before he was born (verse 15; Isa. 49:1; Jer. 1:5; cf. Luke 1:15). His special prophetic vocation was to preach among the Gentiles (verse 16; cf. Acts 9:15; also I Tim. 2:7; Eph. 3:8), and this distinguished him from the other apostles (2:7-8). Because he interprets his commission in such thoroughly prophetic terms, some scholars prefer to speak of Paul's encounter with the risen Lord as a call rather than a conversion. Such a distinction cautions us against interpreting Paul's encounter with the risen Lord in terms of classical conversion experiences, such as those of Augustine or Luther, in which a troubled conscience gives way to a more blissful state of forgiveness. It suggests that we interpret Paul's experience as vocational rather than psychological reversal. But even if Paul does view his former life in terms of rectitude (verse 14), the element of regret, perhaps even remorse, is not lacking (cf. I Cor. 15:9).

Homiletically, this text has often served as the basis for exploring the profound change that occurred in Paul and the difference a genuine encounter with the grace of God can make. It is a theme that bears further treatment, but the preacher needs to ask to what degree the subject being described here was unique to Paul—not only his encounter with the risen Lord but his apostolic vocation. Perhaps another tack might be to explore what actually constitutes a "human gospel" (verse 11). What are the criteria for distinguishing between a gospel that truly comes from God and a gospel that mirrors mere human values?

Luke 7:11-17

The story of Jesus raising from the dead the only son of a widow of Nain (Luke 7:11-17), found only in Luke, is the second of six units in 7:1–8:3 which Luke inserts into the framework of Mark. Except for this and one other major insertion, Luke generally follows the Markan order.

In this account Luke tells his story in a manner clearly dependent on the Elijah and Elisha cycles, early established as two of Luke's favorite prophets (4:25-27). Both Elijah (I Kings 17:17-24) and Elisha (II Kings 4:18-37) restore life to young men. In the case of Elijah, the mother was a widow, the prophet met her at a city gate (Luke 7:12), and after the restoration "he gave him to his mother" (I Kings 17:23), a statement quoted from the Septuagint by Luke (7:15). Luke's story is, however, much less dramatic than its Old Testament antecedents. The form of Luke 7:11-17 is similar to that of miracle stories from Hellenistic circles, but the details correspond to burial practices in Israel at the time: the use of a bier, the procession of bearers and mourners, and the moving of the corpse outside the city wall for burial.

Three aspects of the story deserve special attention: the act of Jesus, the response of the crowd, and the editorial work of Luke. If the preacher attends to all three in the sermon, the order in which they are treated will be determined by the intent and emphasis of the sermon. As for the act of Jesus, both his words to the mother and his restoration of the young man reveal compassion and mercy (verses 13-15) toward the mother. Since the man is her only son and she is a widow (verse 12), he very likely was her sole support. From the moment he saw her until "he gave him to his mother" (verse 15), Jesus' total attention was on the woman. In fact, the story is told so simply and in such subdued tones, it is as though there were no disciples with Jesus, no large crowd with Jesus, and no large crowd in the funeral procession; the storyteller focuses completely on Jesus, the mother, and her son. The raising from the dead is without drama, ritual, or even prayer. The same word of Jesus which from a distance had healed the centurion's slave (verse 7) here is powerful to give life to the dead (verse 14).

In response to the act of Jesus, the crowd is seized with fear and glorifies God. Their expressions of praise are two: "A great prophet has arisen among us!" and "God has visited his people!" (verse 16). The reference to Jesus as a prophet is not uncommon in Luke since Jesus ministers in a manner reminiscent of the prophets of Israel, especially Elijah and Elisha (4:24; 7:39; 13:33; 24:19). And in Acts Luke refers to Jesus as the prophet like Moses (3:22-23; 7:35-37). The phrase "has arisen among us" may be a faint allusion to Jesus' resurrection but more likely is an echo of the language of Deuteronomy 18:15: "The Lord your God will raise up for you a prophet." The expression, "God has visited his people" (verse 16), is also a favorite of Luke (1:68; 9:44; Acts 15:14). Although in the Old Testament, God's visitation may be in wrath (Exod. 20:5) or in mercy (Ps. 106:4), for Luke divine visitation is always an act of grace.

Finally, a word needs to be said about Luke's editorial contribution. Luke's editing appears in two ways.

First, he locates this story of the raising of the dead here in preparation for verses 18-23 which record Jesus' response to the messengers from John the Baptist. That response includes "Go and tell John . . . the dead are raised up" (verse 22).

Second, verse 17 of our lection is not part of the story but is an editorial comment tying this event to the next account: "The disciples of John told him of all these things" (verse 18). That John's ministry was in Judea probably accounts for verse 17 reading, "And this report concerning him spread through the whole of *Judea*," rather than the natural and expected "Galilee." The disciples of John can without uncertainty report back to him what they saw and heard (verse 22). The lectionary does not move next to verses 18-35 but the comparisons and contrasts between the ministries of John and Jesus are very important to Luke and to this church.

39

Proper 6

Sunday Between June 12 and 18 Inclusive
(If after Trinity Sunday)

I Kings 19:1-8; Psalm 42; Galatians 2:15-21; Luke 7:36–8:3

In their own individual way, all of today's texts give expression to and illustrate the human quest for salvation, for the acquisition of truth, for that relationship that fulfills hope, for fellowship with the Divine. Elijah, awash in the torrent of events that his own zeal for the faith had unleashed, flees to the mountain where in the people's memory their ancestors had been given generations ago the law embodying the will of God. The psalm speaks of longing, yearning, thirsting for God that is fed by a discontentment with the normalities of life. In the Epistle text, Paul wrestles with the issue of how humans experience salvation and live out the reality. In the Gospel, yearning leads to adoration and adoration to service.

I Kings 19:1-8

The readings for these next three Sundays are part of a continuous narrative, the account of Elijah's flight to Mount Horeb and his return to Israel. The chapter, however, contains two distinct stories, the first (I Kings 19:1-18) concerning the prophet in the wilderness and the second (I Kings 19:19-21) is the brief report of his return and the selection of Elisha as his successor. On the surface, the parts of the chapter are held together somewhat loosely by an itinerary, a series of brief notices of Elijah's travels and stopping points.

Today's text is the first episode in Elijah's wilderness travels. It stands in sharp contrast with the preceding story, the account of Elijah's contest with the prophets of Baal on

Mount Carmel (chapter 19). It is a story of fire and rain, of life and death. Its backdrop is the royal couple, Ahab and Jezebel, and their support of the Canaanite deity Baal and their persecution of the followers of Yahweh. Elijah wins the contest dramatically, for in response to his prayers Yahweh ignites the fire of the sacrifice and then—in the midst of the drought—brings the life-giving rain. The people acknowledge that Yahweh is God, and the prophet of Yahweh has the prophets of Baal seized and killed (I Kings 19:39-40). In that case Elijah was the majestic, powerful, and successful advocate of Yahweh against Baal. In our text, however, he is a persecuted fugitive, full of self-doubt to the point of despair.

Verses 1-3 provide the transition from the Mount Carmel episode and set the scene for all that follows in the chapter. Ahab, who is said to have been present when Elijah brought the rain and had the prophets of Baal killed, reports all this to Jezebel. She sends a "messenger" to Elijah with her vow—with the typical oath formulas—that she will see the prophet dead before the next day is ended (verse 2). The same Elijah who had commanded fire and rain and had the enemies of Yahweh killed, flees to the south for his life (verse 3). The reference to Beer-sheba indicates that he will soon pass the boundary from the arable, inhabited land into the wilderness, alone.

The next scene transpires under a "broom tree" at some unspecified place in the wilderness. But, like the places where Jacob stopped when leaving and reentering the Promised Land (Gen. 28:10-22; 32:22-32), it is a place of divine encounter and revelation. Asking—literally—"his life [*nephesh*; see the discussion of last week's Old Testament reading] to die," he goes to sleep. What follows are two dream theophanies, but as is often the case in such reports, the line between the dream and waking reality is obscure. The "angel," or "messenger" of Yahweh appears to the prophet (verse 5). The contrast between this messenger and the one sent by Jezebel (verse 2) is, quite literally, the difference between life and death. The first brings a death sentence and the second brings food. The message is a simple one: "Arise and eat." Seeing bread and water, the prophet does as commanded and then sleeps again.

41

When the angel appears a second time, he repeats the command but with some explanation (verse 7). The explanation suggests but does not state a further message, that Elijah is to take a long journey. The prophet again obeys, and the food and water sustain him for the forty days and nights of the trip (verse 8). Only in a final note do we hear of the destination, "Horeb the mount of God."

In addition to the parallels with the journeys of Jacob noted above, the acount recalls the flight of Moses to the wilderness and his encounter with God there (Exod. 2:15–4:31). Moreover, like the people of Israel in the wilderness, who also travel to and from the Mount of God, Elijah's food and water are provided by the Lord.

Two themes in particular present themselves for theological and homiletical reflection. First, there is the journey and the status of the traveler. Elijah clearly sets out into the wilderness as a fugitive. Has he become, by the end of our passage, a pilgrim? At first he is only going away from danger; in the end he is going to a holy place. But the goal of the journey is not emphasized, nor is any new purpose for the trip mentioned. So the encounters with the divine messenger and the acceptance of the life-sustaining gifts take place on the way, when the prophet does not yet know whether he is a fugitive or a pilgrim.

Second, there is the prophet's experience of fear and despair. There under a bush, praying for his own death, he reminds us of that cantankerous prophet Jonah (Jon. 4:1-5). In the case of Elijah, the only explanation given for the change from triumph to despair is the circumstances. In the moment of his success, Queen Jezebel seems still to have the upper hand. The hearers and readers, both ancient and modern, of the story are expected to be those who identify with Elijah and Elijah's God. They learn that even the majestic man of God of Mount Carmel is human. Like him, they have experienced both success and failure, triumph and self-doubt, confidence and fear. Such hearers and readers can understand that flight does not take them beyond the reach of this God, and that fugitives can become pilgrims.

Psalm 42

The psalm for today and the psalm for next Sunday are actually two halves of a single composition that was for some reason separated in two in antiquity. The unity of the two can be argued for on a number of points: (1) an identical refrain appears in 42:5; 42:11; and 43:5; (2) the thought, content, and style of the two pieces are identical; (3) 42:9*b* is repeated in 43:2*b*; (4) Psalm 43 has no title or superscription as one would expect if it were a separate psalm; and (5) many ancient manuscripts present the two psalms as one.

The central concerns of this psalm are despair over the present and a hopeful desire to worship again in the Jerusalem temple. The despair can be seen best in the threefold refrain. In the refrain, the soul of the psalmist is addressed in a form of self-admonition. The soul is questioned ("Why are you cast down, O my soul, and why are you disquieted within me?") and then admonished or encouraged in a personal self-motivating supplication ("Hope in God; for I shall again praise him, my help and my God"). This dialogue of the self with the self may sound a bit peculiar to modern ears and yet all of us engage, at one time or another, in such self-diagnosis or analysis. In a way, talking to oneself indicates a person's ability or at least desire to objectify oneself and gain some perspective on matters at hand.

The person who produced this psalm longs to be again in the presence of God, in worship at the temple. That the composition is entitled "A Maskil of the Sons of Korah" could indicate that the psalm was used by a member of the clergy, a Levite of the order of the sons of Korah. The Korahites were cultic officials especially associated with the music of the temple as well as with other duties (see II Chron. 20:19; I Chron. 9:19, 31; 26:1). Use by a Levitical musician or by Levites would explain many features in the psalm.

The material in Psalms 42–43 shows the following outline: (A) address to God (verse 1), (B) address to a human audience (verses 2-4), (C) self-address (verse 5), (A¹) address to God (verses 6-7), (B¹) address to a human audience (verses 8-10), C¹) self-address, (A²) address to God (43:1-4), and (C²) self-address.

In the address to the Deity (and for the time, we omit Psalm 43 which will be treated with the lections for next Sunday), the imagery of water plays a significant role. In verse 1, water symbolizes the object of the thirsty deer's desire and is identified with God. Like a thirsty animal in a desert, the worshiper longs for God like the deer for an oasis. Here God is seen as the source of solace and comfort, as refreshment to a person distraught by distress. In verses 6-7, the imagery of water plays the opposite role. Here water represents the overwhelming, flooding aspects of life; the torrents that wash away the little dams we construct to provide dry land on which to "lifestead." Note the destructiveness indicated in the terminology—deep, thunder, cataracts, waves, billows. All come from God but all threaten.

The reference to the land of Jordan, Mount Hermon, and the otherwise unknown Mount Mizar are not really clear. Perhaps they are used to symbolize the torrential flow of waters associated with these regions, namely, the sources of the river Jordan. Mount Hermon, over nine thousand feet above sea level, fed the headwaters of the Jordan.

In the addresses to a human audience, the psalmist speaks of adversity and opposition but also recalls the memories of past days. The first address (verses 2-4) reaffirms the longing for God and the desire to worship (to "behold the face of God" denotes worshiping in the temple). The psalm emphasizes the present despair and discomfort of life, the tears of the pious and the taunting of the opponents. References to tears occur frequently in the Psalms (see Pss. 6:6; 39:12; 56:8; 80:5; 126:5). In the Middle East, tears and weeping were not looked down upon as weakness; perhaps the ancients knew that only the damned don't cry. The worshiper also refers to the memories of the past, good memories that may make the present even more painful and yet stimulate expectations about the future. The past memories recall pilgrimages to the temple with their shouts and singing and festival joys. The second address to a human audience reflects on the features of present living—the routines of devotion day and night (verse 8), the sense of being forsaken by God (verse 9*a*), the oppression of the enemy (verse 9*b*), and the psychological wounds that opponents inflict by their jesting over the incongruities between faith and actuality (verse 10).

Finally, there are the self-addresses we have noted earlier: they are encouragements to hope and faith in God.

Galatians 2:15-21

Here we have one of the classic texts summarizing Paul's basic theological position. Yet as important and theologically laden as this passage is, it should not be divorced from its context. It grows directly out of the preceding discussion where Paul has assailed Peter and Barnabas for equivocating on a matter of cardinal importance. In one context Peter would eat with Gentiles as equals, but in the presence of Jewish Christian rigorists, who were unwilling to accept uncircumcised Gentiles as full-fledged members of the covenant, Peter would not eat with Gentiles. Such an action could only imply that they were in some sense only half-Christian, and thus inferior to Jewish Christians. Paul insists that Peter cannot have it both ways. In one context, he cannot behave as if he were a Gentile without any special obligations, yet in another context require Gentiles to conform to Jewish behavior before he will associate with them.

This practical question of the form which Christian fellowship is to take gives rise to the theological exposition in verses 15-21. These remarks are especially directed against Jewish Christians such as Peter and Barnabas. The crucial point being made is that Jews are justified before God in exactly the same way Gentiles are: through faith in Christ. It is not as if there is one method of justification for Jews and another for Gentiles, and the task is to find meaningful ways to relate to each other since they have come to God in separate ways. Rather, there is only one way of truly being made right with God, and this is through faith in Christ. Since Jews and Gentiles alike come to God on the same terms, there can be no distinction between them. They are all equals.

What Jews must recognize is what Paul himself had come to see, and what Scripture itself had already asserted: no one will be justified by works of the law (verse 16; cf. Ps. 143:2; Hab. 2:4; Gen. 15:6). One way of being religious is to meet the requirements imposed by a sacred law, in this case, the Law of Moses. Yet the heart of the Pauline gospel was that this was a misguided pursuit (cf. Rom. 3:20). Works of the law may have value in their own right, but they are not the basis for justification (Rom. 3:28). Indeed, it had never been the case. Just as Abraham had received righteousness through his obediential faith, so had everyone else since, including the Gentiles (cf. Rom. 4:5; 5:1; Gal. 3:6-9, 24).

Since Christ, and not the law, was the means through which God's grace was revealed, it is through Christ that both Jews and Gentiles experience justification. This could only mean that all previous distinctions between Jews and Gentiles had been obliterated. And yet, when Peter allowed old distinctions to govern his conduct, it was tantamount to breaking the law which forbade Jews from associating with Gentiles (cf. Matt. 9:11). If this were the case, Christ would actually be the occasion for sin (verse 17). Moreover, if on the one hand one works to eliminate all distinctions, then reverses position by erecting them again (as Peter had done through his conduct), this in itself is a transgression of principle (verse 18).

For Paul, the true solution to this position of continued ambivalence regarding the law was to understand that union with Christ meant death to the law (verses 19-20). His theology of baptism was to regard it as an event in which the initiate actually participated in the crucifixion *with* Christ (cf. Rom. 6:6-8, 10; 7:6, 4). Since the cross was itself a violation of the law, so did it in effect seal the death of the law (cf. 3:12-13). So closely was his own identity linked with that of the crucified Christ, his life ceased to be egocentric and became Christo-centric (verse 20). The only way in which he could envision life was in terms of the risen Christ living within him (Rom. 14:8; Eph. 3:17). The contours of his life now conformed to the faith of Christ who had given himself in love (verse 20; cf. John 13:1; I Tim. 2:6).

His final word is a categorical either/or: either justification through Christ or justification through the law—not both. Had the latter been possible, the death of Christ would have been unnecessary. To concede this would be to "nullify the grace of God" (verse 21).

The passage echoes themes sounded in Romans (3:9-26) and obviously brings us close to the center of Paul's theology. One exegetical point worth noting is the phrase "faith in Jesus Christ" (verse 16). Some recent commentators have rendered it in its more literal form "faith of Jesus Christ," suggesting a fresh line of interpretation: that rather than being justified by placing our faith and trust *in* Jesus Christ, we are justified by the faithfulness that Christ himself exhibited before God. This places greater stress on the work of Christ in our behalf than on our faith in our own behalf.

Luke 7:36–8:3

The Gospel for today consists of two distinct parts: a woman who was a sinner anoints Jesus (Luke 7:36-50) and women share in the ministry of Jesus (8:1-3). These are the last two of six units Luke has inserted at this point in the Markan order (Luke 7:1–8:3), and although both concern women, to join them too closely can be misleading, as traditions about Mary Magdalene (8:2) amply illustrate. More later.

To understand 7:36-50 it is necessary to review the preceding unit in which Jesus testifies concerning John the Baptist (verses 24-35). Luke says that when Jesus praised John (verses 24-28) all the people and tax collectors justified God for they had received John's baptism, but the Pharisees and lawyers had not, having rejected the purpose of God (repentance and forgiveness) for themselves (verses 29-30). The sharp contrast is between those who accept the offer of repentance and baptism and those who do not, and that is precisely the contrast in our lesson, verses 36-50. The difference is that it now will be precipitated by Jesus, "a friend of tax collectors and sinners" (verse 34), and it will be done at a meal because unlike John, "the Son of man has come eating and drinking" (verse 34). In other words, the speech of Jesus in 7:24-35 will now be acted out in verses 36-50.

All four Gospels record a woman anointing Jesus (Matt.

26:6-13; Mark 14:3-9; Luke 7:36-50; John 12:1-8). Luke's story varies most noticeably from the others even though it clearly has points of contact with Mark's account: Jesus is at table, his host is named Simon, a woman enters the dining area and anoints Jesus with an alabaster flask of ointment. Thereafter, the similarities cease. In all but Luke, the anointing is in Judea, is associated with the burial of Jesus, and the issue is the waste of the ointment. In the text before us the issue is the character of the woman who lavishes upon Jesus her affection and, as becomes evident later, her gratitude for forgiveness.

Luke 7:36-50 can be understood as a drama in four parts. First, there is the setting: Jesus and others are dinner guests of Simon a Pharisee (verse 36). There is no reason to impugn Simon's motives in inviting Jesus, especially in Luke's Gospel in which Jesus' relation to the Pharisees is not so tense (for example, 13:31). We are led, however, because of verses 29 and 34, to anticipate tension over Jesus' forgiveness of sinners. The second part of the drama is the crisis (verses 37-39) created by the entrance of the "woman of the city." That Jesus does not expel her is proof enough to Simon that Jesus is no prophet; if he were, he would know the woman was a sinner. Simon thinks this but does not say it, but Jesus knows Simon's thought, proof by Simon's own criterion that Jesus is a prophet. The third movement of the drama is the solution of the crisis (verses 40-47). By means of a brief parable (verses 41-42) Jesus leads Simon to reflect on the meaning of the difference between his response to Jesus and that of the woman. Her behavior is that of one who has been forgiven. It is important not to construe the awkward verse 47 as meaning that her love earned her forgiveness. On the contrary, because she was forgiven much she loved much. The NEB expresses it quite clearly: "And so, I tell you, her great love proves that her many sins have been forgiven." The fourth and final part of the drama is the christological dispute (verses 48-50). Reminiscent of Mark 2:1-12, the question of Jesus' identity and authority comes into sharp focus and returns the discussion to its beginning in verse 18: "Are you he who is to come, or shall we look for another?"

Luke 8:1-3 begins a new phase of Luke's narrative and

consists of a summary statement of Jesus' missionary tour through cities and villages. The striking item in the summary is that Jesus was accompanied not only by the Twelve but "also some women" (verse 2). These were women who had been healed by Jesus, and some of them were women of position and means, helping finance the missionary tours (verse 3). The one most familiar to us is Mary Magdalene from whom Jesus exorcised seven demons. There is no evidence to warrant identifying her with the unnamed woman of the preceding story. In fact, there is no evidence to justify portraying her as having been a prostitute. Demon possession caused various maladies but not moral or ethical depravity.

Proper 7

Sunday Between June 19 and 25 Inclusive
(If after Trinity Sunday)

I Kings 19:9-14; Psalm 43; Galatians 3:23-29; Luke 9:18-24

In this collection of readings, the question of how God relates to humans may be seen as a unifying theme. The prophet Elijah, on the run, hides away in the recesses of his cave. There he succors his martyr complex and indulges his sense of self-righteousness only to be addressed not in glory but in quietude, in the voice of stillness. In the Galatians reading, Paul argues that one and all are related to God through faith in Christ not by deeds of achievement but by grace, not through law but promise. In Jesus' instruction to his disciples, the way to life is presented as the way of the cross, the way of death. The psalmist engages in self-address with admonishment that hope lies with God.

I Kings 19:9-14

Continuing where last week's Old Testament lection ended, this passage is the account of Elijah's arrival at Horeb and of Yahweh's appearance to him there. The reading breaks off, however, in the middle of the report of the prophet's encounter with the Lord, with next week's text completing the account.

The geographical setting of the story is important. Traveling forty days and forty nights into the wilderness, Elijah has arrived at "Horeb the mount of God" (19:8). What some of the Old Testament sources and traditions call "Horeb"—Deuteronomy in particular—others identify as "Sinai." Horeb was the location of Moses' call (Exod. 3:1). The mountain was the site of the establishment of the covenant and the revelation of the law through Moses.

Historical geography has not been able to locate the place with certainty. The traditional site, Jebel Musa, is deep in the Sinai peninsula and far from any usual route between Egypt and Canaan. Some recent scholarship tends to seek the site near Kadesh-barnea, much farther to the north and nearer the boundaries of Israel. For our text the important point is that the prophet has gone to the holy mountain of divine revelation and takes up residence in a cave.

What transpires is an epiphany of Yahweh to Elijah. The report has two distinct parts, verses 9b-13a and verses 13b-18. The opening formula, "Behold, the word of the Lord came to him," (9b) introduces the first encounter, but it could just as well stand as the heading for the passage as a whole. We are not to forget that it was the *word* of the Lord that was decisive in the epiphany. Both sections of the account consist of dialogue between Yahweh and the prophet. Yahweh speaks (verses 9b, 11a, 13b, 15-18) and Elijah responds (verses 10, 14). The first two exchanges are divine questions and the prophet's responses. Finally, Yahweh's last word (verses 15-18) is not a question but instructions, which Elijah obeys but does not answer.

The questions and answers are virtually identical. When the Lord asks Elijah what he is doing in this place, the prophet responds with words of self-defense and perhaps, self-pity. He cites his zeal ("I have been very jealous," verses 10, 14) for Yahweh, the apostasy of the people of Israel, and insists that he is the only faithful one left, and he has had to flee for his life. Note that he accuses, not Ahab and Jezebel, but "the people of Israel" of violence against Yahweh's altars and prophets. The plural reference to altars is an accurate historical allusion, since worship was not centralized in Jerusalem and all other sanctuaries torn down until the time of Josiah in the seventh century. The reference to the slaughter of the prophets may allude to the persecution by Jezebel noted in I Kings 18:4, 13.

Between the first and second dialogue is the account of the epiphany itself (verses 11-13a). It is parallel in some respects to the appearance of the Lord to Moses (Exod. 33:17-23). Both take refuge in the mountain (a cave or a "cleft in the rock"), and neither is allowed to see Yahweh directly. The account of

51

the theophany to Elijah is consistent with a widespread Old Testament tradition. When the Lord appears, there are awesome and dangerous natural phenomena. Here it is first "a great and strong wind" (verse 11) that even splits rocks, then earthquake (verse 11), followed by fire (verse 12). In every case there follows the refrain, "But the Lord was not in the wind . . . the earthquake . . . the fire." Finally, there was "a still small voice" (verse 12; NEB reads a "low murmuring sound"). Only then does the prophet come to the mouth of the cave and hear the word of Yahweh. That "he wrapped his face in his mantle" (verse 13) reflects the deep awareness in the Old Testament tradition that no one can see God and live (cf. Exod. 33:21; Isa. 6:2-5).

The major issue in this passage is the nature of divine revelation. While awesome and destructive natural phenomena (wind, earthquake, fire) may attend the appearance of Yahweh, the God of Israel is not to be identified with any of these. The story may even contain a polemic against the popular cultic view of the theophany (cf. Ps. 18:12; 68; Hab. 3:3). In any case, the perspective of this prophetic tradition is unmistakable: God reveals himself by means of the word, here the spoken word, and not fundamentally through the manipulation of natural forces, although those forces, to be sure, are set into turmoil by God's appearance. That word is calm, comprehensible, personal, and purposeful. As next week's reading will show, the purpose of the epiphany is to commission the prophet to change history.

Psalm 43

Psalm 43 is actually the third strophe or section of a single composition now designated Psalms 42–43. For general matters regarding the psalm, see the preceding psalms lection.

This unit is composed of the plea addressed to the Deity (verses 1-4) and the self-address or refrain (verse 5). The petition addressed to God is quite aggressive, punctuated by a number of imperatives—vindicate (judge), defend, send out, let them lead/bring. There is, in other words, a move away from the character of passivity found in Psalms 42 to a more extroverted, demanding posture. The responsibility, or at least some of it, for the psalmist's welfare and status is shifted to the Deity who is "commanded" or requested to rectify matters. In addition, God is even accused of dereliction of duty, for not being the adequate source of refuge that he should have been or for even casting away the one who would seek solace in his protection (verse 2).

What the worshiper desires is God's light and truth, that is, for the worshiper and others to see and understand things as they really are (verse 3*a*), and to move in pilgrimage to the temple where God dwells (verse 3*b*). The final goal, the ultimate request is go to the altar (to offer sacrifice) and there to praise God (verse 4). In spite of life's troubles, worship is seen as the means for confronting and overcoming them.

It is possible that we overpersonalize such a psalm as this and try too hard to discover some individual's face beneath the poetic mask. It is entirely possible that this psalm (42–43) was written to be used by worshipers and sung antiphonally as pilgrims set out on their way to some pilgrimage in Jerusalem. The portrayal of the present discontent with life thus forms the backdrop for the expectations of the coming worship (see Pss. 84 and 120).

Galatians 3:23-29

In this final section of chapter 3, Paul brings to a conclusion the fairly extended argument for justification by faith begun in verse 1. From their own experience the Galatians should have known that the Spirit came to them through "believing the gospel message" (3:2, NEB) and not through keeping the law (verses 1-5). In addition, the example of Abraham is instructive: he was reckoned as righteous by God because of his faith in God's promise, not because he kept specific legal requirements, such as circumcision (verses 6-9). All those who similarly believe are Abraham's seed.

In the next section (verses 10-14), we find that righteousness based on law-keeping is ill-founded, primarily because no one can keep the law perfectly. If being accepted by God is a matter of achievement, true acceptance would require flawless performance. Everyone who tries to become religious in this way ultimately finds religion to be a curse. The fact is, we are made righteous not by our achievement but through God's gracious gift which we appropriate through faith.

If Abraham was accepted by God because he believed, justification by faith is the established precedent, antedating the giving of the law by more than four hundred years. This is the way God has always worked—extending a promise to those who act in faith (verses 15-18).

The obvious question arises, "Why then the law?" (verse 19). It served to "make wrongdoing a legal offence" (verse 19, NEB). It was a necessary, yet temporary measure, put in place until the coming of Christ, Abraham's offspring (verses 21-22).

Life under the law had been a life of constraint, indeed a form of bondage (verse 23; cf. 4:4, 21; 5:18). In a sense, the law served as a guardian or custodian whose role was that of temporary caretaker (verses 24-25; cf. I Cor. 4:15). With the coming of Christ, however, the faith-principle was reestablished as the basis for justification. Like Abraham, Christ had demonstrated unqualified faith in God, and thus became the one in whom the divine promise was renewed (3:14). Thus it was in and through Christ that all who live in faith are able to become God's children, the true heirs of the promise (verse 26; cf. 4:5-7).

What results is a new order of existence in which all human distinctions are removed—ethnic, sexual, and social (verse 28). To be sure, this is an eschatological reality but one that has already begun to be realized within the Pauline churches (I Cor. 12:13; Rom. 10:12; Col. 3:11). We already see it beginning to be implemented as Paul instructs his churches about practical matters of faith (I Cor. 7:17-24). And yet, it by no means was fully realized then, nor is it now. The form of the language suggests that this affirmation of oneness in Christ occurred in the context of a baptismal liturgy (cf. I Cor. 12:13; Col. 3:11). Baptism into Christ meant putting on Christ, as one would don a new garment (cf. Rom. 13:14; Eph. 4:24). Besides moral renewal, it implied entering a new world whose ordering principle was oneness in Christ.

Union with Christ created a new form of social existence that sought to embody unity in Christ (John 17:21).

The implication of this is that God's original promise is firmly established; by being Christ's children, we experience solidarity with Abraham who was saved by faith.

This text provides one of the clearest statements of Paul's vision of a new humanity where all distinctions are removed. In Paul's own lifetime, as the debate in Galatians and Romans attests, it was the Jew-Gentile question that came to the fore, and Paul became the champion for a form of religious community in which faith was the fundamental prerequisite for all members. In other ways, we begin to see the removal of sexual and social distinctions, but only embryonically. This continues to be an unrealized vision in the church.

Luke 9:18-24

Today's Gospel is, with typical Lukan modifications, a form of the tradition found also in Mark 8:27-33 and Matthew 16:13-23. In fact, John 6 preserves the same or similar tradition in the account of feeding the five thousand followed by Peter's confession of faith. For Luke and Matthew, Mark has provided the basic framework: the question of Jesus, Peter's reply, Jesus' prediction of the passion, and teachings on discipleship. The preacher will want to be alert, however, to Luke's variations from Mark: the omission of any reference to place (earlier at verse 10 Bethsaida was mentioned); the addition of "as he was praying alone" (verse 18); the omission of the sharp interchange between Jesus and Peter; and the addition of "daily" in the call to cross-bearing (verse 23). Luke's context is also different in that he places this event immediately after the feeding of the five thousand (9:10-17) as does the Gospel of John (6:1-71), while Mark and Matthew record healings, teachings, and another feeding between the feeding of the five thousand and the story before us. Let us then, focus on Luke's account.

First, Luke sets the stage not by naming the place but by focusing on Jesus and the Twelve. Jesus is praying. Luke has already said that Jesus prayed at his baptism (3:21) and the night before choosing the Twelve (6:12). Clearly Luke understood prayer as vital for Jesus and most especially on occasions of critical significance.

Second, Jesus asks his disciples to voice what they have been hearing as the public opinion of Jesus (verse 18). Their answer indicates that the people understood Jesus to be the forerunner of the Messiah (verse 19). In other words, the Galileans placed Jesus in the role we have given to John the Baptist: the prophet to precede the coming of the Christ (Mal. 4:5-6).

Third, Jesus asks the Twelve for their perception of his identity and Peter responds with the designation, "the Christ of God" (verse 20). This title is for Luke more than an elaboration of Mark's "the Christ" (8:29). To relate Christ to God in this way is typical of Luke (2:26; 23:35; Acts 4:26) and consistent with his overall theme: the primary subject of the entire drama of salvation from Eden to eschaton is God. It is God who led Israel, spoke through the prophets, sent John the Baptist, sent Jesus Christ, and sends the Holy Spirit. To focus entirely on Christ or, for that matter, the Holy Spirit, is to break up the story, shatter the continuity, and to turn attention away from the Creator, Revealer, Sustainer, and Redeemer. Or as Paul would express it: of God, through God, and to God are all things; therefore to God be the glory forever (Rom. 11:36).

Fourth, Jesus commands silence about this designation, "the Christ of God" and prophesies for the first time his own suffering, death, and resurrection (verses 21-22). The charge to silence finds its best reason in that prophecy, for it is unreasonable to expect the Twelve, without our vantage point of hindsight, to link meaningfully the category "Christ," with all the hope and blessing surrounding that term, and suffering, rejection by the religious establishment, and death. The popular notion of reverse psychology, that instruction not to tell is the way to get a message spread, is too shallow for this deep and dark prediction. The fact is, even after the resurrection the followers of Christ have had difficulty associating God's Christ with the offense of the cross. There have always been those persons and groups who have embraced Easter while trying to forget Good Friday.

And finally, Luke follows the prophecy of death with instructions on cross-bearing (verses 23-24). All three Synoptics locate these sayings here (Matt. 16:24-28; Mark 8:34–9:1; Luke 9:23-27). That this is editorial placing is evident, especially in two clues. One, these words are "to all" (verse 23) even though the conversation has been private, between Jesus and the Twelve. But the Evangelists are unanimous in asserting that the demands of discipleship are incumbent on all who follow Jesus. Two, Jesus calls for cross-bearing even though he had not indicated his own death would be by crucifixion. By the writer's time, that was the assumed connection between Jesus' suffering and that of his followers. In fact, Matthew assumed as early as 10:38-39, before Jesus spoke of his own death, that "cross" was a meaningful term for the readers. Luke's special accent lies in the word "daily" (verse 23) which interprets cross-bearing as a way of living, a way of negotiating each day as a Christian in the world, not as a call to martyrdom. In case anyone hears in Luke's modification an easing of the demands on disciples, that will be quickly dispelled by reading about or talking with those followers of Jesus in various parts of the world for whom discipleship is a bearing of the cross every day.

Proper 8

Sunday Between June 26 and July 2 Inclusive

I Kings 19:15-21; Psalm 44:1-8; Galatians 5:1, 13-25; Luke 9:51-62

The lections for today may be viewed as sharing in common an exhortation or a resolution to an action or a course of action. The prophet Elijah is ordered out of the solace of his seclusion and back into the arena of Israelite-Syrian politics. Paul admonishes the Galatians to walk under the banner of freedom in Christ and to live in freedom as slaves to one another. In the Gospel reading, Jesus sets his face toward Jerusalem warning those who would follow him that such a pattern of life comes wrapped in the demands of drastic obligations. The psalm, a lament, promises to make thankfulness an ongoing pattern of life.

I Kings 19:15-21

Our reading is an account of piety, politics, and prophetic succession. As indicated in the discussion of last week's lesson, this passage begins in the middle of a unit, the account of the epiphany of Yahweh to Elijah on Horeb (verses 9-18). The awesome appearance of the Lord, then, is the immediate context in which the lection should be read and heard. The broader context is the collection of stories concerning the life and times of the prophet. The reading for the day brings us to the issue at the heart of those stories, the conflict between Yahweh and Baal, between Elijah and the followers of Baal—especially those in Israel's royal palace, Ahab and Jezebel.

This conflict between Israelite and Canaanite religions is both an ancient and a continuing one. When Israel began to establish herself in the land, the fertility religions of Baal and

58

numerous other deities had been practiced in Canaan for centuries. From Israel's perspective, the conflict with the native religion may be seen as a crisis of faith and culture. Which Canaanite practices and symbols could Israel accept and still remain faithful to the God who brought them up out of Egypt? Many said, "None," and that was the official and orthodox answer, in keeping with the first commandment. But Canaanite culture and religion were powerful forces, and as the Israelites became farmers and city-dwellers, it is not surprising that they took over many practices and ideas from their predecessors in the land. Even the kingship, like that of the other nations, represented for many a compromise with culture, for "Yahweh is our king." In the ninth century when Elijah appeared on the scene in the Northern Kingdom, the conflict had become an open one because Ahab's wife Jezebel had officially reintroduced the religion of Baal. Elisha is instrumental in putting an end to that problem, but, as the Book of Hosea shows, it is still alive in more subtle forms a century later.

The first part of the reading for the day (verses 15-18) concerns that conflict between Yahwism and Baalism. It is framed as a speech of Yahweh to Elijah, introduced by the account of the theophany. God's appearance leads to words of commission—similar in some ways to the vocation reports of other prophets—to the fugitive prophet. The prophet's complaints are answered by commands, first to return to the land where his life was in danger. Yahweh instructs him further to anoint two kings, one for Syria and one for Israel, and a prophet as his own successor (verses 15-16). Then follows a somewhat cryptic, oracular interpretation of the purpose for which these three are to be anointed (verse 17): bloodshed. The final sentence (verse 18) at once clarifies the death sentence—presumably for all who have "bowed the knee to Baal" and kissed him, i.e., his image—and rebukes Elijah for his claim that he is the only one left who is faithful to Yahweh (19:10, 14).

There is a poignant note in this commission. Elijah, who has been at the center of the religious and political conflict, is not to see its resolution. That will be for his successor, while his duty is to designate the instruments of the Lord's will.

Like Moses, who was not allowed to enter the Promised Land, he lives with the promise and not its fulfillment.

The second part of the reading (verses 19-21) reports how Elijah responded to the commission, by finding Elisha and ordaining him. Elisha was plowing with oxen when Elijah, without a word, threw his mantle over him. When Elisha runs after Elijah a curious dialogue transpires. Elisha asks to kiss his parents farewell before following Elijah, who seems to deny that the act with the mantle meant anything. But then Elisha returns, kills the oxen and cooks their flesh on a fire made with the yokes, and feeds the people. The goal of the anecdote is reached when we hear that Elisha followed Elijah and "ministered to him" (verse 21).

Actions here speak louder than words. Like many other prophets, Elijah performs a symbolic action, but unlike most others, he does not interpret its meaning. The point, however, is obvious both to Elisha and to the hearers and readers: succession. The mantle is a symbol of the authority that is passed on, as also in the final Elijah episode (II Kings 2:1-14). Note that Elijah does not literally "anoint" Elisha, as instructed in verse 15. There is no Old Testament example of anointing a prophet, and even the designation of a prophetic successor is remarkable. God usually calls prophets directly, but here does so through another prophet. Elisha's action with the oxen is symbolic as well. He signals a break with his previous occupation and hosts a sacrificial meal. That he "ministered to" Elijah suggests that his role in some ways is parallel to that of Joshua in relation to Moses (Deut. 31:7-8, 14-23; Josh. 1:1).

Along with issues of the prophetic role and vocation, the passage raises but does not resolve for us the relation between faith and politics. Both those who feel that religious leaders should be involved directly in politics, and those who feel they should not are likely to find support in this text. On the one hand, Elijah, like all Israel's prophets, was deeply involved in politics to the point of instigating rebellion. Without such zeal it is questionable whether the Yahwistic faith would have survived. On the other hand, his fanatically held faith called forth a bloodbath, which at least one later prophet will condemn (Hos. 1:4-5). Today, in a very different culture, where political and religious institutions are more distinct, we are impelled to struggle with the issues of faith and culture, religion and politics.

Psalm 44:1-8

lament

These verses comprise part of a lengthy psalm of communal lamentation. The psalm was composed for use in worship services after the nation suffered defeat in battle but a defeat which the community felt was not their responsibility but was the result of God's unwillingness to aid them in conflict. This lament (like Pss. 74 and 79) was the opposite of a victory song such as the one found in Judges 5. As a prayer, the entire psalm is speech addressed to God.

The following is an outline of the psalm: a statement of *outline* confidence (verses 1-8), a description of the distress and the defeat in battle (verses 9-16), a statement of the people's innocence and their unwillingness to accept defeat as the consequence of their sin or wrongdoing (verses 17-22), and a petitionary plea for God to activate himself and help his people (verses 23-26). In the latter, God is indirectly accused of somnolence (sleeping on the job), lassitude (wearying on duty), insouciance (lack of concern), and dereliction of duty (forgetting his responsibility). In the last analysis, however, the community appeals for help, throwing itself on the grace of God rather than claiming rights based on privilege or innocence (verse 26).

The psalm moves back and forth between the use of plural and singular first-person pronouns. The plural form ("we, our") indicates community address while the singular form ("I, my") points to individual address. The solution to the problem of who is speaking is found in seeing the king as the speaker when the singular appears (verses 4, 6, 15-16) and the community elsewhere. One should imagine this psalm being used in public worship just after the king and his forces have returned from the field where they were defeated in battle.

The verses in today's lection contain only the opening statements of confidence which in themselves give no indication of the intensity of the lament and the complaints against God that follow. The contents of verses 1-8 are the *1 - 8*

61

certainty of the assurance of victory based on the example of the past (verses 1-3) and the present confidence in God based on the leader's and the people's commitments to the Deity (verses 4-8).

The example of God's past deliverance of his people that serves as the paradigm of the divine commitment to save is the conquest of the Promised Land (verses 1-3). It was Yahweh who drove out the nations, afflicting the occupants of the land but granting freedom to his people, planting them in the land. The victory is not ascribed to the might, the valor, the uprightness, or the superiority of the Hebrews but instead to God's action on their behalf. The land is, in other words, a gift.

From the analogy of the past, the statement of confidence moves to a confessional about the present. The congregation (verses 5 and 7-8) and the royal commander (verses 4 and 6) confess their faith and testify to God that he was the source of their victories in battle and the one who subdued enemies under them.

But all the confidence and confession are only prologue to the "yet" with which verse 9 opens.

Galatians 5:1, 13-25

Rather than seeing an abrupt shift at 5:1 from the so-called theological section to the practical, hortatory section of the letter, chapters 5–6 should be viewed as being much more integrally related to chapters 1–4. Freedom is one of several thematic links between the two sections (cf., e.g., 2:4; 3:28; 4:22, 23, 26, 30; 5:1, 13).

One way of reading chapter 5 is as a theological exposition of freedom, for which Paul has so strongly argued throughout the letter, and which is indeed one of the hallmarks of Pauline theology (cf. Rom. 6:18, 22; I Cor. 7:23; II Cor. 3:17; also John 8:32, 36). Especially is this true of today's epistolary lection.

It may seem odd to us that our text begins by reminding us that Christ has liberated us and that we should be resolute in remaining free. Yet Paul is all too aware of the hazards of being free, and he targets three potential dangers.

First, freedom may turn out to be more difficult than slavery. There is a good chance that, like the long-term prisoner who is finally set free and finds it difficult to shake the habits of servitude, we may actually turn back to "a yoke of slavery" (verse 1). Freedom, after all, poses new responsibilities. Whereas formerly our choices may have been made for us, we now find they are ours—and ours alone—to make. And one advantage to living under law is that our duties and responsibilities can be spelled out in great detail. We may actually be more comfortable having law define our conduct for us instead of exercising our own autonomy in deciding on the responsible course of action to take. Freedom may be attractive initially because we think it will demand less of us, yet we discover that it actually makes greater demands on us. One of the ironies of life is that the life of freedom requires greater effort than the life of servitude. It has to be nurtured, protected, and rigorously pursued. It turns out not to be a lifelong afternoon in a hammock.

Like the Israelites after the Exodus who found themselves actually longing for their former life of servitude, we may find freedom in Christ too much to take. Paul's charge is for us to be resolute in our newfound freedom, to be relentless in our pursuit of freedom, to "stand fast" (verse 1). We are often given this charge to be steadfast, and this in itself suggests that our tendency will be to take the easier course and be lured away to the more comfortable life of slavery (4:9; cf. Rom. 11:20; I Cor. 10:12; 15:1; 16:13; II Cor. 1:24; I Thess. 3:8; II Thess. 2:15; Phil. 1:27; 4:1).

Second, freedom may destroy a sense of community. We are cautioned not to allow our freedom to become "an opportunity for the flesh" (verse 13). This could be thought of as against sexual laxity (cf. Rom. 7:8), but the following verses suggest otherwise. We are called to a life of loving service to each other and reminded that this is the essence of the law (verse 14; cf. Lev. 19:18; Rom. 13:8-10). And verse 15 reminds us of the nursery rhyme: "There once were two cats of Kilkenny; Each thought there was one cat too many; So they fought and they fit, they scratched and they bit; Til, excepting their nails and the tips of their tails; Instead of two cats, there weren't any!"

63

More likely, our text is warning us against an overly individualistic interpretation of freedom. The tendency of the flesh, in this sense, would be the tendency to pursue our own needs and desires, oblivious to the common good. That this was a real issue is seen in the church at Corinth (I Cor. 8–10; esp. I Cor. 8:9). So defined, freedom becomes the relentless pursuit of the individual with no moral commitment to others, and eventually becomes inhumane and self-destructive. In any case, we are reminded that freedom can easily be abused and become a cover for our own evil desires (cf. I Pet. 2:16).

Third, freedom may translate into a form of moral relativism. One objection to Paul's gospel is that it provides an open license to sin (Rom. 6:1-4). In the absence of law(s), how do we develop a responsible ethic?

For one thing, we can recognize the existence of genuine moral conflict within us. Plato portrayed it as the struggle between two horses pulling a chariot. It is sketched in today's text as a war between the Spirit and the flesh (cf. Rom. 7:15, 23; James 4:1, 5; I Pet. 2:11). The two are antithetical to each other (verse 17), for they represent two fundamentally opposed ways of construing reality. "Conflict does not mean peaceful co-existence, let alone co-operation. . . . No co-operation, then, between the two! For how can there be co-operation between total freedom and total bondage? How can the Spirit give assistance to the flesh, or the flesh to the Spirit?" (Barth).

At the very least, we can recognize the existence of two fundamental outlooks, one domain in which the Spirit lives and reigns (cf. Rom. 8:4), the other dominated by the flesh (cf. Eph. 2:3; I John 2:16; I Pet. 2:11). For Paul, life under the law belonged squarely within the latter (3:23; 4:4-5, 21; Rom. 6:14). Essentially, two profiles of existence are sketched. The first set of vices represent the various forms of behavior that result from giving in to the impulses of the flesh, or our own desires (cf. Rom. 1:29-31; 13:13; Matt. 15:19; Luke 18:11; I Cor. 5:10-11; 6:9-10; II Cor. 12:20; Eph. 4:31; 5:3-5; Col. 3:5, 8; I Tim. 1:9-10; 6:4-5; II Tim. 3:2-4; Tit. 3:3; I Pet. 4:3; Rev. 9:21; 21:8; 22:15; also IV Macc. 1:26; 2:15). The set of virtues, or fruits of the Spirit (e.g. Eph. 5:9; Phil. 1:11; Heb. 12:11; James 3:18;

Prov. 3:9; 11:30; Amos 6:13), display the results of living in response to God's own Spirit (cf. II Cor. 6:6-7; I Tim. 4:12; 6:11; II Tim. 2:22; II Pet. 1:5-11).

Since freedom, in the Pauline sense, exists where the Spirit presides (II Cor. 3:17) and provides the norm by which we live, Paul's final charge is to "walk by the Spirit."

Luke 9:51-62

With 9:51, Luke begins a new section of his Gospel, a fact recognized in many English translations by the use of a break in the text between verses 50 and 51. That 9:51 marks a new turn in the narrative is indicated by a time reference ("when the days drew near"), a purpose reference ("he set his face to go to Jerusalem"; cf. a similar expression in the Servant Song of Isa. 50:6-7), and a final departure reference ("to be received up," an ascension expression in Luke and I Tim. 3:16).

Exactly where the section that begins at 9:51 ends is not quite so clear. If Luke is viewed in relation to Mark, then the unit extends sufficiently to include the stories in Luke that are not found in Mark. This means the end would be at 18:14, for at 18:15 Luke resumes following Mark's framework. Others who prefer to call this Luke's "travel narrative" conclude at 19:27 at which point Jesus arrives at Jerusalem. There is a general correctness to calling 9:51–19:27 a travel narrative because the materials in this section are broadly framed as the trip to Jerusalem. However, the place references are such as to make reconstruction of the itinerary impossible. Approximately one-half of the material in 9:51–18:14, while having no Markan parallels, has parallels in Matthew; the other one half is in Luke alone.

It is probably helpful to the preacher to see this section in the larger pattern of Luke's Gospel. The first section of Luke's work was preceded by Jesus' baptism, an event bathed in prayer and given divine attestation (3:21-22). This section is prefaced by Jesus' Transfiguration, again marked by prayer and the voice from heaven (9:28-36). The first began with a rejection at Nazareth (4:16-30), the second, with a rejection in Samaria (9:51-56). Neither rejection stops Jesus' ministry; in fact, in each in embryo is the prophecy of an even larger mission to the Gentiles. For the next four months the Gospel lessons will be taken from this special section, this travel narrative of Luke. While the journey itself cannot be reconstructed, we will be able to experience what Luke wished to convey: the life of discipleship is a pilgrimage, and those who follow can expect to share in the fate of Jesus.

Today's lesson, 9:51-62 consists of two parts: Jesus' rejection by the Samaritans (verses 51-56), and Jesus' terms for discipleship (verses 57-62). While each unit has its own integrity, they should be treated together because verses 51-56 set the tone for the encounters with Jesus in verses 57-62. Understanding the unswerving intensity, the destiny-oriented sense of Jesus setting his face toward Jerusalem and the cross enables the reader to grasp the same intense commitment expected of Jesus' followers. This same pattern occurred earlier in the chapter when Luke placed the demands of discipleship immediately after Jesus' prediction of his death (9:18-27).

Verses 51-56 have a double function. They record Jesus' rejection by Samaritans because his face is set to go to Jerusalem, a statement which at one level testifies to racial tension between Samaritans and Jews, but which at another level says they are not willing to follow one who is on his way "to be received up"; that is, to be killed. But these verses also anticipate the mission of the seventy (10:1-12). Jesus' own ministry, the sending out of disciples by twos, the extension of the mission beyond Judaism, the dependence upon the hospitality of others, the response to those who reject the message, and the movement on to other places, all elements in verses 51-56, provide precedence and dominical authorization for the subsequent mission of the church.

Verses 57-62 provide three examples of encounters between Jesus and would-be disciples as Jesus moves toward Jerusalem as one who has set his face like a firm stone. A threefold pattern was common to storytelling at that time, even though these may have existed earlier as independent episodes. Matthew 8:19-22 records the first two. The pattern here is: "I will follow," "follow me," and again, "I will follow." Given the portrayal of Jesus in verse 51, the reader should not expect Jesus to offer easy options. The call for total and primary loyalty is underscored by setting Jesus' demands over against, not the worst or lowest, but the best and the highest loyalties. Anything less would deny his own destiny and the claims of the kingdom of God. There is no reason, then, for the preacher to search for loopholes in Jesus' absolutes. He is on his way to be received up; shall he deceive his disciples with offers of bargains?

Proper 9

Sunday Between July 3 and 9 Inclusive

I Kings 21:1-3, 17-21; Psalm 5:1-8; Galatians 6:7-18; Luke 10:1-12, 17-20

The biblical story of Naboth's vineyard with its account of the framed charges against the victim and Elijah's denunciation of King Ahab in terms of Naboth's murder could be said to have provided the substance from which Paul deduced the principle—"whatever a man sows, that he will also reap." Although found in a totally different context and employed for radically different purposes, Jesus too draws on the imagery of reaping when, at the sending out of the seventy, Luke has Jesus note that "the harvest is plentiful." The psalm reading without using agricultural and harvest imagery extols God as one before whom "evil may not sojourn."

I Kings 21:1-3, 17-21

Our reading consists of the introduction and part of the conclusion to the story of Naboth's vineyard. The verses are chosen wisely, for they set the scene and then present the resolution of the drama's conflicts, but one could hardly preach on the text without retelling the entire story. It is another account of confrontation between Elijah and the royal household. Usually in the Elijah cycle the confrontation concerns apostasy from the Yahwistic faith because Ahab and Jezebel support the religion of Baal. Here, however, the issue is justice, at the level of what we would call civil and criminal law.

In I Kings 21 a story of conspiracy, perjury, theft, and murder (verses 1-16) prepares the way for the account of Elijah's encounter with Ahab (verses 17-29). Verses 1-4 set the scene for the story of the crimes. It seems to be a simple matter that could be resolved by negotiations: Naboth's vineyard is adjacent to the king's property and Ahab makes a generous offer for it, either a better vineyard or the value in money. Naboth's unequivocal refusal sets the story's tension into motion. He does not explain, but the reasons are implicit in his choice of language. "The Lord forbid" is an oath formula, but more. That this land is "the inheritance of my fathers" reflects not only the fact that the land has been passed down through the generations, but that the family holds the property as a gift of Yahweh. According to the traditional belief, one does not treat such gifts as capital investment or real estate.

The irony of the story is similar to that of David and Uriah's wife Bathsheba (II Sam. 11–12). In both cases, a character's fidelity to traditional religious faith contributes to his death. For Uriah it is the soldier's duty and for Naboth it is his responsibility as steward of the land.

Ahab appears childish and weak. He does not quarrel with Naboth, but returns home and pouts (verse 4). Then the strong character enters the story and plays her part. Jezebel considers Ahab's passivity to be ridiculous (verse 7); after all, he is the king. So she promises to give him what she does not own. Clearly her words and actions assume a view of kingship that conflicts with Israel's understanding. Her perspective is the political counterpart to her religious faith, devotion to the religion of Baal. Kings, standing in a special relationship to the gods, may do as they wish, so she engineers a plot to have Naboth accused of blasphemy against God and the king, thereby depriving his descendants of the right to the land. Two "base fellows" (verse 10) collaborate in what can only be described as premeditated murder. Once the deed is done the queen tells Ahab that the vineyard is his, and he goes to take formal possession of it (verses 15-16).

Having run its course and reached it resolution, the first story turns out to be only an episode in the more important sequence of events. History moves in response to the word of the Lord through prophets—that is the belief both of ancient tradition and of the editors of the Books of Deuteronomy–II Kings. Thus the word of the Lord came—happened—to

Elijah. The narrator does not inform us where the prophet is, except that he is not in Samaria. The word of the Lord (verses 18-19) is a commission in two parts: (1) what to do—go meet Ahab in Naboth's vineyard—and (2) what to say to the king. The opening rhetorical question accuses him of murder and theft, and then there follows a cryptic announcement of judgment.

Without transition the scene changes. Elijah has, as usual, appeared suddenly, and Ahab greets him as he did in 18:17, with an accusation. Elijah's retort is in the most familiar pattern of prophetic address, both in the prophetic stories in Samuel and Kings and in the early prophetic books. First comes the accusation, in direct address (verse 20b). It is less specific than the indictment in verse 19, but it moves the violations beyond the realm of civil or criminal law into the religious, convenantal stipulations. "You have sold yourself"—that is, for the price of a vineyard—" to do what is evil in the sight of the Lord"—that is, murder and the appropriation of a person's "inheritance" are not simply matters for human courts, but violations of Yahweh's will. Consequently, such offenses lead to divine intervention in the form of judgment (verses 21 ff.). The punishment fits the crime. Not only Ahab but also his entire household will die.

We leave the story on that note, but it goes on to detail a specific judgment against Jezebel, and then to a modification of the punishment when Ahab repents.

At the heart of the story lies the most basic theme of prophetic literature, the Lord's response to injustice. Implicit are the concerns with justice. They are considered in various ways. Ahab and Jezebel violate procedural justice—due process—in manipulating the juridical system. They violate distributive justice by taking more than they need and depriving Naboth of his most basic right. But more than that, they violate the substance of justice, which rests on the character of Israel's God as being just. Covenantal stipulations—laws, commandments, traditions about land tenure—mean to show how justice will be established among God's people.

Ancient Israel does not concern itself much with lines between religious faith, politics, and the legal system. All these institutions rest on the conviction that Yahweh seeks justice. Consequently, Elijah—like Nathan before him (II Sam. 11–12)—boldly confronts the head of the government with his sin, with a word that is powerful because it comes from the Lord.

Psalm 5:1-8

Psalm 5 is best understood as a composition produced for use in special legal processes in the temple. When regular courts could not reach verdicts in certain cases, because of the nature of the alleged crime or lack of evidence, special appeal could be made to God, that is, to a process of trial and/or ordeal in the temple under the supervision of the priests (see Exod. 22:7-8; Deut. 17:8-13; 19:15-21; I Kings 8:31-32; Num. 5:5-31).

A feature in the temple ritual was apparently the affirmation of innocence by the one or ones who felt falsely accused, along with a plea to be judged and a request for the opponent or the wicked to be condemned and punished. Along these lines, the following seems an appropriate outline of the psalm: a plea for a hearing and a judgment from God (verses 1-3), a hymnic, confessional praise of God (verses 4-6), an affirmation of purpose and a commitment to worship (verse 7), a request for help (verse 8), a charge against the accusers (verse 9), a plea for those, including the worshiper, who seek refuge and recourse in God (verse 11), and a statement of confidence and confession (verse 12).

Only the first eight verses of the psalm make up the lection for today. These are primarily concerned with the worshipers' plea for help and affirmation of innocence and fidelity. Verse 3 suggests that the hearing and/or adjudication of the legal case occurred in the morning. The RSV translates part of verse 3b as, "I prepare a sacrifice for thee, and watch." No term for sacrifice occurs in the Hebrew text which could just as easily be translated, "I prepare [make ready] for thee, and watch." The preparation could be the worshipers' self-preparation for the sacred suit and hearing, or even the preparation of the case itself. Thus one could translate, "I prepare my case [or the arguments for the defense] for thee, and watch."

Two further items should be noted, especially with regard

to verse 3. First, the morning was probably the time when cases were heard and verdicts rendered (see II Sam. 15:1-6 where David holds court early in the morning and Ps. 101:8, part of the king's oath of office). This explains the frequent references in the Psalms to salvation and redemption coming in the morning (see Pss. 30:5; 46:5; 49:14). Second, the priests probably handed down the verdict of guilt or innocence as if spoken by the Deity (see Deut. 17:8-13). Part of the accused's ordeal may have been to spend the night and sleep in the temple precincts. Here the priests could observe the individual, and the awesomeness and solemnity of the temple's surroundings may have "forced" the guilty to give up any claims of innocence and confess.

Verses 4-6 spoken as hymnic praise of God was a way that the composer of the psalm had for making an individual participant face the consequences of deliberately pleading innocent when guilty. That is, these verses forced the participants to preach to themselves and condemn themselves if guilty. "The boastful [of their innocence] may not stand . . . thou hatest all evildoers [me if I am guilty]. . . . Thou destroyest those who speak lies [like I would be were I pretending innocence]." Today's worship should provide the occasion for the community and the individuals to confront the reality of who they are just as this psalm did for the ancient Hebrews.

Verse 7 implies an assurance that the one pleading innocence would be allowed to worship, that is, to offer a sacrifice of thanksgiving for deliverance.

Galatians 6:7-18

In these concluding words to the Galatians, Paul makes two moves, one characteristic, the other uncharacteristic. First, in typical fashion he provides concluding instructions consisting of a mixture of scriptural teaching, proverbial wisdom, and concrete moral exhortation (verses 7-10; cf. I Thess. 5:12-21). Second, in untypical fashion, he returns to themes treated earlier in the letter and once again becomes polemical, even caustic as he summarizes his own position once for all (verse 11-18).

Exhortation to generosity (verses 7-10). It should be noted that the verse immediately preceding this section is a call to generosity; students should be generous in sharing their possessions with their teachers (verse 6; cf. I Cor. 9:14; Rom. 15:27). Similarly, the final verse of this section urges us to be generous to believers and unbelievers alike (cf. I Thess. 5:15). There is ample evidence to suggest that early Christians felt responsible for taking care of the physical needs of one another (cf. Acts 2:44-45; 4:32-35; I Tim. 5:8; James 1:27), but here they are urged to look beyond their own circle and extend their generosity to everyone (cf. Rom. 12:20; Gal. 5:14).

We should note that this is the context in which Paul reminds us that we reap what we sow. Taking the immediate context seriously may mean that verses 7-8 have an application that is quite specific and are not to be interpreted as if they state a general principle of the religious life. In any case, Paul cautions us not to be naïve and blind to fundamental religious truths (I Cor. 6:9; 15:33; James 1:16; Luke 21:8). One of the most basic of these truths is that God cannot be duped (cf. Job. 13:9). One of the principles by which God orders life is that we reap what we sow (cf. Job 4:8; 15:35; Prov. 11:18; 22:8; Hos. 8:7).

We are presented here with a choice of sowing in one of two fields. This metaphor is captured especially well in JB: "if he sows in the field of self-indulgence he will get a harvest of corruption out of it; if he sows in the field of the Spirit he will get from it a harvest of eternal life" (verse 8; similarly NEB). The options here are as clear and unequivocal as those set before the Israelites: life or death (Deut. 30:15-20). To sow in the field of the flesh is to pursue the path of self-fulfillment, answering only to the call of the *self,* and we are assured that the life so lived finally turns in on itself and leads to death (cf. Rom. 8:6, 13; Eph. 4:22-24; II Pet. 2:12). By contrast, to cast our seed in the domain of the Spirit is to pursue the path of self-abandonment, refusing to yield to the call of the *self* but answering instead to the call of the Spirit. It is the Spirit who summons us to reach outward beyond ourselves, indeed to transcend ourselves. To do so is really to live, now and finally (Rom. 8:6, 13).

So we are urged not to "grow weary in well-doing" (verse 9; cf. II Thess. 3:13, also II Cor. 4:1, 16). This charge is reminiscent of Jesus' parable of the great judgment (Matt. 25:31-46). Its effect is startling because it calls us to account for failing to perform ordinary acts of kindness. Similarly, Paul's charge recognizes all too well that those concrete acts of generosity that are most obviously Christian are precisely the ones we tend to ignore. They are so obvious we cease to do them.

Postscript (verses 11-18). Even as he signs off, Paul returns to earlier themes with a few summary remarks having the same polemical edge as his earlier discussion. To underscore the importance of these final words, he picks up the stenographer's pen and writes in bold print (verse 11; cf. I Cor. 16:21; Col. 4:18; II Thess. 3:17; Philem. 19).

First, he attacks his opponents for grandstanding (verses 12-13). Their primary motive is "to make a good impression outwardly" (verse 12, NIV). The implication is that they insist on circumcision because it is the most popular and least hazardous course of action (cf. Gal. 5:11; Phil. 3:18). What's more, their behavior is inconsistent; they enforce minute ritual observances, such as circumcision, but they themselves violate the law. They do this either by violating the spirit of the law, or simply by not keeping all the commandments of the law (Rom. 2:21-22). If the latter sense is in view, Paul is assailing them for insisting on perfect obedience to the law when they themselves are unable to deliver in this regard. The final barb Paul tosses at his opponents is that they like to boast in their results. For them, converts are trophies to be waved and not souls to be cared for (verse 13*b*).

Second, he defends his gospel and his own behavior (verses 14-16). In these few verses, we have a remarkably compact summary of Pauline theology. The following motifs are worth noticing:

1. The cross is central (verse 14*a*). The only trophy Paul waved was the crucified Christ (I Cor. 1:18-25; 2:2; Phil. 3:3). This formed the center of his preaching and the center of his life.

2. His life is cruciform (verse 14*b*). Paul had not only

reenacted the crucifixion, he had become a co-participant with Christ in the crucifixion (Gal. 2:20). In doing so, the world and its human outlook had died in him, even as it had been unable to lay any claim on Christ (cf. Rom. 6:5-11).

3. Outward religious performance is nothing; inward religious transformation is everything (verse 15). Religious rituals, such as circumcision, have no value in and of themselves (I Cor. 7:19; Gal. 5:6; Rom. 2:25-26). They are nothing. The performance of a religious act, qua religious act, is a meaningless performance, hollow and devoid of significance. What counts is whether it is in any sense transforming, that is, whether it attests an inner change that results in a new creation (cf. II Cor. 5:17; Rom. 6:4; 12:2; also Rev. 21:5).

4. "New creation," or inner transformation, provides the real clue to our identity before God. Those who see and truly understand this constitute the real "Israel of God" (verse 16), and theirs are the eschatological blessings of peace and mercy (cf. Rom. 2:25-29; 9:6-8; also Ps. 125:5; 128:6).

His penultimate word is a word of warning, if not a threat: "I want no more trouble from anybody after this" (verse 17, JB). His gospel is authenticated through his own apostolic sufferings (II Cor. 4:10; 6:4-5; 11:23-24; Phil. 3:10). The real proof of his gospel is the form of life he lives.

To his credit, Paul concludes the letter with a word of fraternal benediction (verse 18; cf. Phil. 4:23; II Tim. 4:22; Philem. 25).

Luke 10:1-12, 17-20

Jesus sending out seventy, two by two, into those towns and villages where Jesus would later come (10:1) is a report peculiar to Luke. Both Matthew (9:35–10:16) and Mark (6:7-11) record the sending out of the Twelve and some of the instructions parallel Luke 10. However, the differences are striking. Primarily, there is the number, seventy (there is almost equally strong manuscript support for seventy-two). We cannot know if Luke is recalling the seventy nations reported in Genesis 10 (seventy in the Hebrew text, seventy-two in the Greek), or the story of the seventy translators who worked for seventy days to give the Gentiles an Old Testament in their own language (Septuagint), or Moses' selection of seventy elders to be his helpers (Num. 11:16-25). Given Luke's fondness for telling his story with echoes and allusions from the Old Testament, it may be safely assumed that Moses' choice of twelve to represent the twelve tribes (Num. 1:4-16) and then his choice of seventy (Num. 11:16-25) lay in the background of Luke's mind. That Luke is also anticipating the mission to the nations and the day of Pentecost when persons gathered "from every nation under heaven" (Acts 2:5) is also clear. In fact, the Gentiles may already be in mind here in the instruction, "eat what is set before you" (verse 8). Food was a critical issue in the spread of the gospel (Acts 11:1-18; Gal. 2:11-21).

Omitted from today's Gospel lesson are verses 13-16, the pronouncement of woes upon certain cities. Even though such words of judgment may have been appropriate afterward when Jesus and his message had been rejected, they hardly fit into a commissioning service. Matthew places these pronouncements in other contexts. We have, then, two portions for our lection: the sending (verses 1-12) and the return (verses 17-20).

The seventy were sent out in teams of two into those places where Jesus would go later. This practice of sending them as emissaries ahead of him began when Jesus set his face toward Jerusalem (9:51-52), continues here, and will appear again at Jesus' entry into the city of Jerusalem (19:28-34). The reader senses not only preparation for Jesus, but also something magisterial or regal about persons running ahead to announce Christ's coming. The instructions to travel light and to take no time for social amenities (verse 4, perhaps an echo of II Kings 4:29) could reflect the conviction that the end is near and all their work is under the shadow of the eschaton. While that element is not lacking, more likely Luke is continuing consistently the tone of intense single-mindedness begun at 9:51. "He set his face to go to Jerusalem" and resumed in stating the strict demands of those who would become disciples (9:57-62). The missionaries were to depend on the hospitality of their hosts, and were not to go searching about for the best room and board (verse 7). Very likely these instructions reflect the practice of some early Christian groups.

Jesus had been rejected in a Samaritan village, but rather than call down fire upon those villagers, Jesus moved on to other places (9:52-56). So were the missionaries to make brief their rituals of departure, making no pronouncements of doom, but rather letting what had been missed by such persons serve as the judgment (verses 10-11). There will be judgment, but that is a word Jesus speaks (verse 12), not the missionaries. It is also significant that to both receivers and rejecters the message is the same: "The kingdom of God has come near" (verses 9-11). The preachers did not wait to see how they would be treated before preparing their sermons, nor did they have different messages for different groups. Relevance and appropriateness are, of course, vital to preaching, but some aspects of the message are noncontingent.

In some ways, the report of the return of the seventy does not seem to fit the sending. The entire unit centers upon exorcisms (verses 17-20) which were not included in the instructions before the teams went out. Perhaps another problem is being addressed here. Upon hearing the report of the seventy that they were successful exorcists (and according to Luke, Jesus' disciples did exorcise demons, Acts 8:7), Jesus makes three statements. The first (verse 18) confirms that in his and their ministries, the end of Satan's power and the reign of God is present. That Satan dwelt first in heaven is stated elsewhere (Job 1:6; 2:1; John 12:31; Rev. 12:7), and Luke's description of his downfall is probably based on Isaiah 14:12-15. The second statement (verse 19) comes from Psalm 91:13, a reference to the promise to the righteous that they shall reign over all the evil and antagonistic powers that seek to destroy. And the third statement (verse 20) warns against overemphasizing their spiritual gifts. Our chief joy should be, not that we have certain gifts and powers, but that God has received and accepted us. Our names are "written in heaven" (Dan. 12:1; Phil. 4:3; Rev. 3:5; 13:8; 20:15). Luke's warning, though softer, is not unlike Matthew's: "Lord, Lord, did we not prophesy in your name, and cast out demons in your name, and. . . . Depart from me . . ." (7:22-23).

Proper 10

Sunday Between July 10 and 16 Inclusive

II Kings 2:1, 6-14; Psalms 139:1-12; Colossians 1:1-14; Luke 10:25-37

The narrative of his ascension to the other world, as one of only two Old Testament characters who are taken without death (see Gen. 5:21-24), completes the readings about Elijah which began following Trinity Sunday. Already in this material, the attention has shifted to Elisha the successor. The Epistle selection inaugurates a series of readings from the Letter to the Colossians. The psalm reading, a portion of a lament, confesses to the all-knowing character of God, the divine inescapability, portrayed as a knowledge of and concern for the individual self. The Gospel reading, on the other hand, looks outward, to the neighbor, to the other self in need.

II Kings 2:1, 6-14

It is a tale of two prophets, the end of one's career and the beginning of the other's. The atmosphere is heavy with the mysterious and miraculous power of God manifested through these two and worked upon them. Elijah was taken up into heaven in a whirlwind, having used his mantle to divide the waters of the Jordan. That places the emphasis upon the older prophet. But the younger prophet loyally followed his master, actually *saw* him taken up, and also divided the waters of the Jordon with the same mantle. That places the emphasis on Elisha. In the broader literary context in the Books of Kings, the chapter makes the transition from one prophet to the next, but it emphasizes the latter, confirming Elisha as Elijah's successor.

Binding the story together is the account of the journey,

the itinerary of the prophets from Gilgal to Bethel to Jericho, across the Jordan and then—for one of them—back again. Elijah had been a remarkably peripatetic prophet all along. These movements heighten the tension and make what would otherwise be a brief anecdote into a story with a plot, that is, the creation of tension, its resolution, and its results.

The plot does not turn on the question of what will happen to Elijah. From the very beginning we know Elijah's fate, that the old prophet will be taken "up to heaven by a whirlwind" (verse 1). Left in doubt is Elisha's future. The ground is laid for an answer in the account of the journey. At each stopping place, Elijah asks Elisha "to tarry" (verses 2, 4, 6), and in every instance the younger prophet vows not to leave him. Were these requests Elijah's way of testing his successor's stamina and devotion? Their effect is to underscore both Elisha's persistence and his unqualified loyalty to his master.

In the background are the "sons of the prophets" (verse 7), here fifty in number. These were members of the prophetic guild, probably under the leadership of a "father" such as Elijah. The allusion to this group is a clue to the institution that would have been most interested in perpetuating the stories of the miraculous exploits of the great prophets.

But Elisha stands out from all the others. Thematically, there is a link with Elijah's commission on Mount Horeb and his designation of Elisha as his successor, the one to carry out God's will for the house of Ahab (I Kings 19:15-21, see the commentary for Proper 8 in this volume). There, too, Elijah's mantle had played a role. But our text for the day makes no explicit reference to that original encounter between Elijah and his successor. One might think that Elijah has forgotten altogether the Lord's instructions to commission Elisha.

Once the two prophets have crossed the Jordan, a dialogue transpires that is the key to the story (verses 9-10). Elijah, aware that the end is near, invites Elisha to make a final request of him. The request, for "a double share" of his spirit asks a great deal, as Elijah points out. (Although according to Deut. 21:17 a double inheritance is the rule for the eldest son.) So Elijah sets a condition: "*If* you see me as I am being taken from you, it shall be so for you; but if you do not . . ." (verse 10). The climax is thus not the description of the manner of

Elijah's departure in verse 11—at the same time graphic and elusive—but the affirmation in verse 12 that Elisha did, indeed, see it. In its resolution we see the story's question clearly: Will Elisha be the successor of Elijah, one fully endowed with "a double share" of his spirit? The presence of that spirit is confirmed when Elisha divides the Jordan with the mantle, just as Elijah had.

Several specific points in the story call for comment. When Elisha cries out to Elijah, "My father, my father! The chariots of Israel and its horesemen," he is using two titles. The first, "my father," indicating respect and affection, stems from his role in relation to the prophetic groups. The second, with its reference to military might, also is applied to Elisha when he is about to die (II Kings 13:15). The phenomena that attend the prophet's ascension suggest both disruptions in nature (whirlwind, fire) and military imagery. They recall the theophany to the prophet on Mount Horeb (I Kings 19). Some aspects of the story parallel the Moses traditions: the parting of the waters and the fact that both Moses and Elijah meet their ends beyond the Jordan and leave to their successors the completion of their tasks.

As there is continuity of authority and power between Elijah and Elisha, so there are contrasts. The former is a solitary individual, always at odds with the royal household. The latter will always seem to have others—prophets, kings, soldiers—around him. He will intervene directly in the political arena, bringing about the destruction of the house of Ahab that Elijah prophesied. Finally, Elisha, even with a double share of his master's spirit, will die an ordinary death.

Psalm 139:1-12

Psalm 139, or portions thereof, is used for two consecutive Sundays. The psalm appears to be a composition produced for use in legal procedures in the temple, when an individual was charged, perhaps falsely, with some particular wrong or crime (see the discussion of Ps. 5:1-8 in Proper 9). In Psalm 139, the wrong appears to be some form of idolatry or turning away from Yahweh the God of Israel. This is suggested by three factors: (1) there is no indication in the psalm of charges about injury or wrong done to humans; (2) the "wicked way" (verse 24) or, in some readings of the Hebrew text, "idolatrous way," suggests apostasy or false worship as the problem; and (3) the plea for action by God in verses 19-24, especially verses 19-22, focuses attention on those who defy God, lift themselves up against him, and hate him, which demonstrates the concern for the proper relationship to the Deity as the focus of the psalm.

The psalm is best understood as the lament of one who feels unduly and falsely accused of infidelity to God. Verses 1-18 speak about the Deity's knowledge of the worshiper, while verses 19-24 are a call for God to judge and slay the wicked. Thus the latter verses would have functioned as one's self-curse if the person praying them fit the category of those upon whom the judgment is requested. At the same time, verses 21-22 are also an affirmation of the worshiper's innocence. The worshiper can claim to hate, with a perfect (or utter) hatred, those who hate God. Although such an expression may shock our sophisticated sensibilities, it was a way of expressing devotion to God, championing the divine cause, and placing oneself squarely in God's camp. Under these circumstances such extravagance in terminology would have been expected in ancient cultures.

Verses 1-18 all speak of or confess the knowledge which God has of the human/individual situation. (Note that the entire psalm is human speech to the Divine; that is, prayer.) Verses 1-6 describe the *insight* God has into the life of the individual. Verses 7-12 describe the divine *oversight* which God has of the individual life. Verses 13-18, the lection for next Sunday, speak of the divine *foresight* which God has over the person from conception to death. In a way, all these sections seek to say the same thing by approaching the matter from different perspectives or slightly different angles. The reason for such extensive coverage of the topic of God's knowledge of the individual is the fact that the supplicant in the legal case was claiming innocence, and one way to do this was to point to the omniscience of God. Had anything been amiss, were there any infidelity, then the Deity would surely have known and taken action.

The insight which God is said to have into the person in

verses 1-5 is expressed in a number of ways, mostly in the form of opposites: sitting down—rising up (inactive—active): inward thoughts—from afar; my path (where I go, my walking)—my lying down (where I rest, my reclining); behind—before. All these are ways of saying that persons in the totality of their behavior are known to God. Even the thought, before it finds expression on the tongue, in words, is known (verse 4). The knowledge of God, the psalmist confesses, is a fathomless mystery (verse 6).

Verses 7-12 affirm that there is no escaping the Deity whose presence (= Spirit) knows no limits and is not subject to the normal conditions of existence. A number of geographical metaphors, again in opposites, are employed to illustrate the point: heaven—Sheol; winds of the morning (to the east) —uttermost parts of the sea (to the western horizon). In all these places, the psalmist says he would find God (see Amos 9:2), or be found by God. The psalm, however, not only affirms the all-pervasive knowledge and oversight of God, but also the universal sustaining quality of the Divine—"Thy hand shall lead me, and thy right hand shall hold me."

For the Divine, according to the psalmist, normal conditions do not prevail. Verse 11 makes this point, a point best expressed in the new NJPSV which, following medieval Jewish exegetes, translates: "If I say, 'Surely darkness will conceal me, night will provide me with cover,'" then darkness does not conceal since for God light and darkness do not determine or set limits regarding knowledge.

Colossians 1:1-14

With this text begins the semicontinuous reading of the Epistle to the Colossians. It is the first of four passages to be read over the next four weeks.

This particular pericope overlaps with the epistolary text for All Saints Day (November 1) in Year B (Col. 1:9-14), and the reader may wish to consult our remarks on this passage in *Year B, After Pentecost*. It also partially overlaps the epistolary text for Proper 29 (Christ the King) in Year C (Col. 1:11-20), treated later in this volume.

Since the Epistle to the Colossians will provide the

epistolary readings for the next four weeks, a few introductory remarks are in order here. Even though the Pauline authorship of this letter is disputed, it stands closer in tone and content to the genuine Pauline letters than do the other disputed Pauline letters, such as Ephesians. It addresses a church which Paul had neither established nor visited, but one started and nurtured by Epaphras, a devoted co-worker of Paul (1:7; 4:12).

The letter is written in response to the threat of false teaching which seems to have consisted of syncretistic, speculative, perhaps even Gnostic elements (2:16, 18, 20-23). Even though we do not know the exact details of the heresy, such as where, how, and with whom it originated, its potential threat was clear. It threatened the unique supremacy of Christ and tended to make of him one among several heavenly figures in the angelic hierarchy. In response to this threat to the supremacy of Christ, the letter presents us with a bold statement of the preeminent superiority and uniqueness of Christ (cf. esp. 1:15-20).

Today's epistolary lection represents the opening section of the Epistle to the Colossians and consists of two parts: the greeting (verses 1-2) and the prayer of thanksgiving (verses 3-14).

Greeting (verses 1-2). The greeting is quite typical of other opening salutations in the Pauline letters (cf. Rom. 1:1; I Cor. 1:1; II Cor. 1:1; also Eph. 1:1; II Tim. 1:1). One of the remarkable features is that here, as elsewhere when he is facing a situation threatened by competitive teaching, he underscores his status as apostle. Similarly, the twofold prayer of grace and peace (verse 2) is quite typical (cf. Rom. 1:7; I Cor. 1:2; II Cor. 1:2; Gal. 1:3; Eph. 1:2; Phil. 1:2; Philem. 3; I Thess. 1:1; II Thess. 1:2).

Prayer of Thanksgiving (verses 3-14). Typically, the opening prayers of the Pauline letters do two things: (1) set the tone of the letter and (2) telegraph to the reader some of the major concerns to be dealt with in the letter (cf. Rom. 1:8-17; I Cor. 1:4-9; II Cor. 1:3-7; Phil. 1:3-11; I Thess. 1:2; 2:13; 3:9; II Thess. 1:3-12; Philem. 4-7). Here, the tone is hopeful and reassuring, as Paul seeks to shore up the faith of a relatively young church. The reference to knowledge, spiritual wisdom and understanding (verse 9) already anticipates later themes (cf. 2:2-3). Also, the opening prayer concludes by pointing to the work of Christ in our redemption (verses 13-14), and this too begins to prepare us for the rich christological sections of the letter (cf. 1:15-20, 27-28; 2:2-3).

In this opening prayer, Paul first recalls the Colossians' life in Christ, and does so in terms of a triad of Christian experiences: their faith in Christ, that is their conversion; their love for all their saints, probably their genuine sense of community and willingness to share their possessions; and their eschatological hope which gave them direction (verses 4-5). These three foci of Christian experience, in varying orders, are often employed by Paul in teaching his churches (cf. I Thess. 1:3; 5:8; I Cor. 13:7, 13; Gal. 5:5-6; Rom. 5:1-5; 12:6-12; also Eph. 1:15-18; 4:2-5; I Tim. 6:11; Tit. 2:2; cf. also Heb. 6:10-12; 10:22-24; I Pet. 1:3-9). In other cases, they occur in pairs: faith and love (I Thess. 3:6; II Thess. 1:3; Philem. 5); faith and hope (II Thess. 1:4); hope and love (II Thess. 3:5; cf. II Cor. 13:13). What's important to notice here is that the manifestation of this Christian triangle among the Colossians is an occasion of ceaseless thanksgiving (verses 3, 9; cf. Eph. 1:14-15; Philem. 4-5).

Second, he recalls how they only recently came to the faith: "It is only recently that you heard of this" (verse 5, JB). But it is important for them to know that the "message of the truth" (cf. Eph. 1:13; II Cor. 6:7; James 1:18; II Tim. 2:15) sounded in them had also echoed through them, and beyond "in the whole world" (verse 6; cf. 1:23; also I Tim. 3:16). The vital link in their faith was provided by Epaphras from whom they had learned the faith (verse 7), who served as their emissary to Paul (verse 7), and whose love for them continued unabated. He had also endeared himself to other churches in the region (4:12-13; cf. Philem. 23).

Third, he prays for the Colossians to grow in their capacity for spiritual wisdom and discernment, especially as it pertains to the will of God (verses 9-10; cf. Rom. 2:18; Eph. 5:17; Acts 22:14; James 4:17; II Pet. 2:21; also Luke 12:47). Coming to proper knowledge of God and growing in that knowledge are part and parcel of the Christian experience (cf. Phil. 1:9; Philem. 6; I Tim. 2:4; 4:3; II Tim. 2:25; 3:7; Tit. 1:1;

Heb. 10:26; II John 1). And yet it is not that we seek knowledge for the sake of knowledge, but rather discernment in knowing how "to lead a life worthy of the Lord" (verse 10; cf. I Thess. 2:12; Phil. 1:27; Eph. 4:1). This means, among other things, "bearing fruit in every good work" (verse 10; cf. Rom. 7:4; II Cor. 9:8; Eph. 2:10; II Thess. 2:17; II Tim. 3:17; Tit. 2:14; also Mark 4:8, 20).

Fourth, he prays for them to receive spiritual strength to be supplied by God (verse 11; Eph. 1:11-19; 3:16; cf. Acts 20:32; 26:18). It is God, after all, who has granted us a share in the eternal inheritance with the saints and has transferred us from the realm of darkness into the realm of light (verse 13; cf. I Thess. 5:4-5; also Luke 22:53). The one in whom our redemption and forgiveness is possible is Christ (verse 14; cf. Rom. 3:24; 8:23; I Cor. 1:30; Eph. 1:6, 7, 14; 4:30; also Ps. 130:7).

Luke 10:25-37

Again we have a lesson from Luke which has partial parallels in Mark and Matthew but which is sufficiently different in form and location (both geographical and literary) to raise the question whether Luke had another source or perhaps had done major editing. Apart from the parable of the good Samaritan which is Luke's alone, the story has parallels in Mark 12:28-31 and Matthew 22:34-40. Mark and Luke set their stories in Jerusalem, in the closing days of Jesus' ministry and in a series of controversies between Jesus and various opponents. Interestingly, at that point in his Gospel, Luke follows Mark but omits this one episode since he had placed his version of it earlier in the travel narrative. In Mark, the questioner is a scribe; in Matthew, a lawyer. In both the question has to do with the greatest commandment and in both, Jesus supplies the answer, complete love of God and love of neighbor (Deut. 6:5; Lev. 19:18). Luke's lawyer asks, "What shall I do to inherit eternal life?" and Jesus has him supply the answer to his own question.

The preacher will want to notice the symmetry in Luke's combination of the conversation between Jesus and the lawyer (verses 25-29) and the extension of that conversation to include the parable of the good Samaritan (verses 29-37). In the first unit, the lawyer asks a question, Jesus responds with a question, the lawyer responds with an answer, and Jesus does likewise. In the second unit, the lawyer asks a question, Jesus responds with a question following the parable, the lawyer answers, and so does Jesus. The questions are important and so are the answers, but Luke's Jesus makes it doubly clear that the kingdom of God is not a discussion, even between two leaders. Twice Jesus says *do* what you know (verses 28, 37). It was not more information that the lawyer needed; rather it was action on his own understanding.

It is evident that the conversation between the two is treated by Luke as the occasion to introduce the parable. The parable itself (verses 30-35) focuses not on both love of God and love of neighbor but on love of neighbor. This is not an isolated instance. Twice Paul said the whole of the law was summed up in the command to love one's neighbor as oneself (Rom. 13:8-9; Gal. 5:14). It is important to notice that the parable and Jesus' question following do not directly answer the lawyer's question. To ask, "Who is my neighbor?" is to ask for a definition of the object and extent of love. Jesus' question as to who proved himself to be a neighbor shifts the attention to the kind of person one is to be rather than to those who are or who are not one's neighbors. This shift need not be understood to mean the parable originally addressed another question and has been set in at this point rather awkwardly by Luke. The question of Jesus lies outside the parable itself (verse 36; the parable ends at verse 35) and is Jesus' corrective to an improper question.

Most likely the parable is one Luke received and, therefore, one might ask, What was its original purpose? or To whom was it addressed? The story assumes its hearers know about priests, Levites, and Samaritans. It also assumes the hearers know the bitter tension between Jews and Samaritans (John 4:9). The Samaritans were descendants of a mixed population occupying the land following conquest by Assyria in 722 B.C. In the days of Ezra and Nehemiah the Samaritans opposed rebuilding Jerusalem and the temple (Ezra 4:2-5; Neh. 2:19).

The Samaritans built their own place of worship on Mount Gerizim. Against such a background of enmity, to have characterized the Samaritan rather than the priest or Levite as the one who proved to be a neighbor must have been to its first audience a shocking turn in the story, shattering their categories of who are and who are not the people of God. For Luke and Luke's church it now serves as an example story to the effect that kingdom people are to act in love, love that has no drawn boundaries, and love which expects no recompense.

Proper 11

Sunday Between July 17 and 23 Inclusive

II Kings 4:8-17; Psalm 139:13-18; Colossians 1:21-29; Luke 10:38-42

The Old Testament and the Gospel lections have in common the theme of hospitality, especially the hospitality of women to men of God. Elisha is the guest of the Shunammite woman and her husband, and the setting for the saying of Jesus is Martha's house where he is a guest. The responsorial psalm, continuing from the one for last week, is the part of a song of lament that gives reasons for God to listen to the petition. It responds to the first reading in its affirmation of life and its meditation on God's knowledge of the psalmist even before he was born. The epistolary reading seems to have no direct links with the other texts.

II Kings 4:8-17

The reading for the day is part of one of four very similar stories of the prophet Elisha in II Kings 4. All of them are accounts of the prophet's miraculous intervention in some situation of human need. The others are the widow's oil (verses 1-7), the purification of the poisonous pot of food (verses 38-41), and the feeding of the crowd (verses 42-44). All are miracle stories, each revealing the power of this man of God. They are part of an old folklore tradition and were doubtless circulated among those very prophetic groups mentioned so frequently in the Elisha narratives. In the broader scheme of the Book of Second Kings, they were set here to demonstrate that the prophet who is to overthrow kings has the authorization of the spirit of the Lord.

The style and mood of the tales of Elisha are different from the collection of stories about Elijah. The quality of Elisha's miracles is more dramatic, and he seems never to be alone but always with prophetic followers and others who witness his powers. Most of the stories are more elaborate and detailed, the narrators dwelling upon details of description and action.

Second Kings 4:8-17 records the first of two miracles performed on behalf of the Shunammite woman. Our reading for the day reports the unexpected gift of a son, and verses 18-37 tell how Elisha revived the boy after he had died. The latter story is a close parallel to that of Elijah's revival of the son of the woman of Zarephath (I Kings 17:17-24; see the commentary on Proper 5 in this volume). In each instance the woman accuses the prophet of responsibility for the trouble and he restores the child to life. The events should not be described as resurrection but resuscitation, for presumably the children will still die one day.

The story of Elisha and the Shunammite woman tells of hospitality, generosity, and gifts that are unbidden and unexpected. The plot turns on the question of how the prophet can repay an act of kindness. Verses 8-11 set the scene. We learn of a wealthy and generous woman who regularly invited Elisha in for a meal whenever he passed through. Apparently a relationship of friendship and respect grew, so she, seeing the prophet's need, discusses the matter with her husband and they prepare a special guest room for his use when he is in the area. The charming details of the description of the "roof chamber"—"with walls"(!), a bed, table, chair, and a lamp (verse 10)—reveal her solicitous concern for his comfort.

Such concern should not go unrewarded, so Elisha instructs his servant Gehazi to ask what he can do for the woman. Remember, we already know that her needs are few, for she is wealthy. Perhaps Elisha could use his influence with the king or the commander of the army. We can only guess at the meaning of this suggestion, but it may refer to royal patronage, special protection, or relief from taxes. But she says she has no needs. Not only does she have sufficient wealth, but she has the support and protection of her clan (verse 13). Then Gehazi hits upon a solution. The woman has no son, and her husband is too old to provide her with one. She had not asked because she knew such a gift was impossible, and—like Sarah in her old age (Gen. 18:9-15)—is incredulous when the promise comes (verse 16). But it happens as Elisha had said it would. The solemn word of the prophet set the events into motion.

What should we do with such a story as this in the context of Christian worship? To rationalize away the miraculous is to deprive the text of its power to stimulate the awareness and expectations of the hearers. We, like the hearers in ancient Israel, are meant to be impressed and to be astounded. While the human characters are front and center, it is the word of the Lord that is effective. One who was hospitable receives a gift, a gift not asked for or expected. It is a gift of life. We may hear the story as a parable of the kingdom. The reign of God is like this, that people welcome one another with concern, and life is the result.

Psalm 139:13-18

As we noted in discussing the psalm reading for last Sunday, Psalm 139 was probably originally used by persons affirming their innocence in a religious trial at the sanctuary after being charged with or accused of some form of religious apostasy or malpractice. As part of the accused's claim of innocence, the psalm calls attention to the many forms that God's knowledge of the individual takes. The author of the psalm—probably most of the psalms were written by members of the priesthood for use in worship—perhaps saw two main functions for this stress on divine knowledge. First, it could force a crisis of conscience on the participant, who, though guilty, was claiming innocence. If she/he had to confess that God knew everything and was familiar with every nook and cranny of a person's life, then the guilty one had to realize that "God knows my sin already." Second, for the innocent, it allowed them to assert their innocence in the strongest possible terms. If there was divine all-knowing familiarity with the worshiper and there was no overt indication of divine judgment and displeasure, then surely the supplicant must be innocent.

Verses 13-18, built on the basis of a theology of creation, stress the divine foresight which God has of the individual from conception to death. God is described as aware of the mystery and manner of the formation of the embryo in the womb (verses 13-15). The process of the development of the child in the womb is described in various ways in the Old Testament. Here God knits together the person. In Jeremiah 1:5*a* the terminology is "formed . . . in the womb." Job 10:10-11 speaks of the process in this way:

> Didst thou not pour me out like milk
> and curdle me like cheese?
> Thou didst clothe me with skin and flesh,
> and knit me together with bones and sinews.

The points the psalmist makes in this context are:

1. God has a knowledge of human origins—"in my mother's womb," "in secret," "in the depths of the earth" (a poetic circumlocution?)—that transcends any other. The divine knows what humans may only speculate about.

2. God is the creator of the individual person. While other biblical texts emphasize divine creation of the cosmos, here the focus is on the microcosm, the individual person.

3. Such knowledge and such creative power mean that God and his works are fearful and wonderful. (The NJPSV in verse 14 reads: "I praise You, for I am awesomely, wondrously made.")

According to the common understanding of the text, verse 16 indicates that before birth God has already foreordained the course of the individual human life. Before the formation of the embryo, God is said to have written in a book the days allotted to the person. (This seems the most natural interpretation of the text, over against an interpretation that sees the nature and members of the unborn child being predetermined.) For other references to the divine book, see Psalms 40:7; 69:28.

God's thoughts—his knowledge—are more numerous than the sand. From him, the guilty cannot hide.

Colossians 1:21-29

Today's epistolary text follows directly upon the magnificent hymn in which Christ is praised as the head of the created order (verses 15-20). When Christ's work is unfolded in terms so dramatic and overwhelming, the difficulty we face is linking ourselves to this heavenly drama. This is precisely the move that is made in our text today, and it is done in two respects: in terms of (1) the readers themselves (verses 21-23), and (2) Paul's own ministry (verses 24-29).

The Impact of Christ on the Church (verses 21-23). First, the Colossian church is portrayed as the community of faith in which reconciliation has occurred. The focus here is congregational: the "you" of these verses refers to the "saints and faithful brethren in Christ at Colossae" (1:2). Paul's remarks here are congregation specific. This is worth noting since we often tend to think of God's work in Christ in terms of the church universal instead of the church local. And yet, here we are reminded that the divine drama takes concrete form within local congregations of believers, even though we all know how ordinary congregational life can be. Like Christ's own incarnation, the ordinary provides the arena in which the incarnation of the gospel occurs.

Our text provides one of the most natural ways for us to establish our identity as a church: contrasting what we once were with what we now are, with Christ as the pivot of change. This form of comparison—once you were but now you are—seems to have been one of the standard forms of early Christian teaching and preaching. On the one side, our past predicament is sketched in terms cold and distant: estrangement, alienation, and hostility (cf. Eph. 2:12-13; 4:18-19; Rom. 5:10; II Cor. 5:18). It was a life of doing evil (cf. John 3:19; 7:7). Our new status, however, is sketched in cultic and forensic terms: holy, unblemished, and unaccused (verse 22; cf. Eph. 1:4; 5:27; I Cor. 1:8; I Tim. 3:10; Tit. 1:6-7).

And how has this radical change occurred? Through reconciliation made possible "by Christ's physical body through death" (verse 22, NIV). Though the syntax is ambiguous, it is God who is the agent of reconciliation (cf. II Cor. 5:18). We should note the stress on Christ's "body of flesh" as the locus of reconciliation. The Gnostic tendency would have been to de-emphasize, even deny, that salvation could have been mediated through Jesus' flesh. The emphasis in the letter on the bodily form of Jesus is in keeping with more orthodox Christian teaching (cf. Rom. 1:3; 8:3; 9:5; II Cor. 5:16-21; Eph. 2:14-15; Col. 2:9, 11; I Tim. 3:16; John 1:14).

Their faith is conditional, however. It requires steadfastness and constant adherence to the gospel (cf. I Cor. 15:58; Eph. 3:17). Even though the gospel was experienced locally, it is universal, having "been preached to every creature under heaven" (verse 23). This is the language of hyperbole, but does underscore the far-reaching impact of the gospel, at least in the eyes of its own proponents (cf. 1:6; Rom. 8:19-20; I Tim. 3:16; Acts 2:5; Mark 16:15).

The Impact of Christ on Paul (verses 24-29). This passage would most naturally extend through 2:5, but even so our text provides intriguing insight to Paul's apostolic self-understanding.

We are struck by the way in which he conceives his apostolic suffering: "In my flesh I complete what is lacking in Christ's afflictions for the sake of his body" (verse 24). He clearly envisions Christ's own suffering as continuing into the life of the church, not as having ceased with his death on the cross. Moreover, he clearly envisions the suffering he undergoes in behalf of his churches as a continuation, in some sense, of Christ's own suffering (cf. 2:1; II Cor. 1:5; Phil. 1:20; Eph. 3:13; also II Tim. 2:20; Acts 9:16). We should probably understand this in terms of the way in which the messianic age was envisioned as a time of tribulation (Matt. 24:8; Acts 14:22). In this sense, the physical suffering of the crucified Christ merely launched a period in which the risen Christ would continue to be identified with those who became members of his body, the church (1:18; Eph. 1:23; 4:12; also Rom. 12:5). Accordingly, the suffering of Christ continues in the suffering experienced by his messengers and the members of his body. It gives us pause to think of Christ so closely identified with his own that his own suffering continues even in his exalted status as Lord.

Christ also becomes the center of Paul's apostolic commission. His call was made through divine appointment (I Cor. 4:1; 9:17; Rom. 15:15-16; also Eph. 3:2, 7). His special commission was to reveal the "mystery hidden for ages" (2:2; cf. Rom. 16:25-26; Eph. 1:9; 3:3-4, 9; I Pet. 1:20), namely that the Gentiles would have a full share in God's salvation (Eph. 3:1-6). The church has become the community in which this mystery is unfolded (Eph. 3:5, 10), and is to be understood as the locus of the presence of Christ, "which is Christ in you, the hope of glory" (verse 27; cf. Rom. 8:10; Gal. 2:20; II Cor. 13:5; John 17:23).

For this reason, Christ forms the center of Paul's apostolic proclamation (verse 28). His hope is that eventually everyone who is "in Christ" will finally become "perfect in Christ" (1:22; 4:12; I Cor. 2:6; 3:1, 18; Phil. 3:15; Eph. 4:13). Here we are called to a level of maturation and formation for which Christ serves as the measure. To bring people to this form of identification with Christ, Paul labors and strives, "helped only by his power driving me irresistibly" (verse 29, JB; cf. 2:1; 4:12; Eph. 3:7, 20; Phil. 4:13; II Thess. 1:11).

Luke 10:38-42

Practically everyone who reads or hears the story of Jesus as dinner guest in the home of Martha and Mary is drawn to the simplicity, the personal interest, the realism, and the ease of identification with one of the sisters. No wonder preachers love it; in a sense it preaches itself in the mere telling.

However, preachers must beware of seduction by apparently easy sermons. Some work needs to be done. Only Luke tells this story, but John joins him in knowing Martha and Mary. John knows them as sisters of Lazarus and locates their home in Bethany (11:1; 12:1-3). Upon the death of Lazarus and also at the dinner for Jesus in their home, their behavior is not unlike that described by Luke: Martha first goes out to meet Jesus while Mary sits in the house (11:20), and at the dinner, Martha serves and Mary anoints the feet of Jesus (12:1-3). In Luke, Mary sits at the feet of Jesus (10:39). The two writers pose a minor geographical problem for the reader, however, in that John locates them in Bethany near Jerusalem while Luke's travel narrative seems to have Jesus on his way to Jerusalem but at this point still in Galilee. Our text also contains a textual problem. Manuscripts are divided on verse 42: "one thing is needful" or "few things are needful, or only one." If the latter is the correct reading,

Jesus is probably telling Martha she is preparing too many dishes; if the former, he is saying that the word of God and not food is the one thing needed. Very likely, this is the point: we do not live by bread alone but by every word that proceeds from the mouth of the Lord (Deut. 8:3; Luke 4:4; John 6:27). If Jesus seems a bit harsh with Martha, it should be remembered that this story follows the sharp turn toward Jerusalem in 9:51, after which Jesus' words to the disciples are rigorous and demanding. The cross awaits all of them on down the road.

The story is a radical one if one notices how Jesus breaks through the social barriers of his time. Jesus is received as a guest in the home of women (Luke does not know or, at least, does not mention a brother). And Jesus teaches a woman. Rabbis did not allow women to "sit at their feet," and yet Mary is clearly pictured here as a disciple. In this regard the episode accords well with Luke's earlier statement about women in 8:1-3. In telling the story, the preacher will want to be careful with the details: it is Martha's house, she received Jesus into her home, and the whole story centers on her and Jesus. She has a sister, Mary, who is described but who never speaks or enters otherwise into the action.

The preacher can be easily drawn into allegorizing the sisters: Martha, the model of the active and busy Christian worker; Mary, the model of the contemplative and reflective Christian. Such portraits can be overdrawn. Perhaps more fruitful might be a consideration of Luke's location of this story. It follows immediately the parable of the good Samaritan and Jesus' injunction, "Go and do likewise" (verse 37). Now Jesus affirms and blesses not going and doing but sitting still and listening. Side by side Luke has placed occasions on which Jesus called for active engagement with human need and being still, listening, and learning. Luke is not making a choice between them nor is he asking the reader to accept one and reject the other. Both the Samaritan and Mary are examples, and both are to be emulated. The burden lies in discerning when to do the one and when to do the other. The Christian life involves, among other things, a sense of timing.

Proper 12

Sunday Between July 24 and 30 Inclusive

*II Kings 5:1-15*ab; *Psalm 21:1-7; Colossians 2:6-15; Luke 11:1-13*

The Old Testament reading reports another of Elisha's miraculous acts, the healing of Naaman, and calls attention to his confession of faith in Israel's God. The responsorial psalm, a king's song of thanksgiving, is a highly appropriate response to an act of divine help for one in trouble. The epistolary text focuses upon faith and its alternatives. The Gospel reading concerning prayer relates to Naaman's eagerness to ask a foreign prophet—and his God—for help, and his reactions to Elisha's instructions, first with reluctance and then with obedience.

II Kings 5:1-15*ab*

This passage is a straightforward story that moves rapidly from beginning to end, but it is by no means simple. Events transpire on several levels. In its characterizations, its allusions to circumstances, and in its unfolding of the plot at least three distinct motifs present themselves. Moreover, while the text can be read as a more-or-less self-contained unit, it takes on new dimensions when seen in the light of its sequel, the remainder of II Kings 5.

First of all, like the accounts in II Kings 4, we have a story of Elisha's miraculous powers, manifest in this case in the healing of a leper. The first scene, which introduces the problem and the main character—other than Elisha, of course—takes place in Syria (verses 1-5*a*). Naaman, a powerful commander of the army and highly regarded by his king, is a leper. As in last week's Old Testament text, the person in need does not ask for help but a third party proposes that the prophet can remedy the situation. In this case it is an Israelite slave girl who serves Naaman's wife. When the commander tells his king what he has heard, the king sends him off to Israel with a letter of introduction. Setting out loaded down with wealth—presumably to pay the prophet—Naaman presents the letter to the king of Israel. The king is fearful and suspicious, thinking that the Syrian king has made an impossible request so that failure to comply will be a pretext for war (verses 5b-7).

But then Elisha, who only now (verse 8) is identified by name, intervenes. Messages go back and forth. He tells his king to send Naaman to him, and the commander rides up in all his splendor. The prophet does not meet Naaman directly, but sends instructions for him to wash himself seven times in the Jordan. This behavior and these too-simple and unexpected instructions infuriate the leper, who knows what kind of healing ritual to expect from a holy man (verse 11). Moreover, he has rivers in his homeland. When the servant persuades Naaman to do as instructed, he is immediately healed (verse 14).

We, like the ancient hearers, are expected to acknowledge that the power of the Lord is manifest in and through a special individual, and that this power works for health. Although the Elisha stories in their eagerness to glorify the prophet sometimes obscure the point, here it is clear that the power to heal belongs to God alone (verse 7).

Second, there is the theme of the needy foreigner, the one who, from Israel's perspective, is an outsider. Through much of their history, Israel and Syria were enemies. The allusion to the Israelite slave girl recalls military conflicts, as does the Israelite king's fear when he hears the letter from his counterpart in Damascus (verse 7). Nationalistic pride rears its head when Naaman speaks disdainfully about the Jordan in contrast to the "rivers of Damascus" (verse 12). But the Israelite prophet heals the foreign general, anticipating a point that will recur over and over in the Gospels, when outsiders—tax collectors and sinners and foreigners, including Roman soldiers—come to Jesus and he accepts and heals them. Here we have at least a hint that Israel's faith has the capacity to cross boundaries, to be inclusive. The point is even more emphatic when one considers the sequel to the story (II Kings 5:19-27). Gehazi, Elisha's Israelite servant, extorts money from the generous Naaman, and is cursed with leprosy. The "great man" has become genuinely great in bowing before Elisha, and Elisha's follower has been shown to be guilty of greed.

The third and central theme concerns faith. At issue throughout is neither the authority of the prophet nor his power to heal, but the human response to the disclosure of that power. The Israelite king's lament in verse 7 begins to introduce the issue of confession, and Naaman is called upon to trust in the power of the God of Elisha (verses 1-12). Suspense is created while we await his response. Will he return home, taking his leprosy with him, when health is so near? Finally, he takes a chance. The high point of the story is not the restoration of his flesh, the hearers had known all along that this would be the result. It is, rather, the confession, "Behold, I know that there is no God in all the earth but in Israel" (verse 15). That is the story's goal. Miraculous healing is, to be sure, for the health of the sick person, but it is also for the purpose of revelation, to make known, even to outsiders, who God is.

Psalm 21:1-7

Many of the psalms were originally composed for temple services in which the Hebrew king was the center of attention. These so-called royal psalms were utilized on various occasions and under differing circumstances. The king's coronation and its annual anniversary celebration were special times in which there was focus on the king's relationship to the Deity, to the nations of the world, and to the responsibilities of national government (see Pss 2; 72; 89; 101; 110).

Psalm 21 was composed for use in worship services held in conjunction with the king's engagement in warfare, or in celebration of his military power. The psalm consists of two basic units. Both take the form of speeches. The first is an address to God and thus a prayer (verses 1-6). Though this section extols the king's reliance upon God, it, above all, reiterates what God has given the king. (If the Hebrew king was present when the prayer was offered, as must have been the case, then the statements of the prayer would have served as words of encouragement to him.) The second unit in the psalm is an address to the king assuring him that God will give him victory and triumph over his enemies and describing the manner of his enemies' destruction (verses 8-12). Verses 7 and 13 appear to be communal or choral responses to the addresses.

Today's lection includes only the first address, namely, the people's speech or address to the Deity. These verses emphasize the Hebrew monarch's reliance upon God, that is, they tend to praise God (the divine king) rather than the Davidic monarch (the earthly king). God is the king's King, the monarch's Monarch. The following points are all noted about the God-king relationship: (1) The king's joy and celebration of his status are really a celebration of God's strength and help (verse 1). The king's strength is thus a manifestation or expression of Yahweh's strength. (2) The king has been treated with special favor, receiving from God his desires and requests (verse 2), although we are not told what these desires and requests were (see Ps. 2:8; I Kings 3:5). (3) The king is the recipient of special blessings and wears a golden crown (verse 3). (4) The king is the special recipient of long life (verse 4). The last part of this verse would suggest that the king was granted immortality—"length of days for ever and ever"—but we are here dealing with court expressions that are not to be taken literally (see Ps. 72:5, 17). (5) The king possesses a reputation and lives in splendor and majesty, that is, above that of the ordinary individual (verse 5). The status claimed by the king is undergirded here by divine justification or divine right. The king must show forth a glory to demonstrate his state of blessedness. (6) Joy is seen as the sign of divine presence (verse 6).

Verse 7 breaks the pattern of address to the divine and speaks of the Deity in the third person. With this shift, the psalm composer moves to proclamation to the king, a little preaching to the royalty, if you please. The king is here said to be (and thus called to be) one who trusts in Yahweh and is immovable.

Colossians 2:6-15

It may be obvious to us that Christ should be the ordering principle of our lives, but it was not to the Colossians. If Christ is merely another member of the angelic hierarchy, as the false teachers apparently claimed, we can see why Paul would need to convince the Colossians to make Christ the sole basis for their lives.

We can consider today's lection in two parts: (1) Paul's appeal for his readers to live according to Christ (verses 6-8) and (2) the basis for the appeal (verses 9-15).

The Appeal (verses 6-8). The appeal has two parts, one positive, the other negative. Positively, Paul urges that the Christ whom we have received should be the Christ in whom we establish our complete identity (verses 6-7). Negatively, he warns against being seduced by systems of thought that are humanly construed and exclude Christ (verse 8).

Before any appeal is made, we are reminded that the fundamental reality is our confession of faith in "Christ Jesus the Lord" (verse 6; Rom. 10:9; I Cor. 12:3; II Cor. 4:5; Phil. 2:13). In accepting the gospel as more than mere human word, indeed as the summons of God (I Thess. 2:13), we receive Christ not only in the sense that we accept the message about him as true but also in the sense that we appropriate him as a living reality (cf. Eph. 4:21).

For this reason, it is possible to "live in him" (verse 6). He becomes the prime Reality in which we establish our identity, the sphere in which we live, the One in whom our lives begin to make sense. Christian existence is existence "in Christ" (II Cor. 5:17). This is where the new creation occurs. With Christ as the One in whom we live, he becomes the trunk in which we are rooted (Eph. 3:17; cf. John 15:1-11) and the foundation on which we build (Eph. 2:20, 22; Jude 20). This occurs as we grow in our knowledge of the faith (II Thess. 2:15), and it becomes an occasion of thanksgiving.

But there will always be competing Christs. We are warned against being seduced by "some secondhand, empty, rational philosophy based on the principles of this world instead of on Christ" (verse 8, JB). This is doubtless Paul's slap at the false teachers in Colossae. The implication is that their religious system was a loosely connected amalgam of quasi-philosophical ideas mixed with cosmic speculation, which was finally devoid of any serious content (cf. Eph. 4:14; 5:6). It becomes clear from our text that, for Paul, Christ must provide the fundamental reference point for any philosophical position or world view that attempts to make sense of reality.

The Basis for the Appeal (verses 9-15). And what is the basis for such an all-encompassing, unequivocal appeal for us to order our lives entirely with reference to Christ?

First, Christ is the full manifestation of deity. "In his body lives the fullness of divinity" (verse 9, JB; 1:19; Eph. 1:23; 3:19; 4:10, 13; John 1:14-16). Because Christ is the complete embodiment of God, we are thereby enabled to experience "fullness of life in him" (verse 10; cf. Eph. 4:15). Since Christ is the fullest possible expression of the reality of God, those who are "in Christ" are able to experience to the fullest the reality of God. Just as Christ is not a partial manifestation of God, neither is our experience of God in Christ partial. Since Christ is the unique embodiment of God, he is preeminent over "all rule and authority" (verse 10, 1:18; 2:19; cf. Eph. 1:22; 4:15; 5:23; I Cor. 11:3).

Second, through sacramental union with Christ we have experienced the "circumcision of the heart," or inner transformation of the heart, and resurrection life. It had long been a hope within Old Testament thought that Israel would experience genuine renewal that was depicted as a circumcision of the heart (Deut. 30:6; Jer. 4:4; 9:25-26; cf. Acts 7:51). In Christian experience, the sacrament of baptism corresponded to the act of circumcision. Here, we are told that in the baptismal act circumcision is now performed by God, not by human hand, and that it is more than mere removal of a small piece of skin. Rather it involves the "complete stripping" of our lower nature, "the body of the flesh" (verse 11, JB, NEB). This is the "circumcision of Christ" (verse 11, RSV), or the "circumcision according to Christ" (verse 11, JB; cf. Rom. 2:25-29).

In the baptismal act, we become a participant with Christ in the cosmic drama of dying and rising (verse 12; cf. 3:1; Rom. 6:4; Eph. 2:6). We should note here that our resurrection with

Christ is envisioned as being already realized, whereas in the undisputed Pauline letters it remains a future reality (cf. Rom. 6:4-11; 8:11). The important point to note is that God has "made [us] alive together with him" (verse 13). The resurrection that God effected in Christ has now been effected within us.

Third, Christ has annulled the power of the law through his own death on the cross (verses 14-15; cf. Rom. 7:4; I Pet. 2:24). Precisely what is meant by the "bond which stood against us" is not clear. The image may be that of nailing a canceled debt to the cross (verse 14, JB). This is seen as a victory over heavenly forces, "the principalities and powers" (verse 15), who are paraded as a public spectacle in the march of triumph (cf. II Cor. 2:14).

Luke 11:1-13

Luke has chosen to assemble in 11:1-13 a number of Jesus' teachings on prayer. There is no reason for the reader to assume Jesus said all these things on one occasion. Collections of materials into sections on controversies, miracles, parables, instructions on conduct, and other themes are common in the Gospels. That these sayings originally had different settings is evidenced by the fact that Matthew parallels Luke 11:1-4 in 6:9-13 and Luke 11:9-13 in 7:7-11. Luke's parable of the friend at midnight (verses 5-8) is not found elsewhere. The clear breaks in the passage yield three distinct units: verses 1-4, 5-8, and 9-13. The preacher is, therefore, justified in not attempting to treat the entire passage in one message. On the contrary, the wealth of the material and the varieties of literary texture (question and answer, the Lord's Prayer, a parable, simple analogies, direct instruction) encourage using several sermons to cover the passage.

Luke has provided an introduction consisting of two parts: the example of Jesus and a disciple's request (verse 1). Jesus at prayer is an image frequent and important for Luke: at baptism (3:21), before choosing the Twelve (6:12), before the first prediction of his passion (9:18), and at his Transfiguration (9:28). Apparently his own prayer life prompted his disciple's request. To be taught "as John taught his disciples" seems to imply that followers of John, perhaps still in Luke's day, were given a certain form for prayer. Such a practice was not unusual for rabbis. It is significant that the text treats prayer as a learned experience and not simply the release of the heart's natural longings.

The form of the Lord's Prayer in Luke (verses 2-4) is briefer than the more familiar and more liturgically extended version in Matthew (6:9-13). It consists of two brief petitions of praise to God and three petitions for the ones praying. It is a community and not a private prayer (us, we), and assumes that the community longs for the final coming of the kingdom. The overall eschatological thrust of the prayer is present in Luke as in Matthew but may be softened a bit in the petition about bread. The difficult word translated either "daily bread" or "bread for the morrow" (verse 3) is in Luke prefaced with a present tense verb meaning, "continue giving us," or "day by day give us," or "each day give us." Apparently Luke has in mind not the bread from heaven at the kingdom's coming but each day's provision of daily food. This would be appropriate for those who were to take up the cross "daily" (9:23) and to go on missionary journeys with no extra rations (10:4-7). Interestingly, the petitioner also asks God to forgive sins (not debts), but in terms of our forgiving others, it is for their "debts" to us (verse 4). It has been suggested that this reflects Luke's concern that possessions not hinder community relationships (6:30; Acts 5:1-11).

The parable in verses 5-8 is difficult to read because it is framed as one long question with the many clauses joined with conjunctions in Semitic fashion. Added to the difficulty is the fact that the listener is to identify at the outset with the one who asks a neighbor for bread, but the question ends with attention on the neighbor who responds to the late-night request. Even more awkward is the fact that parables which begin with, "Which one of you?" have as the clearly implied answer, "No one." These unusual features lead support to the idea that the parable may have originally had another context, perhaps concerning preparedness for the end time, similar to Matthew's story of ten maidens (25:1-13). In its present setting, however, the parable makes the point that if our friends respond to importunate (shameless, NEB) appeals, how much more so will God who desires to give us the kingdom (12:32).

The concluding section (verses 9-13) extends further the line of thought "from the lesser to the greater." This time, however, the analogy is drawn not from one's friends but from one's parents. If earthly parents give good gifts in response to their children's requests, how much more so will God. Luke has egg and scorpion instead of Matthew's loaf and stone (7:9) but with no difference in meaning. Of significance, however, is Luke's "Holy Spirit" (verse 13) instead of Matthew's "good things" (7:11). The gift of the Holy Spirit is vital to Luke's understanding of Jesus (3:21) and of the church (24:49; Acts 1:4, 5, 8; 2:38). The angel's word to Mary that the Holy Spirit would come upon her (1:35) has its completion in Jesus' word to his disciples that the Holy Spirit would come upon them (Acts 1:8). The Holy Spirit creates, sustains, and empowers the church to continue what Jesus began to do and to teach.

Proper 13

Sunday Between July 31 and August 6 Inclusive

II Kings 13:14-20a; Psalm 28; Colossians 3:1-11; Luke 12:13-21

The Old Testament text brings us to the conclusion of the readings concerning the prophets Elijah and Elisha. It reports the latter's death and a symbolic action he performed while on his deathbed. The responsorial psalm is an individual lament in the face of death and enemies, concluding with words of assurance and a doxology. The New Testament lections form a good match, both focusing on the problem of preoccupations with earthly matters. The Gospel text is the parable of the rich fool and the epistolary reading is a series of admonitions concerning life lived in the context of resurrection.

II Kings 13:14-20*a*

Between last week's reading and this one a great deal has transpired in the history of Israel and Judah. Elisha had anointed a new king, Jehu, who overthrew the house of Ahab (II Kings 9–10), thus bringing to a conclusion the Lord's commission to Elijah on Mount Horeb (I Kings 19:15-18). From that point the narrative's full attention turns to kings and armies, with no other mention of prophets until the passage before us. Jehu had died, followed by his son Jehoahaz, who in turn was succeeded on the throne in Samaria by his son Joash (II Kings 13:8-9). From our text we can deduce that Elisha continued to have the respect and affection of the kings in Jehu's dynasty.

In II Kings 13:14-20*a* a sparse narrative framework (verses 14, 20*a*) surrounds a story of prophetic intervention in history by means of symbolic actions. The narrative provides the setting and introduces the characters. Elisha is on his deathbed when Joash comes to see him, mourning over his demise, which comes soon.

Something is missing between verses 14 and 15. In direct response to the king's appearance and his lament for Elisha, the prophet begins to give instructions for the performance of a sign act. What is the question to which the act is the answer? The narrators of the story, in oral tradition and literature, assume that those who hear or read it will know what is happening. Joash has come to make formal inquiry of the Lord through the prophet. His question, like that of the Israelites in the war against Benjamin (Judg. 20:23, 27) and of Samuel (I Sam. 7:9) and Saul (I Sam. 13:9) in the conflict with the Philistines, would have been, "Shall we go up to battle with the Syrians?" The practice of such inquiry stems from the ancient tradition of the holy war. It could have been posed to a prophet or a priest, and might include sacrifices and offerings. The explicit goal is not so much to seek God's help in battle, but to determine the divine purpose. Israel must not go to war without the promise that the Lord will give victory.

Elisha answers on behalf of Yahweh by giving the king instructions for carrying out symbolic actions. Obviously, he is too weak to perform the ritual himself, but the fact that the king is the actor plays an important role in the results. In the description of the first action (verses 15-17) the narrator breaks down the account into a series of steps, with Elisha giving instructions and Joash doing as he was told. Decisive is the fact that the prophet laid his hands on the king's hands (verse 16), thereby showing that the deed is done on behalf of and with the authority of the prophet. Once the king has shot the arrow, Elisha explains the meaning of the action. This is the *Lord's* arrow of victory, signifying a successful battle in Aphek (verse 17).

The account of the second action proceeds in similar fashion, but when the king strikes the ground with the arrows only three times, Elisha is furious. The action has determined the interpretation and the future course of events. Thus the news is ambiguous. Israel will be victorious three times, but conflicts with Syria will persist.

Reports of such symbolic actions are familiar from the prophetic books. Often they are actions performed publicly, such as Jeremiah's going about with a yoke on his neck (Jeremiah 27), Isaiah's parading naked and barefoot in the streets of Jerusalem (Isaiah 20), or Hosea's purchase of a woman (Hos. 3). Frequently, they concern the names of the children of the prophets, as in Hosea 1 and Isaiah 7:10-17; 8:1-4. The reports tend to include an account of Yahweh's command to perform the action followed by an interpretation of its meaning. A report of the actual performance may or may not be given, that being taken for granted.

Prophetic symbolic actions, including Elisha's from his deathbed, are not simply audio-visual aids. They grasp the attention of the audience, to be sure, but they are visual forms of the prophetic word. As such, they are effective, setting into motion the events that they portray. That is, they are effective if the prophet truly speaks for Yahweh, for Yahweh's word has the power to change the future. Elisha's actions are not works of magic, for he manipulates neither dark powers nor the Deity. The actions, like the prophetic words, are a message from God concerning the future.

What then of Elisha's fury when Joash struck the ground only three times? A psychological and rational explanation is tempting: the king's actions revealed that he did not have the will and determination to overpower Syria. That is probably a consideration, for Yahweh's actions are indeed in response to human behavior. But psychological considerations should not obscure the main point. Whether acted out or spoken, the word of the Lord through prophets—and not military might and strategy—determines the fate of the people.

Psalm 28

This psalm begins as a lament, making supplication to God for salvation and destruction of the enemy (verses 1-4). These verses take the form of a prayer addressed directly to the Deity. The psalm concludes, except for the final verse, with praise and proclamation, no longer in the form of a prayer addressed to God, but in human-to-human speech which speaks about God in the third person (verses 6-8).

Two verses do not fall within this general pattern. The first, verse 5, is an oracle spoken neither to nor by the Deity and is best understood as a statement of God's judgment of the wicked and thus an oracle of assurance to the supplicant, probably spoken by some cultic functionary, a priest or a Levite. The second, verse 9, is a prayer of intercession prayed to God on behalf of the community as a whole.

In light of the above considerations, the following seems a likely outline of the psalm and a description of its usage: a supplicant offers prayer to the Deity asking for help (verses 1-4), to which the priest responds, assuring the worshiper of God's fidelity regarding the judgment of those who disregard his actions (verse 5). The worshiper then responds out of a posture of confidence and trust (verses 6-8; verse 8 may have been spoken by the community), and, to conclude, a final supplication is made (verse 9).

The most likely person to have utilized this psalm in its original setting was the Hebrew monarch. Thus the psalm may be classified as a royal lament. The evidence for this is rather slim, namely, the reference to the anointed (the Messiah) in verse 8 which could be the supplicant's indirect reference to himself.

The troublemakers and the distress that precipitated the lament are described in verse 3 as "workers of evil" and those speaking "peace with their neighbors, while mischief is in their hearts." Such general descriptions could cover a multitude of sinners, and point to problems ranging from potentially belligerent national states to personal enemies. If the king is here praying, this would make the psalm and the circumstances in the reading from II Kings 13 similar insofar as contexts of danger are concerned.

The plea for help in verses 1-2 speaks of the consequences of God's failure to help, namely, going down to the Pit, which is synonymous with the expression "descending into Sheol." Both refer to dying, but both expressions are frequently used metaphorically. Elements of lamenting are noted in verse 2: supplication, cry for help, lifting of the hands. The context of temple worship as the place of the psalm's usage is indicated by the last line of verse 2; the Holy of Holies was probably faced while lamenting gestures were made. The Holy of Holies, here called the backroom of the sanctuary, was a cubical room about 30 feet in all dimensions and contained the ark and winged cherubim upon which God sat invisibly enthroned. (The temple, of course, was a very modest building; the central room measured about 30 by 60 feet and was never intended for congregational worship. A vestibule or porch, 30 by 15 feet, served as an entrance portico. Worship and most religious activities were held in the courtyard outside the temple proper.)

Verse 4 is a plea for the destruction of the enemy and requests that their punishment be analogous to their evil, "according to their work," "according to the work of their hands." Common Old Testament views are that judgment should parallel the crime and that evil intent has a way of coming home, so that one reaps what one sows, or even reaps what one intends to sow.

If the words of verse 5 are the assurance for the supplicating king, then they would parallel, in a fashion, the symbolic acts performed by Elisha in II Kings 13.

The transition to thanksgiving is clearly evident in verses 6 ff. Note the reference to the assurance that God has heard (verse 6a) which in itself forms the basis for the joy of celebration and the song of thanksgiving (note Ps. 26:7).

Colossians 3:1-11

Today's text unfolds what we are because of our union with Christ and what we should become as a result of that union. The text is constructed along the familiar distinction between the indicative and the imperative. In the first part of our text (verses 1-4) we are reminded of who we are as a result of our baptism; in the second part of our text (verses 5-11) is sketched for us a profile of who we ought to be as a result of this new identity. (Cf. the paragraph division in RSV, NEB, JB, NIV).

We should also note at the outset that a portion of this text (Col. 3:1-4) also serves as one option for the epistolary lection for Easter in Year A. The reader may wish to consult additional remarks made there in the liturgical context of Easter.

Union with Christ (verses 1-4). We should note the indicative mood in this first section. It is a straightforward declaration. The form of Greek construction used in the opening phrase suggests an accomplished reality: "Since you have been brought back to true life with Christ . . ." (verse 1, JB). Christ was raised, and we have been raised with him. In his resurrection we have become co-participants (2:12; Eph. 2:6). Just as emphatically, the text states, "you have died" (verse 3; 2:12; Rom. 6:3-4). We do injustice to the concreteness of this language if we think of it symbolically, or even metaphorically, even though in one sense it is both. We are being reminded that through our baptism we have actually experienced death and resurrection—not simply *a* death and resurrection, but *our* own death and resurrection.

The actuality of this is seen by the way in which our new identity is described. Our life now "lies hidden with Christ in God" (verse 3, NEB). So closely are we now identified with Christ that it is impossible to think of our existence apart from the Christ-story. Indeed, Christ can be said to be "our life" (verse 4; cf. Phil. 1:21). Is this best described as Christ mysticism, or as our mystical union with Christ? Perhaps. But not in the sense that it plucks us from our ordinary experience and suspends us in some midair, religious moment where past, present, and future merge. To be sure, our text is remarkable for the way it assumes our already having been raised with Christ as a present reality. It stands much closer to later Pauline formulations (e.g., Eph. 2:6) than to earlier formulations where our own resurrection and experience of the exalted Christ is reserved to the future (cf. Rom. 6:4-11; 8:11). Nevertheless, it still retains a future expectation (verse 4). There still remains a form of glorious existence that is not ours until Christ finally appears (cf. Luke 17:30; I John 3:2).

It is a form of sacramental union in which our own concrete existence is reoriented. Through our appropriation of the death and resurrection of Christ, our line of vision is now directed toward the Christ exalted to God's right hand (verse 1; Ps. 110:1; 118:15-16; Matt. 22:44; 26:64; Acts 2:33; 7:55-56;

Rom. 8:34; Eph. 1:20; Heb. 1:3, 13; 8:1; 10:12; 12:2; I Pet. 3:22).
More than this, the object of our deepest desires is now
directed toward "things that are above" and away from
"things that are on earth" (verse 2). It is not as if we become
oblivious to the world in which we live, nor that we live as if
there are not earthly realities. It is rather that our ultimate
desires and values come to transcend the earthly as our own
world and world view is transformed by our perspective of
the risen Lord.

Christ-shaped existence (verses 5-11). For the most part, this
section is a string of imperatives: "put to death" (verse 5),
"put them all way" (verse 8), "do not lie to one another"
(verse 9). A profile of "what is earthly" (verse 5) is sketched
with a list of vices (verses 5, 8; cf. Matt. 15:19; Luke 18:11;
Rom. 1:29; 13:13; I Cor. 5:10-11; 6:9-10; II Cor. 12:20; Gal.
5:19-21; Eph. 4:31; 5:3-5; I Tim. 1:9-10; 6:4-5; II Tim. 3:2-4; Tit.
3:3; I Pet. 4:3; Rev. 9:21; 21:8; 22:15). If we can make any
distinction at all, the first list focuses more on personal vices
(verse 5), the second on social vices (verse 8). All such
behavior stands under the coming wrath of God, or "makes
God angry" (verse 6, JB; cf. Rom. 1:18; Eph. 5:6; also Matt.
3:7). These are also the character traits of the "old nature"
(verse 9, RSV, NEB), or the "old self" (JB, NIV), literally the
"old humanity."

The metaphor of "putting off" and "putting on" suggests a
picture of taking off one set of clothes and donning a new
wardrobe, which is probably exactly what happened in early
Christian baptism. But it is more than a matter of outward
attire or outward behavior. The putting on of a new self
occurs as a process of renewal oriented finally toward the
image of the Creator (verse 10; Gen. 1:26-27). It takes the form
of "being renewed in knowledge" (verse 10; cf. Rom. 12:2; II
Cor. 4:16; Tit. 3:5). The more we seek the true knowledge of
God that transforms us into the divine image the more the old
self gives way to the new self. What actually emerges is a new
creation, not only within the individual who experiences this
profound change, but within the social order where "Christ
is all, and in all" (verse 11). Its transforming impact is to
remove all distinctions (verse 11; cf. Gal. 3:28; I Cor. 12:13).

We do well to note the way in which our text moves from

individual appropriation and transformation to a new social reality, and this may well provide at least one homiletical suggestion. One tendency is to appropriate this text only in terms of individual ethics, especially if we read it as one of the classical expressions of Christ-mysticism. The individual element is there, but the text moves well beyond this as it pushes us to a form of behavior that is both individually and corporately transforming.

Luke 12:13-21

The parable of the rich fool is found in the New Testament only in Luke, but it occurs elsewhere in Near Eastern lore and also in the Gospel of Thomas (Logion 63) in a simpler form. In fact, the Gospel of Thomas also has the conversation of Luke's verses 13:14, but it stands without context or elaboration (Logion 72). In characteristically Lukan fashion, the interpretation of the parable is at the beginning (as other examples, see 18:1 and 18:9).

The parable comes as the beginning of a section on the attitude of disciples toward possessions; here the subject is covetousness (verses 13-21), followed by teachings on anxiety (verses 22-34). The section comes rather abruptly as a change of subject. The shift, which amounts to an interruption, is provided by a question from someone in the crowd. The brief exchange between the person with the request and Jesus and Jesus' warning about covetousness constitute a pronouncement story (verses 13-15). The parable that follows is not inextricably joined to the pronouncement story and could be told effectively in a great number of settings. However, verses 13-15 do influence how one hears the parable.

The parable of the rich fool is a story pointing out the folly of covetousness, the failure to see the distinction between what one has and what one is. Covetousness was a violation of the Law of Moses (Exod. 20:17) and the teaching of the prophets (Mic. 2:2) and seems to have been a widespread problem in the early church (Rom. 1:29; Mark 7:22; Col. 3:5; Eph. 5:5; I Tim. 6:10). It exists in many forms, sometimes as the desire to possess what belongs to another, and at other times the desire to accumulate when one already has enough to meet one's needs. Some persons, however, seem unable to know what is enough until they reach the point of too much, and often, too late. This inordinate craving to hoard as a guarantee against insecurity is not only an act of disregard for those in need but puts goods in the place of God. Luke calls it not being "rich toward God" (verse 21; Paul calls it worshiping and serving "the creature rather than the Creator," Rom 1:25); and both Colossians (3:5) and Ephesians (5:5) label covetousness "idolatry."

The preacher will want to be careful not to caricature the farmer in the story. There is nothing here of graft, manipulating the market, theft from neighbors, or mistreatment of workers. The man is not a criminal and to state or imply as much would be to miss the point. His land produces bountifully; the soil, sun, and rain join in making him a wealthy man. He makes an economic decision and replaces his old barns with larger ones. He is, after all, not wasteful and careless. If, then, he is not unjust, what is he? He is a fool, says the parable. He lives completely in and for himself. He talks neither to others nor to God; he talks to himself, he congratulates himself, he plans for himself. He dies suddenly and "the things you have prepared, whose will they be?" (verse 20). Luke could well have repeated here an earlier statement of Jesus: "For what does it profit a man if he gains the whole world and loses or forfeits himself?" (9:25). Paul probably would have remarked at the close of the parable, let those who possess things live as though they did not possess things (I Cor. 7:29-31).

Again and again, Luke will raise the subject of possessions, holding up as the standard for the Christian community the voluntary sharing of one's goods. This, Luke says, was the message of John the Baptist (3:10-14) and of Jesus (6:30; 16:19-31), and was the practice of early Christians (Acts 4:34-37).

Proper 14

Sunday Between August 7 and 13 Inclusive

Jeremiah 18:1-11; Psalm 14; Hebrews 11:1-3, 8-19; Luke 12:32-40

The readings for today are rich and diverse. In the Old Testament text the message of the Lord to Jeremiah at the potter's house sets out the alternatives for Israel, obedience and salvation or disobedience and judgment. Psalm 14 ends up as a prayer for the Lord's deliverance and the restoration of the people, but along the way it bewails corruption and evil. It might thus serve either as warning or as confession and repentance. A series of readings from Hebrews begins with the famous passage characterizing faith. The Gospel lection concerns the Kingdom, containing words of assurance, admonitions to lay up treasure in heaven, and exhortations to be ready for "the Son of man is coming at an unexpected hour" (Luke 12:40).

Jeremiah 18:1-11

The prophet Jeremiah was active in the seventh century B.C., from about 627 B.C. until the second capture of Jerusalem by the Babylonians in 587 B.C. He would have witnessed the Deuteronomic religious reform under King Josiah and the last decades of Judah's history before the Exile. The prophet was deeply involved in the political affairs of the time, and more than once he found himself in trouble with the authorities.

The Book of Jeremiah is a long and complicated one, containing materials of diverse sorts and origins. There are prophetic addresses in poetry, prose speeches, narratives about the prophet, and Jeremiah's complaints, very similar to the Psalms of individual lament. There are announcements of judgment on Judah and on foreign nations, announcements of

114

salvation, and more or less sermonic speeches calling for obedience to the law or repentance. We know already from the story of Jeremiah and Baruch (Jer. 36) that the prophet did not write the book, but that it originated as a collection of his speeches dictated to the scribe. Close reading has shown that the book continued to grow long after Jeremiah's time. Much of it was edited, and significant portions added, by Deuteronomic writers during the Babylonian Exile. Deuteronomic editing may be present in the text for today, especially in verses 7-12.

This report of Jeremiah's revelation in the potter's house is paired in the context with the account of a symbolic action concerning pottery (Jer. 19:1-13). It begins with an introduction that refers to the prophet in the third person. Jeremiah hears the Lord's command to go to the potter's house (verse 2), and he obeys, observing the potter at the wheel reworking a "spoiled" vessel into another one (verses 3-4). Then he reports, in the first person, the word that the Lord revealed to him. Everything that follows (verses 6-12) is a divine speech to the prophet, which he would have been expected to transmit to the people.

In terms of both style and contents, there are three parts to the speech. First (verse 6) there is the direct application of the analogy of the potter and the clay to the relationship of Yahweh to the house of Israel. This is in the form of a rhetorical question, and its point is that Yahweh can do as he will with Israel. Various aspects of the metaphor may be central: the Lord's power, Israel's frustration of his design, the Lord's judgment, or his will to make something worthwhile of the people. The second part of the address (verses 7-10) sets out a series of alternatives, conditions that will determine the way Yahweh acts, not just toward Israel but toward any nation. The emphasis here is on Yahweh's capacity to "repent" (verse 10) of evil if the people turn from their evil ways, or of good if a nation is disobedient. The third part (verses 11-12) applies these possibilities directly to Judah and Jerusalem, warning of evil and calling for repentance.

Thus in its present form the metaphor of the potter and the clay stresses repentance, both divine and human. God, who can shape a people as he wills, wills to be affected by how they behave toward him. If the analogy itself suggests omnipotence, the remainder of the passage underscores God's responsiveness to human actions and makes human beings fully accountable for what happens to them.

Psalm 14

A few psalms or portions of psalms appear more than once in the Old Testament. For example, Psalm 18 also appears as II Samuel 22. Psalm 14 recurs as Psalm 53, although with a few minor alterations, the most obvious being the use of the divine name Yahweh in Psalm 14 and the use of Elohim in Psalm 53. We really have no explanation as to why some material was repeated in such similar form other than the fact that, for some reason, it fitted well in two places. So far as the Psalms are concerned, however, we have little more than conjecture to go on in explaining why any of them appear in the order they do.

Psalm 14 is clearly a lamenting or complaining psalm which protests about the widespread prevalence of evil in the world. Most of the lament psalms in the Psalter are true prayers, that is, they are addressed to the Deity about some particular trouble or general condition and they request the Deity to rectify matters. Psalm 14, however, has no verses addressed directly to God; the Deity is spoken of throughout in the third person. Thus the psalm is not a prayer. It would be interesting to know how this psalm was used in worship. Who is speaking? The king? The high priest? An ordinary worshiper? Someone who has been mistreated by the wicked?

The psalm has something of a didactic or teaching flavor about it. There is a descriptive, reflective quality about it, with its pessimistic depiction of the human situation. This descriptive character is further expanded in some copies of the ancient Greek version of the Old Testament which adds the following between verses 3 and 4:

> Their throat is an open sepulchre,
>   with their tongues they have used deceit;
> the poison of asps is under their lips:
>   whose mouth is full of cursing and bitterness;
> their feet are swift to shed blood:
>   destruction and misery are in their ways;
> and the way of peace they have not known:
>   there is no fear of God before their eyes.

116

This insertion is paralleled by Romans 3:10-18. Perhaps Paul copied this from the Greek or the Greek translator of the Psalms or a later copyist incorporated the material from Paul's letter.

If we take this psalm as a "homily" on the wicked, what does it say? (1) Verses 2-3 imply that all humans are corrupt, all are bad, all are perverse. No one does what is right. The two expressions "act wisely" and "seek after God" are to be understood as synonymous. Thus the psalmist places everyone under a blanket condemnation. (2) The basic human problem as seen by the psalmist seems to be practical atheism, the assumption in the heart that "there is no God" or that God does not care or take human actions into account (verse 1). Such a position makes the person into the sole authority of what is acceptable or permissible. For the author, such behavior was corrupt, resulting in abominable deeds, in failure to do the good. (3) Real knowledge of the way things are should lead one to do the good and worship God (verse 4). Because of this lack of knowledge, people live without respect for one another, consuming one another with the casualness with which one would eat bread. There is wrongdoing, but even worse, there is no guilt or remorse. (4) In spite of all appearances to the contrary, God is still in control, and is a refuge to the poor and the oppressed (verses 5-6). The "poor" and the "righteous" are those opposed by the powerful. (Here the writer denies the absoluteness of the claim that all humans are bad that was expounded in verse 2.) (5) The final two verses are an expression of hopeful eschatology: someday, the human condition will be as it should be.

Hebrews 11:1-3, 8-19

For this and the next three Sundays, the epistolary readings are taken from Hebrews 11–13. The first ten chapters of the Epistle to the Hebrews provided the semicontinuous epistolary readings for Propers 22–28 in Year B, and the reader may wish to consult our introductory remarks to the epistle made in connection with Proper 22 in *After Pentecost, Year B*. Since this epistle is used extensively in

117

various liturgical settings, the reader may profitably consult the Scripture Reading Index for additional material.

Today's text is taken from the first part of the well-known eleventh chapter of the Epistle to the Hebrews, which provides an impressive list of faith exemplars. Our selection brackets the examples of Abel, Enoch, and Noah (11:4-7), and highlights the faithful examples of Abraham and Sarah. It opens, however, with the classic definition of faith that has come to be identified with this Epistle.

Faith Defined (verses 1-3). For the author of Hebrews, "faith is being sure of what we hope for and certain of what we do not see" (verse 1, NIV). Or, stated in a slightly different fashion, "Faith gives substance to our hopes, and makes us certain of realities we do not see" (NEB). The two parts of this definition may very well serve to encompass the two dimensions of the present and the future. On the one hand, faith gives us a grasp of the future that renders it as hope (cf. Rom. 8:24-25). We are thereby able to look forward expectantly, firmly assured that the future to which we are summoned has genuine substance. On the other hand, faith also enables us to interpret the present in terms of realities we cannot see (cf. II Cor. 4:18).

To sharpen the definition, we might compare this understanding of faith with that of Paul, but we should not distinguish too sharply between the two. For both, faith is obedient response (cf. Rom. 1:5), but Paul seems to lay greater stress on the element of trust and utter dependence, whereas Hebrews stresses the element of steadfast commitment to the divine promise. In Hebrews, faith is the faithfulness "which one shows to God and his promise by holding fast to what was once seized, and by allowing it to be normative for one's behavior. The concept contains both aspects: Assent to the divine promise, and the persistence with which this assent is maintained in assurance of the future. Marked stress on this second aspect alongside the first characterizes the uniqueness of Hebrews' conception of faith (Strathmann). As the author of Hebrews views faith, it is this constancy in clinging to the divine promise, even when it became dim, that consistently characterized our ancestors (verse 2).

Also important to note is the insistence that our understanding of faith is reflected in our theology of creation (verse 3). Drawing on the biblical account of creation (cf. Gen. 1; Ps. 33:6, 9), our author stresses that the universe came into being through an act of divine speech. Out of this spoken word of God sprang the visible from the invisible (Rom. 1:20). To account for what we see in the world of creation, faith looks to God as the one in whom unseen reality became visible reality. In this view, the origin of all we know and see cannot be conceived, known, or explained apart from the creative act of God. We begin, then, with the way we construe the created order as a clue to whether we can make sense of what we see in terms of what we cannot see, whether in fact we have the capacity for faith.

Faith Exemplified (verses 8-19). Abraham and Sarah became the paradigms of faith in a variety of New Testament witnesses (cf. Rom. 4:3-25; 9:9; Gal. 3:6-9, 15-18; James 2:21-24; cf. I Pet. 3:6). Singled out in today's text are their capacity to shape a vision of the future informed by the promise of God and to project themselves forward into that future. We should note the number of times the word "promise" occurs in our text (cf. verses 9, 11, 13). For Abraham, it was his singular response to the call of God (Gen. 12:1-4), the promise to possess a land (Gen. 15:7), and his willingness to become a foreigner in another land (Gen. 23:4, 12; 26:3; 35:27). But more than this, he followed the promise as an itinerant, a pilgrim, living in tents (Gen. 12:8; 13:12). But in this transitory mode of life his faith pushed ahead toward a more permanent dwelling—the city of God with lasting foundations (cf. 12:22; 13:14; Rev. 21:10-22; also Wisd. 13:1). What emerges is an assured promise sustained by hope.

Sarah also lived in response to the divine promise, and was able to become pregnant even though she was well beyond age (Gen. 17:19; 21:2; also Rom. 4:19-21). This miracle of birth is explained by her conviction that God is a faithful God (verse 11; cf. I Cor. 1:9; 10:13; II Cor. 1:18; I Thess. 5:24; II Thess. 3:3; II Tim. 2:13; Heb. 10:23; I John 1:9; Rev. 1:5). Consequently, from one person an innumerable host of descendants came (verse 12; cf. Gen. 22:17; 32:13; Exod. 32:13; Deut. 1:10; 10:22).

In retrospect, what Abraham and Sarah (and Abel, Enoch, and Noah as well) exemplified was faith that responded to promise without seeing it come to full fruition (verses 13-15). Living in hope, but not in fulfillment, they became strangers and exiles (cf. Gen. 23:4; I Chron. 29:15; Ps. 39:13; 119:19; I Pet. 1:1; 2:11; Eph. 2:19). Theirs was a pilgrim existence that moved where it was led by God.

In no sense is the vision of faith in today's text a static vision, as if steadfastness means clinging to a stake driven in the ground. It is rather a steadfast clinging to a divine promise that moves us through time and history. Even if we stay in one place, the promise of God calls us to leave and move on to new horizons. "Faith thus becomes a confident wandering" (Kaesemann). We move in response to the summons of God, and in so doing move from one alien existence to another. As we move, what was once invisible to us becomes visible, even as we move into another world that is new to us. Initially, we find ourselves returning to the land we left, but in the venture of faith it lays less and less claim on us. What we finally find most compelling is a sure vision of what we hope for and a firm conviction of what we cannot see.

Luke 12:32-40

The preacher has been served such neat, well-defined units from Luke (the good Samaritan, Martha and Mary, the rich fool) that it may have been forgotten that one of the early tasks in studying a biblical text for preaching is to ascertain the limits of the passage. Where does it begin and end, does it have a center, and can it be lifted out for study and proclamation without tearing it? Today's Gospel lesson invites the preacher back to that discipline. English translations tend to make two paragraphs of our text: verses 32-34 and 35-40. Commentaries discuss verses 32-34 along with verses 22-31. An unaided reading of the text leads to a preliminary judgment that verse 32 belongs with 31, verses 33-34 continue the discussion of possessions but move in a new direction, and verses 35-40 provide a new focus for reflection. Looking to the parallels in Matthew offers little help. Matthew parallels Luke's verses 32-34 at 6:29-31, does not have Luke's verses 35-38 at all (instead he has the parable in 25:1-13), and parallels verses 39-40 at 24:43-44. Mark 13:35-36 is similar.

The decision by the preacher can perhaps best be made thematically. Verses 32-34 deal with possessions and verses 35-40 concern being prepared for the Lord's coming. While the two themes could be joined in a single message, the preacher may prefer to treat only one. Either path taken is valid, and Luke's message need not be violated in the process.

Our lection offers first the conclusion to the section on possessions (12:13-34). Within that section Jesus deals with covetousness (verses 13-21) and with anxiety (verses 22-32). As the teaching on anxiety comes to a close, the reader is urged to trust God who knows our needs and, instead of seeking things, to seek God's kingdom (verses 30-31). And then, as if to quiet any anxieties created by these teachings against anxiety, Jesus says, "Fear not, little flock, for it is your Father's good pleasure to give you the kingdom" (verse 32). In other words, seeking the kingdom is not a futile search for that which is being withheld. On the contrary, seek the kingdom with confidence that God desires to give it to you.

With verses 33-34 the discussion of possessions comes to a close on a positive note. No longer warning about covetousness and anxiety, Jesus calls for a demonstration of freedom from both in the generous giving of alms. Like Judaism before it, the Christian community assumed responsibility for the needy (16:9; 18:22; 19:8; Acts 2:44-45; 4:32-37; 9:36; 11:27-30). Concern for the poor was a priority in both Jewish and Gentile Christianity (Gal. 2:10). There is no reason those who traveled light on missionary tours (10:4) should be burdened with surpluses when at home.

Verses 35-40 turn the reader's attention to the matter of preparedness for the Lord's coming. All the teachings we have now considered for several weeks are not forgetful of 9:51: Jesus' time to be received up was at hand and he set his face toward Jerusalem. Neither, says Jesus, are they to be forgetful of the Lord's return. Actually, teaching concerning the parousia continues through verse 48, but verses 41-48 are

121

addressed to Christian leaders, prompted by Peter's question in verse 41. Versus 35-40 pertain to all. It consists of two brief parables (verses 35-38, 39-40) in which the Lord is portrayed as a master returning home from a wedding feast and as a thief entering the house at an unpredictable hour. The first parable is a very positive picture with servants ready and waiting. Their lamps are burning and their loins are girded (the long outer garment is gathered up at the waist), the very image of readiness for work or for a journey (Exod. 12:11). Upon them is pronounced the Lord's beatitude, for even after the passing of a great deal of time (until Luke's own day), they remain prepared. The second parable offers a picture more frustrating than positive. The householder is unable, of course, to stay awake all the time, but he is also unable to know when the thief will come. But readiness in the kingdom cannot be based on calculations. Rather readiness is being busy at one's Christian duties; when that is the case, the uncertainty of days and hours is no cause for anxiety.

Proper 15

Sunday Between August 14 and 20 Inclusive

Jeremiah 20:7-13; Psalm 10:12-18; Hebrews 12:1-2, 12-17; Luke 12:49-56

With the exception of the reading from Hebrews, the dominant mood of today's lections is somber. Both the Old Testament reading and the responsorial psalm are individual laments or complaints. Jeremiah complains because he suffers under the burden of the word of the Lord. With hopeful petitions and expressions of confidence, verses 12-18 of Psalm 10 conclude a complaint concerned about the success of the wicked. The passage from Hebrews 12 is filled with words of encouragement and hope, while the Gospel lection has Jesus announcing a time of trouble and division, and pointing out how difficult it is to interpret "the present time" (Luke 12:56).

Jeremiah 20:7-13

Even though the prophetic tradition remains far more interested in the words of the Lord through the prophets than in the individuals themselves, the Book of Jeremiah presents us with a great deal of information about the prophet, some of it quite personal. This information comes mainly in the form of reports of Jeremiah's activities, either by himself or third parties. The text before us today gives an instance of another kind of material, found almost exclusively in Jeremiah among the prophetic books, the prophet's complaints about his life and experience with the word of God. These personal prayers—often called the "Confessions of Jeremiah" (see Jer. 11:18-23; 12:1-6; 15:10-21; 17:14-18; 18:18-23; 20:7-13, 14-18)—provide insight not only into

123

Jeremiah's thoughts and feelings, but also into the institution of prophecy in Israel.

For all its highly personal tone and language, this passage is indebted to a prayer tradition in Israel. This confession, like most others in Jeremiah, closely resembles the individual lament or complaint Psalms. Like most prayers, they begin with an invocation of the name of God ("O Lord," verse 7). They contain complaints that describe the person's suffering (verses 8-10) and reproach Yahweh for the trouble (verse 7). The one who prays wants God to understand the situation and take responsibility for it. Often there is a confession of sin (Ps. 7:3-5) or of innocence (Ps. 17:1-5), all in order to give God every reason for responding favorably. That element is not present here, but Jeremiah does affirm that he has done his best (verses 8-9). The heart of such prayers often is a petition for divine help, giving reasons for God to respond. In this case, as in many others, the petition is a plea for vengeance on those who oppose the prophet (verse 12). Frequently, we hear an affirmation of confidence in the Lord (as in verse 11), and sometimes at the end of the prayer an expression of assurance that the prayer has been heard and God will act (verse 13). This last element is directly related to the priestly salvation oracle pronounced in a prayer ritual, not unlike words of absolution or assurance following confession in Christian worship.

Jeremiah's cry of anguish is distinctive in both its passion and its cause. His suffering is a direct result of his vocation. His complaints concern his call to proclaim the word of Yahweh. He confesses to inner anxiety and compulsion. Because proclamation of Yahweh's word has led to ridicule and persecution, he tries to hold the word in, but cannot. It burns in his heart and exhausts him (verse 9).

Jeremiah's complaint does not exaggerate the trouble he has experienced; it was real and continuing. His words of judgment hardly were calculated to make him popular, and he was ridiculed when the judgment was slow in coming. Often his life was in danger. The passage immediately before this prayer (20:1-6) reports how Jeremiah was beaten and thrown in the stocks. He was also hauled before court with the charge of blasphemy (Jer. 26), and on another occasion beaten and put in prison (37:11-21). Small wonder that he complains.

We must keep in mind that he complains to God. That he addresses God with such strong accusations ("thou hast deceived me") is an embarrassment to many readers, and some commentators speak of his language as almost blasphemous. But this is not blasphemy. Jeremiah, like other Israelite faithful, knew that no thought or emotion was forbidden in prayer. To the contrary, one may speak honestly and directly to God. Note that while Jeremiah prays for relief, he knows that he cannot escape his calling, and he does not.

Prophets reacted differently to the experience of the word of Yahweh. When Ezekiel was handed a scroll filled with "words of lamentation and mourning and woe," he ate it and it was "as sweet as honey" (Ezek. 2:10–3:3). Jeremiah is horrified at the judgment he has to proclaim. But all prophets agree that they have been grasped by Yahweh (cf. Amos 7:15), and that their words are no longer their own.

Some human anguish stems from the experience of the absence of God. Not so in Jeremiah's case. It is the very presence of God—specifically, the word of God—that troubles him so deeply, so he prays to be left alone. Some anguish stems from the hiddenness of God's purpose. Not so in Jeremiah's case. He knows God's purpose all too well. Some anguish stems from lack of vocational clarity. Not so in Jeremiah's case. It is his very vocation, unavoidable despite all his efforts, that places such a burden on him.

Psalm 10:12-18

All of us have been taught that the interpretation of scripture should pay attention to the context of the pericope at hand. These verses present some particular problems in this regard. On the one hand, the reading for today is only a portion of Psalm 10 which would appear to be the text's immediate context. On the other hand, Psalm 10 itself appears to be part of a larger composition since Psalms 9 and 10 seem originally to have formed a single composition.

The evidence for the unity of Psalms 9–10 is as follows: (1) some ancient Hebrew manuscripts and ancient versions (the

Greek and Latin) treated the two as a single composition; (2) the two poems are based on an alphabetic (or acrostic) structure, in which the lines and verses of the composition work through the Hebrew alphabet, from "A to Z" we would say; the alphabetic structure, which has not been preserved totally (a few lines are missing), extends over the two psalms; (3) Psalm 10 has no title, as one would expect in Psalms 3-41; (4) Psalm 9 would end with a *selah* if taken by itself, the only psalm where this would be the case; and (5) there is much similarity of contents and expressions between the two psalms (compare 9:9 with 10:1, 9:19 with 10:12).

An outline of Psalms 9–10 contains the following features: (1) a vow to God to offer thanks (9:1-2), (2) a statement of confidence addressed to God (9:3-6), (3) confessional proclamation addressed to a human audience (9:7-9), (4) confessional statement addressed to God (9:10), (5) a call to the congregation to praise God (9:11-12), (6) appeal for God to help the supplicant (9:13-14), (7) proclamation (by a priest?) on the judgment of the wicked (9:15-18), (8) an appeal to God for action (9:19-20), (9) a complaint against God and a description of the triumphs of the wicked (10:1-11), (10) an appeal to God for divine intervention (10:12-15), (11) a confessional affirmation (10:16), and (12) a statement of confidence addressed to God (10:17-18).

The villains throughout the psalm are the wicked powerful who oppress the powerless and the poor. In preaching from this text, which focuses on the plea for the enemy's destruction, the minister might want to summarize the charges made about the oppressor, limiting the survey to Psalm 10. (1) The wicked are schemers who act in arrogance (verse 2). (2) They boast of their ambitions and goals (verse 3a), while (3) giving no regard to God (verse 3b). (4) Their thoughts and actions demonstrate that they are practical atheists, since they live as if "there is no God" or as if God were blindfolded (verses 4 and 11). (5) They prosper, making judgments and peddling influence in high places, out of reach of their opponents (verse 5). (6) They are cocksure and confident, believing themselves immune to the normal processes of life (verse 6). It should be stressed that a constitutive feature of most evil is the assumption of being an exception. Once people place themselves in the category of the "that-doesn't-apply-to-me [us]," it becomes possible to rationalize and justify almost anything. (7) The wicked are full of "oaths, deceit and fraud" (NJPSV) or, we would say, their words cannot be relied on and deviousness is a way of life (verse 7). (8) The powerful feed upon, not one another, but the poor—like a robber in ambush, a lion secreted in his lair, a hunter with a net (verses 8-11).

Against this typology of the wicked, one can understand the plea. In verse 12, God is asked to rise up, to lift up his hand. Both expressions can be seen as reflective of military imagery. The Ark of God was carried into battle, hailed by the shout, "Arise, O Yahweh" (see Num. 10:35-36). For lifting up the hand as a military action, see II Samuel 20:21; I Kings 11:26. Verse 14 calls the Deity to account and to defend his own cause: "Why should the wicked man scorn God, thinking You do not call to account?" (NJPSV).

The appeal to previous actions and to theological claims provides a means for the psalmist to remind the Deity of his responsibility and commitment to the case of the powerless (verse 14). Here the powerless are the hapless ("the poor victim," NEB) and the fatherless (probably children born out of wedlock rather than actual orphans). Elsewhere, the powerless who are a special concern of the Deity are the widows, the fatherless, and the sojourner (non-native) (see Isa. 1:17; Jer. 7:6).

The desire of the psalmist is for the destruction of the evildoer; "to break the arm" was to render powerless, inoperative (verse 15). Verse 15b asks that no unrequited sin be left unpunished. (Verse 16 looks like a late interpretation inserted at a time when the oppressed were identified with the Jews and the oppressors with such foreign powers as the Assyrians, Babylonians, or others. This made the structure reflected in the psalm, originally an intra-communal affair, into a Jewish-Gentile phenomenon.)

In the conclusion, the psalmist assumes the audacity to tell God what he will do (verses 17-18). Perhaps building here on a creedal statement of the facts of their faith, God is pictured as one who would "listen to the entreaty of the lowly" (NJPSV), giving them internal confidence and vigor ("strengthen their heart") and an external confidant who would allow them to get it off their chest ("thou wilt incline thy ear") and champion the cause of the ill-born (the fatherless) and the ill-treated (the oppressed) until tyranny should disappear.

In preaching from this psalm, two additional things should be noted: (1) griping, bitching, and complaining are assumed to be characteristic of the lowly and the oppressed; crying out against the structure of oppression is seen as normal, healthy, and the means to get things changed; and (2) God is especially associated with the bottom rungs of society, as a God whose responsibility is to liberate.

Hebrews 12:1-2, 12-17

The first part of today's epistolary lesson overlaps the text (Heb. 12:1-3) used on Wednesday in Holy Week in Years A, B, and C. The reader may wish to consult our remarks in each of these years in the *Lent, Holy Week, Easter* volumes.

Both parts of today's lection are linked by the race metaphor, which is frequently used in the New Testament to illustrate aspects of the life of faith (cf. I Cor. 9:24-26; Phil. 3:14; II Tim. 2:5; 4:7; also Phil. 1:27-28; I Tim. 6:12; Jude 3). In the opening section, the image of the athletic contest, or more specifically the foot race, provides an effective metaphor for including the host of examples cited in the previous chapter. They are envisioned as the "great cloud of witnesses" who have completed the race and now watch as we run the same course of faith. As every runner knows, what is required, above all, is the ability to hold out till the end—endurance, or perseverance (*hupomone*, cf. 10:36; Luke 8:15; 21:19; Rev. 2:2-3, 19; 3:10; 13:10; 14:12). We should look to Jesus "who leads us in our faith and brings it to perfection" (verse 2, JB). If the race metaphor is still in view in this exhortation to focus our attention on Jesus, perhaps we should think of Jesus as "pioneer and perfecter" in athletic terms as faithful starter and finisher.

With the race metaphor before us, we are urged in the second section to lift our drooping arms, strengthen our weak knees, and find a straight and level course so as not to inflict further injury on ourselves (verses 12-13). The language is supplied by Isaiah 35:3-4, where the image seems to be that of tired, exhausted POWs rather than fatigued athletes (cf. also Job 4:3; Sirach 25:23). It is a universal image—the person "bone tired," weary to the point of collapse, walking with arms drooping by the side, legs ready to give way at the knees. It may be fatigue from hoeing cotton all day, fighting fires all day, standing at the operating table all day, or assembling parts all day, but it is fatigue all the same. The last thing we want is another hill to climb (cf. Prov. 4:26-27).

What is being combatted here, however, is not general fatigue, but fatigue that besets the life of faith. Struggle is part and parcel of this contest (verse 4), and it inevitably entails discipline (verses 5-11). For all sorts of reasons, we can be tempted to forsake the life of faith. We may grow weary through sheer boredom, or we may find ourselves fighting enemies and battles that take their toll on us physically and mentally. The resistance may be open assault and physical abuse we experience at the hands of demonic archenemies. The fact is, as long as faith is genuine it meets resistance both from without and within, and can become debilitating. In the face of the enervating effects of living in faith for the faith, our text summons us to react in strength.

But how is this to be done concretely? The final section of our text supplies at least a partial answer.

First, there is a general exhortation for us to strive for peace and purity of life. It is one thing to be troubled, quite another to be a troublemaker. If we live in faith, we will make enemies, but we need not try to make them. At the heart of Christian faith should be the insatiable appetite for God's *shalom* (cf. Matt. 5:9; Mark 9:50; Rom. 12:18; 14:19; II Cor. 13:11; I Thess. 5:13; II Tim. 2:22; I Pet. 3:11 = Ps. 34:12-16). The true vision of God must also include the pursuit of holiness, the quest for a character shaped by God's own otherness (cf. Matt. 5:8; I John 3:2).

Second, we are called to implement the peaceful and pure life by being watchful. The text enjoins us to "see to" certain things. This is a call to collective sensitivity, to a form of community discipline in which we are urged actively to seek some things and actively avoid other things. The community of faith is here being summoned to be self-conscious in shaping its identity and retaining that identity. Three things are called for specifically:

1. We should see to it that "no one fail to obtain the grace of God" (verse 15). The community of faith should not be oblivious to the needs of its own members, but have active concern for one another that keeps anyone from slipping away (10:24-25).

2. We should see to it that no internal evil is allowed to destroy the community. No "root of bitterness" should be allowed to take root and become noxious poison that kills everything and everyone. For Israel this poisonous weed was idolatry, the failure to maintain unalloyed allegiance to the one God, Yahweh (cf. Deut. 29:17-19).

3. We should see to it that no one forsake the life of faith for a life of sexual immorality or "degrade religion" (verse 16, JB). Esau provides the classic example of the latter—someone who is unable to see that his birthright ties him to the divine promise, and thus sells it for a bowl of soup (Gen. 25:33-34; 26:34-35; 27:30-40). As Esau shows, only in retrospect do we realize what we lose by jettisoning our religious heritage.

Luke 12:49-56

Let us remind ourselves that the time between Pentecost and Advent provides the opportunity to treat continuous readings which give the preacher and the listeners a sense of the narrative and the overall impact of a writing. During this time one also becomes impressed with the structure and movement of the document and the unusual patterns to the material. It is certainly a time for a church to disabuse itself of any notion that a Gospel is written as a biography in chronological order.

Luke 12:49-56 is a clear illustration of unusual patterns in the text. Verses 49-53 are spoken to disciples; verses 54-56 to the multitudes. For verses 49-50 the other Gospels have no parallel but for verses 51-56 Matthew does. Matthew's version of verses 51-53 is found in 10:34-36 and verses 54-56 are paralleled in 16:2-3. However, Matthew seems to have been aware of Luke's verses 49-50, because Luke's unusual phrase "to cast fire" (verse 49) echoes in Matthew's "to cast peace" (10:34), translated "to bring peace" in the RSV. For our purposes here, we will consider the word to the disciples (verses 49-53) and the word to the crowd (verses 54-56). This is not to separate entirely the two units. Even a casual reading gives one a sense of Luke's reason for joining them: both reflect a disturbed and disturbing present with even more unsettling events on the horizon.

Verses 49-50 express the burden of the one who has set his face toward Jerusalem because the hour of his death, resurrection, and ascension is at hand (9:51). Jesus is ready to enter that dark hour and have it accomplished. Referring to his passion as a baptism is found elsewhere (Mark 10:38). The apocryphal Gospel of Thomas contains two interesting expressions about the "fire" of Jesus' ministry. "Jesus said, 'I have cast fire upon the world, and see, I keep it until it burns up'" (Logion 10), and "He that is near me is near the fire; and he that is far from me is far from the kingdom" (Logion 82). The joining of baptism and fire in our text may be a reflection of the preaching of John the Baptist concerning Jesus: "He will baptize you with the Holy Spirit and with fire" (3:16). Luke later joins the symbols of Spirit (wind) and fire on the occasion of his followers being baptized with the Holy Spirit (Acts 1:5; 2:1-4). But all that waited upon Jesus' "baptism" of a different kind: suffering and death. Then the fire he would cast on the earth would judge, cleanse, and inspire (Zech. 13:9; Mal. 3:2-3).

Jesus' words in verses 51-53 remind the reader of old Simeon's prophecy when the child was being dedicated at the temple: "Behold, this child is set for the fall and rising of many in Israel" (2:34). The decision to follow Jesus, as we have already seen, can disrupt even family obligations (9:57-62). Here it is stated more sharply: taking on a primary loyalty to Jesus creates a breakup of old loyalties, even those as close as family ties. The picture of family tensions here is taken from Micah 7:6, but unlike Micah and Matthew's version (10:34-36), the division is not a case of the younger against the older. There is in Luke no sense of social revolt but of Jesus "making a difference" in the sharpest meaning of that phrase. How the reader understands this and similar passages depends to a large extent on how one understands the condition of the church addressed by Luke. If it were somewhat accommodated to the culture, placing loyalty to Jesus somewhere among its other loyalties, then verses 51-53 are very confronting. But if that church were already experiencing the price being paid, even in the home, for following Jesus, then these words are comforting. The church could find some peace in the knowledge that Jesus himself had said it would be this way.

In verses 54-56 Jesus chastises the crowds for being expert at predicting the weather on the basis of signs and yet being blind to what is really going on among them. It is not fully clear to what Jesus refers in the phrase "interpret the present time." He could be referring to the social and political unrest fomenting. Pilate had already violently crushed a small threat of revolt (13:1-3). The rebellion that would eventually become war, destroying Jerusalem and the temple, was already afoot. More likely, however, Jesus is referring to his own ministry as, in Matthew's wording, the sign of the times. But the two were related in the mind of Luke and other Christian writers. The rejection of Jesus' offer of the way of the kingdom was understood as bearing directly on the calamities to befall the nation politically. Luke's picture of Jesus weeping over Jerusalem "because you did not know the time of your visitation" (19:41-44) says it all most vividly.

Proper 16

Sunday Between August 21 and 27 Inclusive

Jeremiah 28:1-9; Psalm 84; Hebrews 12:18-29; Luke 13:22-30

As is often the case in this season with its semicontinuous readings, these lections offer diverse themes and issues for the preacher's consideration, although all of them may be related to the question of what God has in store for the future. The Old Testament reading is part of the account of Jeremiah's conflict with Hananiah, and raises the question of true and false prophecy. Psalm 84, as a hymn praising Zion and expressing the psalmist's desire to be in the house of the Lord, is a fitting anticipation of the passage from Hebrews, which looks toward that heavenly Jerusalem. The portentous sayings in Luke warn that the door to the Kingdom is a narrow one, and expectations will be reversed.

Jeremiah 28:1-9

Historical considerations are important in understanding this story about two prophets. The fourth year of the reign of Zedekiah (verse 1) would have been 594/3 B.C., that is, between the first sack of Jerusalem by the Babylonians in 597 and the second, and more complete, destruction of the city by the same army in 587. In the period between the two disasters, there seems to have been a continuing debate in Jerusalem about how Judah should respond to the Babylonian control. Those in power favored rebellion, but Jeremiah advocated nonresistance. This debate over international politics stands in the background of Jeremiah 27–28.

As the expression "in that same year" in verse 1 reminds us, Jeremiah 28 is a direct continuation of the events reported in the previous chapter. Chapter 27 tells how Jeremiah had performed a symbolic action, wearing a yoke on his neck and

133

proclaiming that Judah should submit to the yoke of Babylon, for Yahweh himself had given nations into the hand of Nebuchadnezzar (27:6). This symbolic action and its interpretation provided the occasion for a public debate (28:1-9), Hananiah's symbolic action of breaking the yoke (28:10-11), and Jeremiah's prophecy against the other prophet (28:12-17).

Hananiah, the narrative is careful to point out, was a prophet, and he confronted Jeremiah with a prophetic announcement in the name of Yahweh: "I have broken the yoke of the king of Babylon" (verse 2). He goes on to announce that the Exile will end within two years, the looted treasures of the temple will be returned, and King Jehoiakim will be set free (verses 3-4).

Here, then, is the issue. Two prophets, both speaking and acting in the same manner, announce the word of the Lord, but they contradict each other directly. How can the hearers—the priests and all the people standing there—know which is the true prophet? Moreover, there are immediate political and military implications of what each prophet says is the will of God. The one calls for submission to the Babylonian yoke and the other calls for rebellion.

Jeremiah's response to Hananiah's announcement of good news is surprising: "Amen! May the Lord do so" (verse 6). It is possible that these words are sarcastic, but more likely Jeremiah genuinely holds out the possibility that he is wrong and Hananiah is right. Surely he has never taken pleasure in crying doom and destruction. The prophets of Israel expected surprises from their Lord. For the moment he does not react with a word of Yahweh, but appeals to a rational argument based on a pragmatic principle. The pragmatic principle had been stated in Deuteronomy 18:21-22: you will know the true prophet when what he says comes to pass. Pragmatic, yes, but hardly helpful in the moment when one has to decide. Jeremiah then points out the evidence of history as he reads it, namely, that prophets who prophesied war, famine, and pestilence turned out to be right. So to the first principle, fulfillment of the word, Jeremiah adds a second, true prophecy announces judgment. Those that announce salvation are prophecy lies (see also Jer. 14:11-16).

Elsewhere Jeremiah suggests that false prophets are those who "speak visions of their own minds" (23:16-17).

The Book of Deuteronomy indicates another, more theological, criterion by which to test the veracity of prophets. If a prophet gives a sign or a wonder, and what he says does indeed come to pass, and then he calls for the people to serve other gods, he is a false prophet and should be put to death (Deut. 13:1-5). This, finally, is the best the Old Testament can offer on the problem; test what all prophets say against the heart of the faith, that which calls for singleness of devotion to the one Lord. Any word that leads away from that devotion is false.

Our account of the confrontation between Jeremiah and Hananiah would have been put into its final form by the Deuteronomistic editors of the book. They worked not long after the second destruction of Jerusalem which Hananiah said would not come to pass, and they wrote for the exiles in Babylon whom the false prophet said would return within two years. One of their concerns here was to show that the fault for the Exile lies with false prophets whose optimistic nationalism led people astray. By pointing out the causes they sought to avoid a repetition of the disaster.

Psalm 84

Two issues dominate this psalm: pilgrimage to Zion and worship in the temple. The psalm can be understood as a composition written for singing as pilgrims journeyed to attend a festival in Jerusalem. (Many scholars, however, understand the psalm as a composition by someone who could not make the trip to Jerusalem. Thus it is a psalm of homesickness for Zion. This interpretation seems unlikely to me.)

Psalms were no doubt sung by pilgrims on the journey to Jerusalem. Psalm 42:4 speaks of the throng making its way in procession to the house of God "with glad shouts and songs of thanksgiving." Isaiah 30:29, speaking of the good time to come, says: "You shall have a song as in the night when a holy feast is kept; and gladness of heart as when one sets out to the sound of the flute to go to the mountain of Yahweh."

Psalms 120–134 are a collection of songs to be sung on pilgrimage.

One might expect that on pilgrimage antiphonal singing might take place. That is, the leader of the pilgrimage group and the pilgrims would engage in singing to lift the spirits, pass the time, and express the "tourist" atmosphere of the occasion as well as the genuine religious sentiments. This may help explain some of the variations in address in Psalm 84. The following verses are addressed to the Deity—1, 3-7a, 8-10a, 12—while the others speak about the Deity—2, 7b, 10b-11. Perhaps the two portions of the psalm were sung by two different groups in the pilgrimage party or by the leader, with the pilgrims responding.

Verses 1-2 manifest the temple veneration, almost a mystical devotion to the temple, from two perspectives. Verse 1 appears as an objective assertion, or as an affirmation external to the worshipers: "How lovely is thy dwelling place, O Lord of hosts!" The temple was, of course, the "house [home] of God," and here one has the type of accolade that might be made in value-judging a human's place of residence—"What a lovely place you have!" From the external affirmation, the psalm turns to the internal emotion associated with the temple (verse 2). Longing, fainting for, yearning for, singing for joy about are feelings associated with the temple courts. We Christians, and Protestants in particular, have difficulty sharing or understanding the almost sensual happiness and joy associated with festival observances in the temple. Such observances combined high pageantry, feasting and dancing, and the sense of the divine presence with the atmosphere of a country fair and community reunion. Old acquaintances were renewed, past experiences shared, and new relationships acquired. At the same time, one participated in the cultic services and sacrifices that were seen as restoring and preserving world order.

Verses 3-4 give expression to this devotion in terms of a fantasied identification. How glorious it must be for the birds who nest in the temple precincts, near the altars! The birds—here sparrows and swallows—did not nest in or even beside the altars (the altar of sacrifice in the courtyard and the altar of incense in the building) but near them. "Those who dwell in thy house" may refer to the birds, but also the phrase could denote the temple servants, some of whom were always in the temple.

Verses 5-7 speak about factors associated with the pilgrimage—finding refuge (strength) in God and contemplating the roadways or pilgrim paths to Jerusalem. The presence of pilgrims in the valley of Baca ("thirst" or "weeping") transforms it into an oasis, just as the early fall rains, which could begin in September before the fall festival, moisten the soil, hot and arid from the rainless summer. As the pilgrims move closer to Jerusalem, their numbers swell ("from strength to strength") as parties from other areas join together.

Verses 8-9 are, in some ways and when analyzed closely, a bit peculiar. Verse 8 contains references in the first person singular ("my"), while verse 9 uses the plural ("our"). Again, this may be explained by antiphonal usage. The prayer for the welfare of the king ("thine anointed") is not so much out of place if we think in terms of a monarchical society and the close association between the Davidic king and the temple/Deity.

Two analogies are drawn in verse 10 to describe the joy of worship in and a visit to the temple. One day there is better than a thousand somewhere else. Verse 10b seems, in Hebrew, to give the following sense: "I would rather serve insecurely at the threshold of the temple than to dwell at ease in the tents of wickedness." Better nothing and servitude in the sanctuary than plenty and wealth elsewhere.

In the last analysis, the psalm turns to a praise of God in verses 11-12, since because of God the temple is what it is. It is God who gives and provides and does not withhold.

Hebrews 12:18-29

Today's text divides in two halves. In the first part, the two covenants are contrasted (verses 18-24), and in the second part we are urged to pay heed to the God who has instituted the new covenant (verses 25-29).

The two covenants contrasted (verses 18-24). We are actually presented here with two routes for our pilgrimage, each with a different destination: Mt. Sinai and Mt. Zion. We should note the language used to introduce each way: "For you have not come to . . ." (verse 18) is clearly contrasted with "but you have come to . . ." (verse 22). The language of coming, or journeying, suggests a pilgrimage, and probably continues the race metaphor introduced in verses 1-2, and continued in verses 12-13.

First, we have sketched for us the way that has been, or should have been, abandoned, from which we have turned away (verses 18-21). It is the way of Mt. Sinai, understood here as that which can be touched. This emphasis on the palpable recalls the earlier contrast between the earthly and the heavenly tabernacle (8:1-6; 9:11-12; 10:19-20). Sinai is thus identified with the earthly reality of the tabernacle that was experienced with the senses, for the Israelites were warned against touching the holy mountain (Exod. 19:10-15).

But more than this, we are reminded that the giving of the Law on Sinai was a terrifying moment. The sights ranged from blazing fire to total darkness. Dark clouds were accompanied by bolts of lightning and peals of thunder. With the wind and storm, there was the divine voice that filled the heavens, accompanied by the blast of trumpets (Exod. 19:12-22; 20:18-20; Deut. 4:11-12; 5:22). So overwhelming was this divine epiphany that Israel was petrified (verse 20; Exod. 20:18-20). Even Moses himself experienced this encounter with God as a moment of terror (verse 21; cf. Deut. 9:19). All this by way of saying that Sinai is an unnerving experience that sends shivers through the soul.

Second, we have sketched for us the way of Mount Zion, the destination to which the pilgrimage of the new covenant leads us (verses 22-24). It is sharply contrasted with Sinai because it links us with heavenly realities, notably the "heavenly Jerusalem" (cf. Gal. 4:24-26). Here we have presented the eschatological vision expected by the prophets (Joel 2:32; Isa. 4:5) and embodied in apocalyptic hopes (Rev. 14:1-2; 21:1–22:5).

What we find here is Paradise in every sense: the city inhabited by the living God (11:10; 13:14; Rev. 21:2), the heavenly Jerusalem (Gal. 4:26; Phil. 3:20; Rev. 21:6); the heavenly court of angels (Rev. 5:11; Dan. 7:10); "the full concourse and assembly of the first-born citizens of heaven" (verse 23, NEB, cf. Luke 10:20; Phil. 4:3; Rev. 3:5; cf. Exod. 32:32; Isa. 4:3); God the universal judge (Rom. 2:6; II Tim. 4:8; James 4:12; 5:9); the spirits of the righteous who have been perfected, perhaps through martyrdom; Jesus the high priest and mediator of the new covenant (cf. 7:22; 8:6-10; 9:15-20; 10:29; 13:20; also Luke 22:20); and the sacrificial blood of Christ that surpasses the blood of Abel, that is, the blood of forgiveness not the blood of revenge (9:13-14; I Pet. 1:1-2; cf. Heb. 11:4; Gen. 4:10).

An appeal in the form of a threat (verses 25-29). In the second part of our text, we hear both an appeal and a warning; or rather an appeal made as a warning. The tone may surprise us in light of the fearful picture painted in verses 18-21, but the tone is stern. We are warned not to refuse the voice of God. Israel may have heard the divine voice on earth, but we hear it echo through the heavenly city, and we do well not to ignore it (verse 25; cf. Heb. 2:2-3; 10:28-29). Ultimately, the divine voice will shake both earth and heaven. This is a clear reference to the final dissolution of the cosmos, and this eschatological upheaval will supercede all previous moments when God's voice shook the earth (cf. Judg. 5:4-5; Ps. 68:9; 77:19; 114:7; Hag. 2:6, 21; also Matt. 24:29).

In the face of this cosmic shaking, the only secure way is to be a part of the unshakable kingdom (verse 28; cf. Isa. 66:22; Dan. 7:14-18). The proper response is to worship God (9:14; Rom. 1:9; cf. Deut. 11:13) in a way that is pleasing (11:5-6; 13:16, 21; II Cor. 5:9). The final note is a sober reminder of God's destructive power (verse 28; 10:31; Deut. 4:24; 9:3; Isa. 33:14; II Thess. 1:7-8).

Within the context of Hebrews, this sharply etched contrast between earthly Sinai and heavenly Zion is understandable, but the preacher will think carefully about this terrifying portrait of Sinai and ask whether it does full justice to the Old Testament. An additional tension is the rejection of the way of fear, as symbolized by Sinai, in the first part of our lection, and the threatening note on which our passage ends. What cannot be denied, of course, is the truly captivating, paradisal vision of the new covenant sketched in verses 22-24. It is every bit as powerful as the much grander version in the book of Revelation and lends itself equally well to preaching.

Luke 13:22-30

The preacher who has been following the Gospel lessons from Luke, especially since 9:51 about two months ago, may by this time begin to feel what the listeners are feeling: these demands of discipleship are heavy. Recall some phrases from those texts: set his face to go to Jerusalem; leave the dead to bury the dead; whoever puts the hand to the plow and looks back; carry no purse, no bag, no sandals; shake the dust off your feet; go and do likewise; one thing is needful; beware of all covetousness; sell your possessions and give alms; be ready, for the Son of man is coming at an unexpected hour; I came to cast fire upon the earth, not peace but division. If there is a sense of an accumulated burden, rather than providing comic relief one Sunday or otherwise pulling the punch of Jesus' teachings, the Gospel and discipleship might be served by having a focus and summary sermon. This is to say, draw it all together in terms of Jesus' situation and with a few clear images give these past few weeks a single focus.

This seems to be exactly what Luke is doing in 13:22-30. Much has been said since he set the context in 9:51: Jesus sets his face to go to Jerusalem because his hour of departure is near. Since he is on the way to the cross, what is he going to say to would-be followers? We have been listening to what he said. Now Luke feels it is time to remind the reader of the context, and so he does. "He went on his way through towns and villages, teaching, and journeying toward Jerusalem" (verse 22). Someone among the hearers asks a question, a familiar way of launching material in Luke (11:1; 12:13; 13:41; 13:1). The question is not that person's alone, unless that person has been following Jesus since 9:51. More realistically it is the question of the reader or hearer of 9:51–13:21. The ear and heart are heavy and only one question forms in the mind: "Lord, will those who are saved be few?" (verse 23).

What follows is a composite of teachings of Jesus which summarize what has been taught thus far about discipleship.

That verses 24-30 are composite is indicated by the fact that Matthew has parallel versions but scattered in six different locations in his Gospel. The composite nature of this section is also evident by the internal disjunctures and shifts. For example, verse 24 speaks of entering by a narrow door, indicating the discipline required, the difficulties of getting in the kingdom. Here one recalls the more familiar narrow gate and hard way of Matthew 7:14. However, "door" in the next verse represents an entirely different image. The master closing the door refers not to a narrow entrance but to that eschatological moment when the time of opportunity is ended. Luke's words in verses 25-27 seem to echo the parable of the wise and foolish maidens of Matthew 25:1-13. The following image of a great ingathering of outsiders sits less comfortably here than as Jesus' words to Israel after he healed a Gentile soldier's servant (Matt. 8:10-12). And the closing verse (30) is a floating saying, found as the terminus to many teachings (Mark 10:31; Matt. 19:30; 20:16).

All of this is to say, What about Luke's intent in this section? If one overlooks the composite nature of it for a moment, one clear picture comes into focus. Jesus, Luke reminds the reader, is on his way to Jerusalem. Given the stringent demands for discipleship, will only a few be saved? Jesus says the opportunity to enter is there but the door is narrow and demands more than casual interest. However, even that narrow door will not always be open. There is an eschaton, the closing of the door of open invitation. When it is closed, it is closed, and certainly will not be reopened for persons who have no more claim than that Jesus once visited their town, or preached in their streets, or they knew members of Jesus' family, or once saw him in a crowd. And added to the pain of having missed their opportunity will be the sight of a large ingathering of persons from other nations who heard and believed. Hence, some of the first will be last and some of the last will be first.

Heard in this way, Luke 13:22-30 puts it all into focus for Israel, for Luke's church, and for us, and gives all of us an opportunity to reflect on where we stand.

141

Proper 17

Sunday Between August 28 and September 3 Inclusive

Ezekiel 18:1-9, 25-29; Psalm 15; Hebrews 13:1-8; Luke 14:1, 7-14

All of today's texts converge on the themes of sin and righteousness and their effects. The Old Testament lection presents Ezekiel's argument that all will be held responsible for their own sin or righteousness, the prophet's characterization of the righteous life, and his call for repentance. The responsorial psalm, in specifying who is worthy to enter the temple, likewise characterizes the life of the righteous person. The passage from Hebrews gives admonitions for Christian behavior, and the Gospel text contains a parable concerning humility and the exhortation to invite in the poor, the maimed, the lame, and the blind.

Ezekiel 18:1-9, 25-29

In Ezekiel we meet a prophet who was active in Babylon during the Exile. That he was taken in the first group of exiles with King Jehoiachin and the nobles in 597 B.C. suggests that he was among Jerusalem's aristocracy, a conclusion borne out by what we learn of him from the book. He received his call in Jehoiachin's fifth year (Ezek. 1:2), that is, 593. While Ezekiel was a prophet, especially in the tradition of Hosea, Isaiah, and Jeremiah—whose works he seems to know—his message has affinities on the one hand with priestly concerns and on the other hand with apocalyptic expectations. He was deeply steeped in Israel's legal tradition, including the substance of the laws in Exodus 20–24, the Book of Deuteronomy, and the Holiness Code (Lev. 17–26). His vision reports, in terms both of style and imagery, suggest those of later apocalyptic literature.

Ezekiel 18 records a disputation of the prophet with an audience of the Judean exiles. He addresses them directly throughout, and frequently cites their own words as he opposes them. On the surface, the occasion for the dispute is their repetition of the proverb, "The fathers have eaten sour grapes, and the children's teeth are set on edge" (verse 2). But the saying is just the tip of the iceberg, reflecting some deep problems. The exiles are dispirited, believing themselves caught in the cycle of sin and judgment, living under a curse set into motion by their ancestors. Ezekiel uses the form of debate to correct their views, teaching a different understanding of sin and punishment. But we should not let his repetitious and legal arguments obscure the main goal of the chapter. He holds out "life"—the full, abundant life in the presence of God (verses 9, 21, 22, 27, 28, 32)—to the despairing people, arguing that the sins of the fathers are not visited upon the children, and that even the sinner can repent.

The passage presents three distinct but related themes, any one of which merits consideration by the preacher:

1. The most obvious point is Ezekiel's reaction to the proverb, which amounts to an assertion of individual responsibility. The proverb (see also Jer. 31:29), of course, comes from a tradition often expressed in the Old Testament, including in the Decalogue: "visiting the iniquity of the fathers upon the children to the third and the fourth generation" (Exod. 20:5; Deut. 5:9). Harsh as it is, there is some truth to the saying. Children do, indeed, often suffer for the sins of their parents. But the legal tradition also held individuals responsible for their behavior. The problem is that Ezekiel's compatriots have taken the proverb as the full interpretation of their situation in Exile and thus live in resignation, bearing the iniquity of their ancestors. Thus, for all the warnings about death to the individual sinner, the news is good: You are set free from the effects of the sins of your parents.

2. Then there is Ezekiel's description of the life of the righteous person. More than a dozen points are listed (verses

143

5-9) in the form of case law, "if he does. . . ," and most of them are negative in form, noting what the righteous one does not do. The catalog is not meant to be exhaustive, but it is well worth pondering. None of these provisions is new. Most of them can be found in the Old Testament legal corpus, especially Leviticus 17–26 and Exodus 21–23. They concern a wide range of matters, from false worship to cultic purity to matters of social justice, including generosity to the poor. All are summed up at the beginning and end (verses 5 and 9) in the word "righteous." As Psalm 15 (the response for the day) clearly shows, such righteousness was the criterion for admission to the house of the Lord, and thus to the full life.

3. Next there is the call to repentance. The disputation of which our reading is a part does not reach its goal until Ezekiel 18:30-32. Throughout the argument stressing individual responsibility, the prophet has indicated that both the righteous ones and sinners may turn from their ways and have the consequences of that new direction (verses 26-27). In the concluding paragraph this motif becomes an explicit call to repent. Herein also the justice of God is manifest, that sinners may turn and have that full life. Not only are the effects of sin held in check, limited to the effects for the individual, but even a sinner is called to get "a new heart and a new spirit" (verse 31). In answer to the challenge to God's justice (verse 25), Ezekiel hears God affirming, "For I have no pleasure in the death of anyone . . . so turn, and live" (verse 32).

Psalm 15

This psalm provides an excellent follow-up to last Sunday's lection. That reading was a psalm focusing on pilgrimage and worship in the temple. Psalm 15 was originally used as an entrance liturgy by pilgrims entering the sanctuary. Like the parallel reading from Ezekiel, it offers a series of qualities characteristic of the ideal worshiper.

The psalm opens with a question, perhaps asked by pilgrims as they reached the temple gates, Who can enter the sacred precincts? It is asked here in a graphic and metaphorical form as if access was to be permanent (verse 1).

Admittance to the courts of the temple is the concern of the questions.

The remainder of the psalm is an answer to the question, probably spoken by cultic officials (the Levites? the priests?) inside the precincts. The requirements for entry are given in a series of ten characteristics. It should be noted that, in antiquity, temples did not operate on the principle, "Everyone welcome, all come." Certain persons (cripples and deformed, those with improper parentage) and persons at certain times (when unclean from contact with some pollutant, women during menstruation, persons with certain skin ailments) were not admitted into the sanctuary (see Deut. 23:1-8).

The characteristics of those who might enter were probably proclaimed to the worshipers as the proper qualities of life; pilgrims couldn't be checked on an individual basis, and some of the characteristics noted are as much attitudes as action. Two features about the requirements in the psalm are noteworthy. (1) The requirements articulated all fall into the category of what we would today call moral qualities and interpersonal attitudes. None of the characteristics would fit into the category of purity laws and regulations, such as having recently touched a dead body or eaten unkosher food. (Note how the two are intermingled in Ezek. 18.) (2) The qualifications given in the psalm are ten in number. (Ten was a round figure, and lists of ten could be memorized by ticking off the list on one's fingers. The Ten Commandments may once have been used in such gate or entrance liturgies, perhaps being written on two stone slabs or the posts of the temple gates.)

The following is a listing of the ten requirements:

1. Walks blamelessly and does what is right (behaves according to the accepted mores and standards of the society)
2. Speaks truth from the heart (shows integration of the internal will and external actions; does what one says and says what one thinks)
3. Does not slander with his tongue (does not attack others verbally and falsely so as to destroy them)
4. Does no evil to his friend (does not physically harm his fellow human beings)

145

5. Does not take up a reproach against the neighbor (does not participate in or perpetuate gossip or spread rumors)
6. Despises a reprobate (dislikes those who turn their back upon God or society)
7. Honors those who fear God (the positive counterpart to the preceding negative)
8. Swears to one's own hurt and does not change (one's word and oath were kept, even if keeping them brings injury and cost to oneself)
9. Does not put out money at interest (does not use another person's need to one's advantage; see Deut. 23:19-20)
10. Does not take a bribe against the innocent (would not do wrong even if paid; see Exod. 23:8; Lev. 19:15; Deut. 16:19)

Those who live up to such standards are declared blessed, unshakable, immovable (verse 5c). This final formulation is interesting. The focus of the conclusion is no longer on such a person who has access to the holy place but on such a person who has the quality of life and integration of social characteristics that make for stability of life.

Hebrews 13:1-8

In this final reading from the Epistle to the Hebrews, we have a set of concluding admonitions. This miscellany of Christian advice, which actually extends through verse 21, reminds us of similar lists of exhortations we find at the end of other New Testament letters (cf. I Thess. 5:12-22; also I Cor. 16:13; II Cor. 13:11-13; Gal. 6:1-10; Phil. 4:4-13; Col. 4:1-6). The recommendations here follow no set order nor do they explore a common theme, but move from one topic to another. Let us consider them in turn.

Love for fellow Christians (verses 1-3). The first call is for "brotherly love" (*philadelphia*, verse 1), sharply stated in NEB: "Never cease to love your fellow-Christians." Earlier, the readers are urged to cultivate a genuine sense of community among themselves (10:24). This was a regular concern within early Christian communities (cf. Rom. 12:10; I Thess. 4:9; I Pet. 1:22; II Pet. 1:7). At times, it was advice that was especially needed since Christian communities sometimes found themselves threatened by internal strife ranging from minor disputes (Phil. 4:2; also 2:1-4, 14-15; I Cor. 1:10:13) to

146

more searing dissensions (II Cor. 10-13; I John 4:20-21; also 7-12). These various bits of encouragement at least reflect a sober realism among New Testament writers. They knew only too well the sheer difficulty of living together in community and did not naïvely assume that Christians would automatically love one another.

Concretely, love for fellow Christians meant extending hospitality to strangers, most likely to fellow Christian travelers (Rom. 12:13; I Peter 4:9). As an incentive, we are reminded of those Old Testament instances where Yahweh appeared in the form of strangers (Gen. 18–19; Judg. 5:11-24; 13:3-25; Tobit 5:4-28). Such display of concern for strangers was important enough to become a criterion for leadership in the churches (I Tim. 3:2; Tit. 1:8), as well as for determining who could be assisted financially by the churches (I Tim. 5:10). It was more than simply accommodating passersby, but specifically had to do with hosting itinerant Christian preachers, teachers, and other faithful workers (Matt. 10:11-14; Luke 10:4-12; Acts 17:5-9; 21:4, 7, 16-17; Rom. 15:28-29; 16:1-2; I Cor. 16:10-11; Phil. 2:29; Philem. 22; III John 5-8, 10). Even though the practice could be abused (II John 10; Didache 11–12), it was nevertheless expected that traveling Christian teachers would be well received by other Christians.

Another way of showing love was to visit fellow Christians imprisoned, or ill-treated in other ways, for the sake of the gospel (10:34; 11:36). Doing so is to take seriously the teaching of Christ (Matt. 25:31-46) and to exhibit genuine empathy (I Cor. 12:26).

Marriage and sexual morality (verse 4). Even though Jesus was celibate, he taught a high view of marriage informed by the biblical account of creation (Matt. 19:3-9; Gen. 1:27; 2:24). This view was sustained in the early church in spite of ascetic tendencies that placed severe strains on marriages (I Cor. 7). So well regarded was marriage that it could become an analogy for the relationship between Christ and the church (Eph. 5:21-33). Fidelity to marriage vows excluded fornication and adultery, and our text takes a typical hard line against violators (cf. I Cor. 6:9-10; Gal. 5:20-21; Rev. 21:8; 22:15).

Contentment and reliance on God's care (verses 5-6). We are instructed not to "live for money" (verse 5, NEB). Being locked into the love for money is recognized in the New Testament as one of the cardinal vices (I Tim. 6:10), and serves to disqualify one from a position of leadership (I Tim. 3:3). The seduction of riches and their debilitating effects become a major theme in Luke-Acts (cf. Luke 12:13-21). To counteract the compulsive desire to acquire possessions and find our sense of security in them, today's text calls for a sense of contentment grounded in reliance on God's fidelity (Phil. 4:12; I Tim. 6:8). It is the God who faithfully promised to care for Israel (Gen. 28:15; Deut. 31:6; Josh. 1:5) and to whom the psalmist confidently looked for sustenance (Ps. 118:6; 27:1-3) on whom Christians rely for life and sustenance (Matt. 6:25-33; Rom. 8:31-39).

Loyal respect for Christian leaders (verse 7). Early Christian communities appear to have been organized in a manner similar to Jewish communities where there were duly appointed or selected leaders to oversee various aspects of community life (cf. Acts 11:30; 14:23; 15:2-3; 20:17; 21:18). These included a body of presbyters, who at the earliest stages were also designated as bishops, and their role of oversight appears to have been limited to single congregations of believers (cf. Acts 14:23; 20:17-38; Phil. 1:1; I Tim. 3:1-7; Tit. 1:5-9). Other leadership roles also emerged as some became deacons and deaconesses (Acts 6:1-7; Rom. 16:1; Phil. 1:1; I Tim. 3:8-13). Whether today's text is enlisting respect (and obedience, 11:17) for duly appointed elders is not clear, since this terminology is absent. The leaders who are to be remembered, respected, and imitated are those who have "spoken the word of God," thus who have been teachers (cf. Acts 4:29, 31; 8:25; 11:19; 13:46; 14:25; 16:6, 32; Phil. 1:14). Elders had the responsibility to teach (Acts 20:28; I Tim. 3:2; 5:17; Tit. 1:9), and may very well be in view here. But this just as easily may be a call to respect those whose leadership has been proven through their teaching and service (cf. I Cor. 16:15-18; also Luke 22:26). Whoever they are, their manner of life is expected to be exemplary as a model for imitation (6:12; cf. I Cor. 4:16; 11:1; Gal. 4:12; Eph. 5:1; Phil. 3:17; 4:9; I Thess. 1:6; 2:14; II Thess. 3:7, 9).

Reliability of Christ (verse 8). Even though today's lection ends with this bold declaration of Christ's immutability, the context suggests that it actually belongs with what follows (verses 9-11). Nevertheless, even in its detached form, it provides a strong concluding note for this lection. Reminiscent of an opening motif of the letter (1:12; cf. 7:24), this reassuring claim attributes to Christ what Israel had predicated of God: One who is the same through the ages, unaffected by time (Ps. 102:27).

Luke 14:1, 7-14

Verse 1 provides the setting for Luke's material through verse 24. "Table talk" was a fairly common literary device for gathering into one place several independent units. In verses 1-24 there are four stories that do not depend on one another for their meaning: verses 1-6, 7-11, 12-14, 15-24. Even if Luke is here using a literary device for joining pieces of tradition, this is not to say the setting of a meal was an unimportant detail for him. On the contrary, meals were of profound theological significance for Luke. Bread was important; in fact, where some eat and some do not eat, the kingdom is not present (16:19-31). Breaking bread was important; in fact, the real test of whether the church included persons who were different was not at the point of baptizing them but of eating with them (Acts 11:1-3). Fellowship meals were central in the church's life together; in fact, the risen Lord "was known to them in the breaking of bread" (24:35). Let no one think, then, that Luke's locating many of Jesus' teachings "at table" was only "a nice little touch."

Both verses 7-11 and 12-14 concern self-seeking, in the one case as guest, in the other as host. Upon observing the scramble for places of honor, Jesus advised choosing the lowest place, far removed from the head table. In so doing, one avoids public embarrassment and may, on occasion, be called up to a higher place, providing one a moment in the spotlight of public admiration. In and of itself this is of no religious significance but rather is sound practical advice on social behavior. However, Luke says Jesus spoke it as a parable (verse 7), meaning Jesus is not simply discussing etiquette. That Jesus has in mind kingdom behavior is made explicit in the closing statement: "For every one who exalts himself will be humbled, and he who humbles himself will be exalted" (verse 11). This pronouncement occurs frequently in the Gospels (Matt. 18:4; 23:12; Luke 18:14).

In dealing with this and similar teachings of Jesus, the preacher will be alert to the devious ways in which the ego can convert Jesus' words into a new strategy for self-exaltation. Modesty can be exaggerated and humility can be a form of pride. It would be too bad if this teaching generated a mad rush for the lowest seats with all the competitors all the while glancing toward the head table, waiting to be called up.

Verses 12-14 address the host, and again Jesus is not giving lessons on social graces. The point is, hosting can be a way of making others feel they are in your debt, so they in turn will reciprocate when preparing their guest lists. The cycle of seeking a return on one's behavior toward others repeats itself, for common sense dictates that self-interest not offer self or goods to persons who cannot repay. In the kingdom, however, God is always host, and we extend God's invitation to those who cannot repay. After all, who can repay God? Jesus, therefore, is calling for behavior that lives out this conviction about the kingdom; that is, inviting to table (quite different from sending food to) those who have neither property nor place in society. Luke's fourfold list: the poor, the maimed, the lame, and the blind (verse 13) is repeated in the next story (beyond our lection). In that passage containing the parable of the banquet (verses 15-24) these people from the fringes are guests at the banquet, replacing those who failed to attend because they had other things to do. From the Song of Mary (1:46-55) to the end of his Gospel, Luke is careful to remind us that these, too, are kingdom people.

Proper 18

Sunday Between September 4 and 10 Inclusive

Ezekiel 33:1-11; Psalm 94:12-22; Philemon 1-20; Luke 14:25-33

The texts for the day, diverse as they are, intersect at several points. Ezekiel 33:1-11 reports the prophet's call to be a "watchman" for Israel and affirms that the faithful performance of his duty is a matter of life and death. In the Gospel lesson, Jesus stresses the difficulty of the conditions for discipleship. The responsorial psalm echoes the right note from the first reading concerning the Lord's purpose in calling a watchman, that the Lord seeks to bless even those whom he chastens. Philemon concerns a runaway slave who apparently has repented and wishes to return to his owner.

Ezekiel 33:1-11

A new section of the Book of Ezekiel begins with this text. The arrangement is more or less chronological, with the turning point identified in 33:21-22 where the news is given that Jerusalem has fallen. Since Ezekiel received his initial call in Jehoiachin's fifth year (593), this would have been the second capture of the city in 587 B.C. But the book's arrangement is also theological, and likely reflects a change of emphasis in the prophet's role and message. Before 587 he proclaimed judgment and warning concerning the coming disaster. Now the words are more and more focused on the life and fate of the Judeans in exile, calling for their obedience to the law and warning them of the consequences of disobedience. Moreover, the message increasingly focuses upon the announcement of salvation beyond the judgment.

Our reading begins a unit that is not concluded until 33:20. Following the introductory formula for the word of the Lord in verse 1, the entire unit is presented as a speech of Yahweh

151

directly to the prophet. The Lord addresses the prophet as "son of man," which simply means "human being," "mortal." There are three distinct parts to the speech: (1) in verses 2-7 Yahweh describes the case of a "watchman" ("sentry" is a more precise and inclusive translation) appointed in time of war; (2) verses 8-9 apply the case to Ezekiel, whom the Lord commissions to be a sentry; and (3) verses 10-20 present the Lord's responses to questions posed by the people of Israel, questions concerning divine justice and the effects of sin.

The style of verses 2-7 is casuistic, like case law in presenting a series of connected conditions, from more general to more specific, with the results of each condition stated. The imagery comes from warfare. If, in time of war, the people elect a sentry, and if danger comes, and if the sentry warns someone by blowing the trumpet, and if that person heeds the warning then life is the result. But if not, then the person is responsible for his own death. But if the sentry does not sound the alarm, and someone dies, then he is held accountable. In fact, such a sentry is guilty of murder. Note that the ground is already laid for the theological application of the extended metaphor when the prophet points out that Yahweh is the one who brings the sword (verse 2; cf. Amos 3:6), and the one who imposes the death sentence on the negligent sentry (verse 6).

Verses 7-9 begin with the explicit commission of the prophet as a sentry for the house of Israel and then, literally, lay down the law to him, again in casuistic form. (Ezekiel 3:16b-19 is an exact parallel.) Instead of seeing the sword coming, however, this sentry hears a word of the Lord and must proclaim the warning. If the Lord announces death to the wicked, then Ezekiel must warn that person. If he fails to do so, he is guilty of a capital crime. But, like the sentry for the city under the sword, his responsibilities have their limits. The prophet does not cause the disaster, and once he has given his warning, he has saved his life.

Verses 9-20, a close parallel to last week's lesson from Ezekiel 18, are in the form of a disputation between Yahweh and the people. The dispute assumes that the people have heard and accepted the sentry's warning, but now raise questions about what to do and what to believe. Their words mingle confession of sin with complaint. They are trapped in the effects of iniquity. Now the divine purpose is made plain. The threat of judgment and the sentry's warning are to provoke the repentance that results in life.

The text evokes reflection on two distinct issues. The first concerns the vocation and role of the prophet as sentry for the people. While other prophets as well had seen themselves as watchmen (Isa. 28:1; Jer. 6:17-19; Hab. 2:1), the role described here represents a development of earlier understandings of the prophetic role, in two ways: (1) prophets had been called not primarily to warn but to announce, and thereby to set into motion, the Lord's judgment (Amos 1:2; Isa. 6:1-13; Jer. 1:4-10); and (2) most earlier prophets mainly addressed the people as a whole, but now Ezekiel is to warn individual sinners. His duty is pastoral, to shepherd persons to life. Most important is the combination of urgency and limits in the prophetic role. Faithfulness to the call to be a sentry is, quite literally, a matter of life and death. But once the prophet sounds the warning, his duty is done. There is no way that he is responsible for the sinner's failure to heed his cry.

Second, when the prophet reported to the people what he had heard, as he surely did, what kind of message was it? In reporting his call to be a sentry he already begins to sound the warning. The purpose of the passage, then, is found in verse 11: the Lord, who has no pleasure in the death of the wicked, calls for the people to turn back and find life. What is God's purpose? He brings the sword upon the city and sets death before the sinner. But the one who brings judgment also provides the means to avert it, to frustrate his own plans. The Lord wants to be given every opportunity to repent. Thus announcement of judgment becomes warning to avoid it. The Lord's sentry, through sounding the warning and calling for repentance, is an instrument of divine grace.

Psalm 94:12-22

This lament wrestles with the problem of undeserved distress and suffering. The troubles that plagued the user seem not to have been limited to a particular person, but appear to have been widespread and communally endured. Before analyzing the psalm's response to such troubles, we should note a few things about its structure.

The psalm opens with a plea to God for action (verse 1-2) and includes a complaint against the Deity (verse 3). The situation of distress, or the trouble, is described to God in verses 4-7. The evil situation seems to have been caused by native Israelite leaders or rulers who oppressed the people, especially the powerless elements of society. So far, the psalm has been addressed to the Deity in the form of prayer. Verses 8-11 are human-to-human speech. Those addressed are called the "dullest of the people! Fools . . ." ("most brutish people; fools"; NJPSV). Who is speaking? Who is being addressed? One can assume that the worshiper or perhaps a priest here addresses either the co-sufferers or else the oppressors. The points made in verses 8-11 are: (1) God as creator, the one who planted the ear and formed the eye, still hears and sees, and (2) God who disciplines (chastens) nations and teaches knowledge through such discipline certainly knows the thoughts of humans who before him are only a breath any way. That is, God is still in control and capable of executing actions against the oppressors.

Verses 12-13, the opening of today's lection, returns to the form of prayer, as the worshiper makes a semi-optimistic assessment of the hard days and oppression now being experienced. Suffering is seen as chastisement (or discipline), a form of instruction, which allows the sufferer to endure the days of trouble. Suffering in this case, however, is seen as only temporary, that is, until a pit is dug for the wicked (either by themselves or by God) and the trouble-makers (see verses 4-7) are destroyed. The chastisement is thus seen as a form of discipline in the interim between trouble and salvation. The sense of the text is better seen in the NJPSV than in the RSV:

> Happy is the man whom You discipline, O Lord,
>   the man whom You instruct in Your teaching,
>   to give him tranquility in time of misfortune,
>   until a pit be dug for the wicked.

A return to proclamation occurs in verses 14-15 where, apparently, the priest confirms the final point of the preceding prayer: God does not abandon or forsake his people; justice will prevail for the righteous.

The worshiper's response to the proclamation of verses 14-15 is twofold. First, there is the worshiper's statement to a human audience (or the priests) acknowledging trust in God and affirming that if God had not been his/her helper, death would long ago have been the worshiper's destiny (verses 16-17). It is God who stands between the afflicted and the wicked. Second, there is the worshiper's confessional statement addressed to God which affirms that it is the Deity who has seen him/her through troubles both external (the foot that slips) and internal (the heart laden with pain), verses 18-19. Verses 20-21 again suggest that political powers or powerful persons are the cause of the misery. (The translation of verse 20 is highly disputed. Compare the RSV with the NEB: "Shall sanctimonious calumny call thee partner, or he that contrives a mischief under cover of law?")

The psalm concludes with the worshiper's reassertion, to a human audience, of confidence in the divine (verse 22) and in God's eventual correction of the situation (verse 23). Note that verse 23a assumes that it is the wicked persons' iniquity that will come back on them—their own actions will be the means of their destruction, and God will oversee the process by which retribution works itself out.

In their preaching on this psalm, ancient Jewish rabbis spoke about the positive aspects of discipline and chastisement. Through discipline, they said, God gave good gifts to Israel—the Law, the world to come, and the Land of Promise. Chastisements, they argued, were really better than offerings and sacrifices since offerings come out of a person's property, but chastisements fall upon a person's body.

Philemon 1-20

Of all the Pauline Letters, this brief note to Philemon most resembles the personal letters preserved among the papyri from the ancient world. The circumstances that occasioned the letter are well known. Onesimus, the runaway slave of

Philemon, had made his way to the city where Paul was imprisoned, probably Rome (verses 1, 9-10, 13, 23). There he had become a Christian through the direct influence of Paul. As his "father in the gospel" (verse 10), Paul assumed responsibility for his welfare and considered it in his best interest to return him to his master Philemon, a resident of Colossae (Col. 4:9). What we have here is a letter of recommendation in which Paul appeals to Philemon to receive back his runaway slave "no longer as a slave but more than a slave, as a beloved brother" (verse 16).

Even in its brief form, the letter follows the same basic structure as other Pauline Letters: greeting (verses 1-3), a prayer of thanksgiving (verses 4-7), the appeal (verses 8-21), closing greetings (verses 23-24), benediction (verse 25).

The portrait of Philemon that emerges within the letter is especially revealing. We are told that the church met in his house (verse 2), which displays a level of hospitality that distinguished a select group of early Christians (cf. Acts 16:15, 31; 17:6-7; 18:1-8; Rom. 16:5; I Cor. 16:19; Col. 4:15). It is also a probable indication of his high social position. Not only did he make his home available for the service of the gospel, but he followed suit with his own life, for he is described in intimate, yet highly respectful terms, as a "beloved fellow worker" (verse 1).

The extent and quality of his service is also reflected in the prayer of thanksgiving (verses 4-7), which is unusual compared with other Pauline thanksgivings in that it is couched in the second person singular, and thus addressed directly to Philemon. We are told of his faith in the Lord and love for the saints (verse 5; cf. Col. 1:4; Eph. 1:15; also I Cor. 13:13), as well as the joy and comfort he has brought to Paul (verse 7). He has been a source of refreshment to the saints (verse 7).

In view of the fact that Paul will later ask Philemon a favor, we are not surprised at this laudatory tone. But it need not be interpreted purely as a strategic move to enlist Philemon's favor. The overall tone actually suggests that Philemon is a benefactor of the church. Between the lines we should perhaps see references to his generosity on behalf of the church. If so, his "love for the saints" (verse 5), the joy and comfort he has brought Paul (verse 7), and the refreshment he has given the saints (verse 7) may be softly couched expressions for the money he has given to the church. Accordingly, Paul's prayer that the sharing of his faith (verse 6), or "your fellowship with us in our common faith" (NEB), may be a prayer for his continued financial support in making possible the promotion of the knowledge of the gospel (Note: *koinonia*, or "fellowship" in reference to financial contributions in Acts 2:42; Rom. 15:26; II Cor. 8:4; 9:13.)

It is conceivable, then, that Philemon has also been a financial supporter of Paul (verse 7), to the point that Paul can consider him a "partner" *(koinonos)* in the gospel (verse 17; cf. Phil. 1:5). There is also the intriguing, cryptic remark in verse 19 that Philemon is indebted to Paul for his "own self." Paul might have been responsible for saving Philemon's life, but more likely it suggests that, like Onesimus, Philemon had been converted by Paul.

What emerges from the letter is the portrait of a well-to-do Christian, a convert of Paul, who has given both himself and his property in the service of the church. Because of his generous temperament, Paul seems confident that he will accept Onesimus back and thinks it unnecessary to pull rank in making this appeal (verses 8, 14). His appeal is made to love for love's sake (verse 9). The special appeal that Onesimus be received as a Christian brother (verse 16) also reflects a mood of confidence (verse 21). Even though he would return as a slave, it is to a relationship that has begun to be transformed by the gospel (cf. I Tim. 6:2; I Cor. 7:22).

An equally informative portrait of Onesimus emerges from the letter. As a young convert he has endeared himself through his service so that Paul can refer to him as "my very heart" (verse 12). Elsewhere, he is called "faithful and beloved brother" (Col. 4:9). We should also note the well-known pun in verse 11: at one time useless *(achreston)* but now useful *(euchreston)*. Here too we have a picture of someone setting out on the road of Christian service, urged on by the encouragement and support of Paul, his father in the gospel, and Philemon, now his brother in the gospel.

As we have seen, one homiletical possibility is to do a character study of Philemon, supplemented perhaps by the portrait of Onesimus. On another level, the letter raises the question of equality in Christ (Gal. 3:26-28; I Cor. 12:13), and how this was addressed by Paul and the early church. Although it is a debated question, the letter is not an appeal for Philemon to set Onesimus free, but rather to accept him back as a slave, albeit one who is now a Christian brother. Whether this was Paul's standard practice will depend on how one interprets the controversial phrase in I Corinthians 7:21. The preacher will need to consider the degree to which the gospel even in the first century began to call into question oppressive social practices, and the way Paul's letter to Philemon is related to this.

Luke 14:25-33

Luke provides a transition from the semiprivate conversation of Jesus in 14:1-24 to Jesus' reentry into the public arena. Verse 25 tells us two things about the teachings that follow: they are addressed to the crowds, and they will be in response to their enthusiastically joining the company of Jesus and his disciples. Jesus speaks here to those who come to him (verse 26), not to those called out from the crowd to join him. In other words, we have a repeat of the situation in 9:57 where a volunteer comes to Jesus saying, "I will follow you wherever." It is important to read what follows as Jesus responding to the enthusiasm of those who seem unaware that he is moving toward the cross and that his disciples are not exempt from their leader's burden.

The structure of our text is as follows: verse 25 is transitional and introductory; verses 26-27 state the demands of discipleship, paralleled in Matthew 10:37-38 as part of the charge to those being sent out; verses 28-32 contain twin parables; and verse 33 repeats in digest verses 26-27. In fact, the unit is built on a refrain: "whoever does not . . . cannot be my disciple" (verse 26), repeated in verse 27, and after the parables repeated again in verse 33. The negative form of this refrain expresses the caution and warning to the hasty volunteers who may be caught up in the movement toward Jerusalem as though it were a march or a parade. To persons already cautious Jesus has already spoken his word: drop everything and come immediately (9:59-62).

The repeated call to cross-bearing (verse 27; earlier at 9:23; Mark 8:34-35) is here joined to the unusual demand that one hate one's family and even one's own life (verse 26). The key to understanding this teaching is the word "hate." It is a Semitic way of expressing detachment, turning away from. It is not the emotion-filled word we experience in the scream, "I hate you." Were that the case, verse 26 alone would shatter all the calls to love, to understand, to forgive, to care for others, especially one's own family (I Tim. 5:8), found throughout both Testaments. Hating one's own life is not a call to self-loathing, to throw one's body across the doorway and beg the world to trample on it as though it were a doormat. Paul labeled as valueless such "rigor of devotion and self-abasement and severity to the body" (Col. 2:23). Rather, what Jesus is calling for is that those who follow him understand that loyalty to him can and will create tensions within the self and between oneself and those one loves, and in such a conflict of loyalties, he requires primary allegiance.

The two parables which follow (verses 28-32) say, in effect, "Now sit down and decide if that price is more than you will pay." The first parable is drawn from rural life and the building of a tower in the vineyard from which to watch for destructive animals and thieves. The second is from the royal capitol where decisions of war, peace, and compromise are made. But with peasant or king the same fear of embarrassment should create caution. No one should take on more than can or will be carried through to completion. The questions are two, Do I have the resources and will I commit them fully to this purpose? For prospective disciples the willingness to make full commitment *is* the one needed resource. Without that all other resources are insufficient.

Proper 19

Sunday Between September 11 and 17
Inclusive

Hosea 4:1-3; 5:15–6:6; Psalm 77:11-20; I Timothy 1:12-17;
Luke 15:1-10

desperation/hope

desperation The two selections from Hosea sound the dual notes of
desperation and hope. On the one hand Israel is censured for
forgetting Yahweh, and yet there is a ray of hope that Israel
will repent and return to Yahweh. The selection from the
Psalter echoes the theme of a God who has been at work
among the people to redeem them. The epistolary lection
redemption also underscores the redemptive work of God as one who
bestowed grace on Paul the persecutor. In a similar vein, the
Gospel reading speaks of a merciful God who rejoices over
the sinner who repents.

Hosea 4:1-3; 5:15–6:6

Hosea, a contemporary of Amos, Isaiah, and Micah, was
active in the last decades before the fall of Samaria to the
Assyrians in 722/21 B.C. He is the only northern prophet
whose words have been saved in a book, although his
predecessors in Israel included Elijah and Elisha. As a
northern prophet, Hosea confronted distinctive problems.
Not accepting the Davidic dynasty, Northern Israel experienced turmoil in the monarchy. This turmoil was particularly
acute in the period just before the fall, with some kings
lasting only a few months. The North was more vulnerable
than the South to foreign invasion and domination, and,
likewise in part due to geography, seems to have been more
susceptible to the influence of the Canaanite fertility cult. A
century earlier Elijah and Elisha had put an end to the
worship of Baal, but the problem persisted in various forms

160

in Hosea's day. Consequently, in addition to the crimes of social injustice, Hosea attacked syncretistic worship. In fact, he considered Israel's divided loyalty to be the root of all other problems. His prophetic addresses and symbolic actions included indictment of the people because of their sins, announcements of judgment, and also announcements of salvation.

Our reading for the day combines two distinct units. The passage from Hosea 4 marks the beginning of the second major section of the book, the collection of speeches in chapters 4–14. (Chapters 1–3 are mainly reports of symbolic actions concerning the prophet's wife and children.)

Hosea 4:1-3 is similar in form to a great many other prophecies of punishment from the eight-century prophets. More specifically, as indicated in verse 1, the speech is a prophetic "lawsuit"—a better translation of the Hebrew *rib*, "controversy" in the RSV—against the people of Israel. The unit begins with a call to hear the word of Yahweh, identifying the addresses (see also Amos 3:1; 4:1; 5:1). What follows is unusual in that it is not a direct quotation of the words of Yahweh. First, there is the accusation or indictment (verses 1b-2). It is stated negatively and positively, the first general and the second listing specific crimes. Then, with the transition "therefore," punishment is spelled out for all the land. The movement throughout is from causes to effects.

Rich theological language abounds in this passage. The terminology for Israel's failures comes from the covenant tradition. "Knowledge of God" is not just cognition, but signifies a deep personal relationship (Hos. 4:6; 6:6; 11:3). "Faithfulness" and "kindness" refer to stability and trustworthiness in a relationship; the latter (*hesed*), often translated "steadfast love" (Hos. 6:6), can be understood as "covenant loyalty." When Hosea lists the specific violations that follow because these qualities are absent, his hearers would have recognized his allusions to the Decalogue (Exod. 20:1-17; Deut. 5:6-21). Disloyalty to the covenant leads to crimes against the neighbor.

When the address moves from crimes to their effects, there is a problem in the translation and interpretation of the Hebrew tenses. The RSV, like most translations, reads

faithlessness to lawlessness

present tense, "the land mourns," but it could be understood as future, "the land will mourn." What is clear is that faithlessness leads to lawlessness, which in turn leads to a cosmic ecological crisis. Because of human disloyalty, the land and all the world's creatures—animals, birds, and fish—suffer and disappear. Hosea leaves it there, without a call to repent and without an expression of hope.

The other unit, Hosea 5:15–6:6, uses a different form to address similar issues. Its background is cultic ritual. Yahweh vows that he will withdraw until Israel genuinely confesses its sin and seeks him (5:15). Then the prophet quotes a penitential song sung by the people (6:1-3). Is such a song sufficient? It does call for a return to the Lord, and it expresses confidence in him, but instead of acknowledging their guilt the people look to a quick end to punishment. At this point in the cultic ritual the priest would have spoken an oracle of salvation from the Lord. But Hosea hears the Lord cry that their "love" is as fleeting as the morning mist (verse 4). For that reason he has sent prophets with death-dealing words of judgment (verse 5). Finally, the Lord calls for covenant loyalty and the knowledge of God instead of burnt offerings (verse 6; cf. Amos 5:21-24; Isa. 1:10-17).

✳ That, then, is the heart of both of these texts: God expects uncompromising loyalty to the covenant. No amount of worship—songs and sacrifices—can substitute for that loyalty. And when the people are disloyal, both human relationships and the created order are thrown into chaos.

Psalm 77:11-20

This psalm divides in two major sections: verses 1-10 are characterized by lamenting and descriptions of distress, while verses 11-20 are hymnic in character. Unlike most laments, this psalm contains no plea or appeal for God to act, no request for the destruction of enemies. The tension created and the predicaments noted in verses 1-10 are transcended or bypassed in the praise of God in verses 11-20. It is as if the troubles and distresses were accepted and the attention was focused on God and the divine action in the past. Perhaps the psalmist felt that to describe and praise

162

God's past activities was a means of expressing hope for a repeat of such actions in the future.

The description of the distress and trouble in verses 1-10 takes two forms. The first is an address by the worshiper to a human audience which expounds the worshiper's weariness with ever-present (but unspecified) trouble and indirectly accuses God of dereliction of duty and failure to respond to entreaty and request (verses 1-3). The second section, in verses 4-10, is direct address to the Deity which continues both the lament and the charges against God. Nighttime is described as a very troublesome time for the supplicant, a time when sleep would not come and the hours were spent rehearsing the past and trying to determine when and why things went wrong. The worshiper repeats those haunting thoughts that gnaw at the psyche of religious people when life goes awry: Has God completely rejected me? Am I suffering from some capricious action of the divine? Were all those promises without foundation? Has God forgotten me? Am I, like Job, the object of some hidden, celestial game whose rules and objectives I may never know? The NEB translation of verse 10, admittedly a difficult verse to interpret, says quite nicely one such sentiment:

> "Has his [God's] right hand," I said, "lost its grasp?
> Does it hang powerless, the arm of the Most High?"

The first half of this psalm was obviously composed for use in worship by a person severely depressed. If the latter half is viewed as the manner in which the priests allowed the worshiper to confront that depression, then several things become obvious. (One should recall, even though it goes against the widespread methods of interpreting the psalms, that the psalms were probably written by members of the temple staff for the use of worshipers. In contexts of what we would call pastoral counseling/care, a psalm, the needs of the worshiper, and the form of the cultic service were set so as to minister realistically to particular human and communal needs.)

1. The remainder of the psalm (verses 11-20) shifts completely away from the particulars of any individual situation. The worshiper and the psalm shift to transperson-

al, almost cosmic and mythological concerns, to conditions and situations at the founding of the world and the origins of Israel. (An interesting parallel from Mesopotamian culture is the fact that the "dentist," when extracting a person's tooth, went through a liturgy which involved reciting a short account of the creation of the world.) Such a move may have been a way of distracting the person from his immediate problem or a means of focusing his faith on God's past and glorious acts so as to assure the person that God was still and always had been in control. (The minister here should note, however, that even if there was this desire to instill or reawaken faith in the cosmic dimensions of divinity, this did not override the necessity of the person to give expression to his depression and his hostile feelings toward God.)

note

(2.) The material shifts from lament and protest to hymnic form. In giving help to such a worshiper, the priests must have known that to focus continually on the individual's particular problems and sleepless nights would get nowhere. The person's "little story," that is, the character and quality of the person's particular life, was best dealt with in the hymnic affirmation of God's and Israel's "great story." (The same thing happens in the Book of Job, where God, in answering Job, never points to or responds to Job's particular problems but transposes the issues to a higher, cosmic key.)

(3.) No appeals are made, no personal requests are formulated. The worshiper was apparently dismissed to live in the light of the hymn.

Verses 11-20 combine images and perspectives drawn from the creation of Israel, when God led the people out of Egypt (verses 14-15), and from the creation of the world, when God triumphed over the chaotic waters and chaos monsters and, amid thunder and lightnings and the trembling and shaking of the earth, God established order and led his people like lambs (verses 16-20). In light of such a vision of divine activity, now what was your problem?

I Timothy 1:12-17

With today's epistolary text, we begin the semicontinuous reading of the Epistles of First and Second Timothy that extends through the next six Sundays. As a way of introducing these lessons, we provide here some general *Pastoral epistles* remarks about the Pastoral Epistles.

These two letters, along with Titus, have been designated "Pastoral Epistles" because of the explicit attention they give to the pastoral care of churches. Even though they are attributed to Paul, their Pauline authorship is widely disputed, and consequently are generally regarded as pseudonymous letters. Among the reasons for questioning their Pauline authorship is the difference in vocabulary and style reflected in the letters. A number of terms and phrases prominent in the undisupted Pauline Letters are absent here, and a number of terms and phrases absent in the undisputed Pauline Letters are present here.

It has also been noted that the Pastorals demonstrate a different set of concerns. Not only is the mood of the letters different, but the agenda is different as well. There is a more prominent interest in institutional questions, such as the protocol for worship (I Tim. 2:1-15), the characteristics and responsibilities of church leaders (I Tim. 3:1-13; 6:22), instructions for ministers (I Tim. 4:1-16; 6:11-16; II Tim. 2:1-3, 20-26; 3:1-17; 4:1-5), and practical concern for administering to the needs of persons (I Tim. 5:3-16). Also prominent is the attention given to heretical teaching (I Tim. 4:1-16; 6:3-10; II Tim. 1:13-18; 2:17-19) and the corresponding emphasis on preserving the soundness of the apostolic faith.

What all this suggests is that these letters stem from a period when the church is moving from a more fluid form of organization to a more highly structured, institutional form of organization. These are also the kinds of instructions one would expect after the death of someone as prominent and influential as Paul. Here we see the concern to continue the Pauline legacy, to maintain fidelity to Pauline traditions, and these letters clearly stand within the Pauline trajectory (II Tim. 1:3-14). Their viewpoint is one of praise for Paul and there is a consistent interest in perpetuating a favorable memory of Paul. Most likely, what we have in these letters are some genuine Pauline reminiscences that have been preserved among his disciples and have been written, codified, and applied to their own situation.

In today's epistolary text, we have a Pauline prayer of thanksgiving. It echoes many themes found in the undisputed letters, although there are some new motifs as well.

Commission *Paul's apostolic commission* (verse 12). To be entrusted with the gospel qualified Paul as a steward in the true sense (I Cor. 4:1), and consequently he gives instructions to his churches as one who was found trustworthy (I Cor. 7:25). The source of his strength lay with the risen Lord (Phil. 4:13; II Cor. 12:9-10; II Tim. 4:17; cf. John 15:5), whom he encountered in the Damascus road experience (Acts 9:15; Rom. 9:21-23; Gal. 1:16; Rom. 1:5).

former life *Paul's former life* (verse 13). One of the firm historical features of the Pauline portrait is his conduct prior to his apostolic call. It is attested in both his own writings and the later account of Acts (Gal. 1:13; I Cor. 15:9; Phil. 3:6; Acts 8:3; 9:1, 21; 22:4, 19; 26:10-11). Here, the insistence is that he acted in ignorant unbelief (cf. Acts 3:17; 13:27; 17:30; Luke 23:34). The confession that he is the "foremost of sinners" (verse 15) strikes a new note, since he does not speak in such starkly remorseful terms in his undisputed letters. Instead, he prefers the less implicating phrase "the least of the apostles" (I Cor. 15:9-10). Moreover, his conscience appears to remain quite robust when he recalls his previous conduct (cf. Phil. 3:3-11).

Paul's experience of grace (verses 14 and 16). By his own account, his apostolic commission was a gift of grace (I Cor. 15:9-10). The Christ-event could hardly be described in terms other than grace overflowing (Rom. 5:20). In today's text, this comes to be embodied in a "faithful saying" (verse 15), a phrase unique to the Pastorals (I Tim. 3:1; 4:9; II Tim. 2:11; Tit. 3:8). Its content is perhaps the remnant of a liturgical confession and is thoroughly christological: "Christ Jesus came into the world to save sinners" (cf. Matt. 9:13; Luke 15:2; 19:10; John 3:17; I John 4:7).

exemplar *Paul as an exemplar* (verse 16). Here Paul is presented as an instance of the patience of Christ and is held up as an example for others seeking eternal life (II Tim. 1:13; cf. II Thess. 3:7). In the Pastorals, Paul's conduct becomes exemplary (II Tim. 3:10-11).

The doxology (verse 17). The prayer concludes by offering

praise to God as the King of the Ages (Tobit 13:7, 11-12; Ps. 145:14), immortal (Rom. 1:23), invisible (Col. 1:15; Heb. 11:27; John 1:18; 5:37; 6:46; 14:9; I John 4:12), one (2:5; 6:15; I Cor. 8:4-6; John 5:44; cf. II Kings 19:15, 19; Isa. 37:20).

Luke 15:1-10

Now that we are halfway through the "ordinary time" between Pentecost and Advent, peculiar advantages to continuous readings through a Gospel become evident to both preacher and listener. The structure, movement, and special accents of a given writer come more clearly into focus. Less and less time is needed to call attention to the structure of a particular lection because patterns have begun to emerge. Such is the case with Luke 15:1-10.

Today's Gospel reading consists of three parts: (1) an introduction (verses 1-3); (2) a parable (verses 4-7); (3) a second parable (verses 8-10). These two parables are the first two of three (verses 11-32). Offering materials in triplets is fairly common in Luke (9:57-62; 11:42-52; 14:18-20; 20:10-12). The second and third parables are peculiar to Luke, but the first has a parallel in Matthew (18:12-14), even though the differences between Luke and Matthew are significant, as we shall see. The two parables in our reading say essentially the same thing, a case of repetition apparently for emphasis. We find such doubling of stories elsewhere at 5:36-39 and 14:28-32.

The introduction (verses 1-3) provides the setting and the transition to Jesus' response to that situation. Jesus is attracting tax collectors (collaborators with the Roman government in collecting revenue from their own people) and sinners (not simply a moral description but a term for religious and hence social outcasts). Pharisees and scribes murmur: "This man receives sinner and eats with them" (verse 2). The situation is not an unfamiliar one in the Gospels (Mark 2:15-16; Matt. 9:10-11; Luke 5:29-30). The word translated "receives" could actually mean that Jesus is hosting these persons and not simply present with them at someone else's dinner. But regardless of who is the host, the issue is table fellowship which demonstrates how fully Jesus

table fellowship

welcomes and accepts sinners. Breaking bread together was the act of full embrace and a critical matter for both Jesus and the early church. Earlier (7:31-35) Luke had pinpointed as the key issue in the rejection of John the Baptist and Jesus the table practices of the two men. John ate no bread and drank no wine; that is, he had table fellowship with no one. Jesus, on the other hand, ate and drank for which he was labeled "a glutton and a drunkard, a friend of tax collectors and sinners." The dinner table was central to that culture.

Before moving to Jesus' response in the two parables, we may well caution ourselves about making broad and hasty judgments against the Pharisees. Their position reflects a warning firmly fixed in the Old Testament (Prov. 1:15; Ps. 1; Isa. 52:11) about associating with evil persons, a warning Paul found useful in dealing with moral issues in the Corinthian church (II Cor. 6:14-18). In addition, their stance concerning fellowship with sinners has been taken by most parents who do not wish their teenagers to be unduly influenced in wrong directions. It is easy enough to sit at a safe distance and cheer on Jesus as he receives sinners and socializes with them; it is not so easy to be his disciple in the matter. The point is, the Pharisees stand in a reasonable and long-respected position; Jesus' behavior is radical and disturbing. The church which calls him Lord still finds it so.

The parables of the lost sheep and the lost coin (verses 4-10) are identical in structure, the second serving to reinforce the first. Matthew tells the parable of the sheep but does so in a context of instructions to disciples about responsibility toward fellow disciples especially new ones, who may stumble or go astray (18:1-14). The sheep is not lost in Matthew but "goes astray" and is restored to the fold (verses 12-13). In Luke the sheep is lost; that is, it represents the sinner (verse 7), such as can be found in Jesus' presence. So strong is the love for the lost sheep that the ninety-nine are left in the wilderness while the lost one is being sought. Such love takes risks in order to find the lost, which would not have been the case if the ninety-nine lay safely sheltered in a fold, as one old gospel song has it. Of course, the sheep and the coin do not repent or return; the precise application of that theme awaits the third parable (verses 11-32). What is

finding

central in these two as well as in the third is the joy of finding, a joy so abundant it calls on others to share in it. Such is heaven's joy at the coming of sinners, and Jesus calls upon his critics to join him and heaven in celebrating the presence of tax collectors and sinners. That joy, expressed in the next parable as a party for the prodigal, is not only the heart of the gospel, but also its offense. After all, does not forgiveness from a distance look very much like condoning?

Proper 20

Sunday Between September 18 and 24
Inclusive

Hosea 11:1-11; Psalm 107:1-9; I Timothy 2:1–7; Luke 16:1-13

In the Old Testament reading we have the well-known and quite moving portrait of Yahweh, the ever-patient father, attempting to raise the recalcitrant child Israel. It is a poignant scene as Yahweh withholds his anger and extends compassion to Israel. A similarly moving portrait of the steadfast love of God is sketched in Psalm 107, a psalm of thanksgiving. The epistolary reading provides us with liturgical instructions as it urges the church to be universal in its outlook, and especially in its prayers. The Gospel reading is the intriguing, and always unsettling, parable of the dishonest steward, who is praised, among other things, for his sagacity and decisiveness.

Hosea 11:1-11

This passage, for good reason one of the best-known chapters in the Old Testament, reflects in extreme form the style of the Book of Hosea and brings us to the heart of what is distinctive in the prophet's message. Like Hosea 11, most of the book is characterized by sudden shifts of speaker, addressee, mood, and content, to the point that it is often difficult to determine where units of speech or literature begin and end. Frequently, the interpretation of a saying will hinge on the answers to such questions. Moreover, the message of the prophet included both judgment and salvation. How are the two related, and what is the last word? In the final structure of the book, due in large measure to the work of those who collected and edited the prophet's words, the relationship is chronological—first comes judg-

170

ment followed by salvation. In our text for today, however, we find something different.

Hosea 11 is a divine soliloquy in which the prophet hears Yahweh meditating and deliberating on his relationship to the chosen people. Although the mood frequently shifts dramatically, there is continuity of metaphors and images and progress of thought from beginning to end. The structure consists of three parts: (1) verses 1-7 amount to a prophecy of punishment, first stating Israel's apostasy in the context of God's saving acts (1-4) and then announcing military defeat and return to captivity (5-7); (2) in verses 8-9 we overhear Yahweh questioning himself and changing his heart; and (3) finally, in verses 10-11 there is an announcement of salvation.

From the beginning we are led to expect something different. Yahweh recalls the Exodus from Egypt, often mentioned by Hosea (2:15; 12:9; 13:4), but here he employs the metaphor of a parent's care for a child. Like a father calls a son, or a mother teaches a daughter to walk or takes her in her arms, so Yahweh cared for Israel. The language of love dominates the recital. But for all of this care and concern, Israel was unfaithful, turning to worship other gods (verse 2). Prophets frequently used the history of salvation to accuse the people of their failure to act responsibly. The deeper the relationship, the more serious is its violation. Consequently, justice calls for punishment (verses 5-7), such as Hosea frequently proclaims in word and symbolic action (e.g., 1:2-9).

Once the sentence has been pronounced, the divine judge deliberates within his heart (verses 8-9). Yahweh asks himself how he can "give up" Israel—make an end to the covenant—and bring destruction. Meditating on such a fate tears at his heart, the seat of the will, and evokes his compassion, so the Lord vows not to allow his anger to work itself out in destruction. That is the dramatic high point of the passage, that the Lord's compassion overthrows his wrath, that the will to love overcomes the—to be sure, justified—will to punish. The drama is not acted out on the plane of history but in the very heart of God.

But the theological high point comes in the reason for this

change of heart. The turning of the Lord's will is not due to human activity. Typically, prophetic announcements of salvation do not give human works as reasons for the good news. The reason is, "for I am God and not [a human being], the Holy One in your midst, and I will not come to destroy." On the highest and most generous scales of human justice, Yahweh was justified in executing punishment, but divine justice transcends human capacities for either justice or love. Indeed, the radical difference between God and human beings lies not in power, but in the capacity to withhold judgment, to love even those who have been unfaithful (cf. Hos. 3). After this, the announcement of salvation in verses 10-11 is anticlimactic.

Hosea simply presents this soliloquy without calling for a response. What is its effects on its hearers? Certainly it reminds them of the history of their God's care for them and confronts them with their own faithlessness. But how can one react to the divine compassion, to God's radical change of heart? That is the question the prophet leaves with all who read or hear this text.

Psalm 107:1-9

Psalm 107 is a thanksgiving psalm but a thanksgiving psalm with unique features. Neither a communal nor an individual psalm; it was composed for use in a special thanksgiving ritual. Persons who had been involved in various dangers—lost on a caravan journey, imprisoned, sick, or endangered at sea—and had vowed and made promises to God in the midst of their life-threatening experiences were given the occasion to offer thanks and fulfill their vows.

The psalm calls upon these redeemed (verse 2) to celebrate their redemption, namely to celebrate their being saved from death in the desert, in prison, from sickness, at sea, offering thanksgiving to God and testimony before the congregation (see verses 22 and 32). Thanksgiving services were times of merriment and indulgence (recall the celebration at the return of the prodigal son in Jesus' parable). Sacrifices made for thanksgiving were primarily eaten by the worshipers; in fact, they had to be consumed on the day of the sacrifice or the day following (see Lev. 7:11-18).

The psalm is composed of an introduction (verses 1-3), four sections focusing on four different categories of celebrants (verses 4-9, 10-16, 17-22, 23-32), and a hymnic epilogue (verses 33-43). Within each of the four central sections, a double refrain occurs. The first (verses 6, 13, 19, and 28) reports that those in peril cried out to Yahweh and he delivered them from their distress. The second (verses 8, 15, 21, and 31) calls upon the redeemed to give thanks to God for his love and redemption.

Verses 4-9 concern those who became lost in the desert, unable to find an oasis or settlement but whose salvation was granted by God who satisfied their thirst and filled the hungry.

I Timothy 2:1-7

This text also serves as the epistolary reading for Thanksgiving Day, Year B, and the reader may wish to consult our remarks in *Year B, After Pentecost.*

As a part of instructions given concerning worship (2:1-15), these verses focus specifically on prayer. The emphasis, however, is different from other New Testament passages about prayer. The teachings of Jesus, for example, contained in the Sermon on the Mount not only provide a model prayer but caution us not to pray merely as a form of visible piety (Matt. 6:5-15; Luke 18:10-14). To those less accustomed to religious prayer, he teaches the importance of simply asking, reassuring us that God does in fact answer our requests (Luke 11:1-13). Other passages urge frequency in prayer (Acts 2:42; Rom. 12:12; Eph. 6:18; Col. 4:2; I Thess. 5:17).

In today's text, there is yet a different emphasis. If there is a single theme running through our text, it is universality. The text opens by urging us to pray for everyone (verse 1). This is reinforced by the insistence that God's love is universal and that God wills the salvation of everyone (verse 3; cf. Rom. 11:32; Tit. 2:11; II Pet. 3:9). In the early Christian creed embodied within our text, Christ's death is seen as a ransom offered for everyone (verse 6; cf. II Cor. 5:15; also Matt. 20:28;

John 3:16). And finally, the passage ends with a reference to Paul's appointment as a preacher, teacher, and apostle to the Gentiles (verse 7; Acts 9:15; Rom. 1:5; 15:16; Gal. 1:16). His apostolic charge was to extend the Good News to everyone (Rom. 1:16-17).

These are words well worth hearing, for it is all too easy for the church to turn in on itself. We can find ourselves praying only for our own kind, for those whom we know, even for those whom we love, like, or prefer. Our text challenges us to break through this ecclesiastical parochialism, as does Jesus' injunction, "Love your enemies and pray for those who persecute you" (Matt. 5:44; cf. also Lev. 19:34; Rom. 12:14; Luke 23:34; Acts 7:60; I Pet. 3:9; Luke 6:35). This is difficult, of course, because our prayers tend to relate to what is close to us—our concerns, our friends, acquaintances, and loved ones, our spaces and places. But as localized as the love of God and Christ are, as directly as they address us in our own needs, they are not confined to who we are and where we are. Neither should our prayers be nearsighted. This is one fundamental point of our text.

There are, of course, other themes as well. It is also a call for us to pray for leaders of government—"kings and all who are in high positions" (verse 2). It is a sentiment in keeping with other New Testament passages that call us to respect civil authorities (Rom. 13:1-7; Tit. 3:1; I Pet. 2:13-15). A similar tradition of civil respect is also found in the Old Testament (Ezra 6:10; Bar. 1:10-11; Jer. 29:7). The motive here is stability. Peaceful government means peaceful living and the opportunity for "full observance of religion and high standards of morality" (verse 2, NEB). Since those in such positions of authority would have been non-Christian, this too should be seen as an extension of the universal impulse of the passage, even though the motive is one of self-interest.

Perhaps we should note that the passage only calls for supplications to be made in behalf of ruling authorities. Unlike other passages (e.g., Rom. 13:1-7), it does not actually enjoin submission. This is a distinction worth making since it would be naïve to assume that Christians will also bow before kings and princes with no questions asked. Being prayerful for political leaders is one thing, being blindly submissive to them is quite another.

Apart from these instructions on prayer, we should also note the theological motifs. As noted earlier, embodied within our text is what appears to be an early Christian confession (verses 5-6). Similar to other two-part confessions (e.g., I Cor. 8:4-6), this one mentions the one God (cf. Rom. 3:30; Eph. 4:5-6; Deut. 6:4-5), but primarily focuses on the redemptive work of Christ, our mediator with God (cf. Heb. 8:6; 9:15; 12:24; Gal. 3:19). Our passage is also unusual in its description of God as "Savior," although this is typical of the Pastorals (1:1; 4:10; Tit. 1:3; 2:10; 3:4; cf. Jude 25).

Luke 16:1-13

Except for verses 16-18, the entirety of Luke 16 is devoted to teachings concerning possessions. As we have already seen (12:13-21, 32-34), this is a subject of primary concern to Luke, not only in his record of Jesus' teaching, but as early as the preaching of John the Baptist (3:10-14) and as late as the church subsequent to Jesus (Acts 2:43–6:7). The discussion in Luke 16 consists of two parts, verses 1-13 and 14-31, each part controlled by a parable, and each parable beginning, "There was a rich man" (verses 1, 19). Both parables are found in Luke alone. In the first part only verse 13 has a parallel elsewhere; Matthew places this saying in the Sermon on the Mount (6:24).

Vital to the interpretation of parables is the discerning of the limits of the parable itself; that is, exactly where does the parable begin and end. Obviously, such a task is primary when one is seeking to isolate a story as Jesus told it, but it is equally basic to discovering to what use or for what purpose a particular writer preserves the Jesus tradition. By knowing where the "quotation" from Jesus ends (and begins, although beginnings are usually clear), the interpreter then can recognize the comments on the story which are offered by the Gospel writer. These comments reveal how the Evangelist understands and uses Jesus' words. Parable scholars generally agree that the Evangelists do not insert

175

comments within a parable but preserve it intact, placing their own interpretations before or after.

All of this is to bring into focus the primary difficulty faced by the preacher-interpreter of Luke 16:1-13: Where does the parable of the shrewd steward end and what is Luke's point in telling it? That Luke has given us a parable with appended sayings is generally agreed, but there is no common judgment as to where one ends and the other begins. The beginning of verse 9, "And I tell you," seems clearly to be a saying of the Lord and, therefore, offered by Luke as Jesus' own interpretation of the parable. If that is the case, then the parable means that disciples are to handle material things so as to secure heaven and the future, not here and now. Such instruction would be another way of stating what was said at 12:33: "Sell your possessions, and give alms; provide yourselves with purses that do not grow old, with a treasure in the heavens that does not fail." The same idea is in Mark 10:21 and parallels. A strong case can be made, however, for ending the parable at verse 8*a*. Verse 8*b* seems clearly an interpretative generalization and not really a part of the parable. On the basis of this judgment, that verse 8*b* is a commentary on the story, what does the parable mean? Just as the master of the steward commended him for his shrewdness, so the children of light (I Thess. 5:4-5) can learn something from the shrewd people of this age. And what is to be learned? Verse 9 answers that: handle possessions so as to gain not lose one's eternal habitation.

Given either of these reconstructions, it is evident that Luke has joined to this parable a string of sayings of Jesus concerning possessions which evidently existed in other contexts. When read in isolation, verse 8*b* is a self-contained thought, as is verse 9. Verse 10 is even more distant from the parable, having nothing to do with being shrewd or prudent in securing one's future, but rather arguing from the lesser to the greater, that one's behavior in small matters prophesies behavior in matters of major importance. Verses 11-12 follow generally the same line of thought while verse 13 makes an abrupt shift from lesser-to-greater reasoning to an all-or-nothing pronouncement. Luke has done here what was done at 11:1-13. At that point the subject of prayer was introduced and Luke joined to the topic a collection of Jesus' sayings on prayer. So here on the subject of possessions. The preacher obviously has some decisions to make in order to ensure that one sermon is preached, not many, and that the hearer is not overloaded by that sermon.

Two comments about the parable itself. First, that the steward was dishonest is unrelated to the story's focus, but the listeners will probably need some help in being assured that is the case. Second, as to how the steward managed the books to secure his future, two possibilities exist: (1) he subtracted his own commission as a way of reducing the bills, but in which case he would not have been dishonest; and (2) the debtors did not know he had been fired, thought the reductions were legitimate, and praised the owner who in turn commended the steward. This latter description seems best to fit the story.

Proper 21

Sunday Between September 25 and October 1 Inclusive

Joel 2:23-30; Psalm 107:1, 33-43; I Timothy 6:6-19; Luke 16:19-31

The bounty of God's love is reflected in the eschatological vision sketched by the prophet Joel in today's Old Testament reading, which concludes with the promised outpouring of God's Spirit. Yahweh is similarly praised in the final section of Psalm 107 as the one who gives life to the earth and the people of the earth. God is also lavishly praised in the middle section of the epistolary reading, which otherwise focuses on riches by viewing them within the much more important perspective of life before God. Both the Old Testament reading and the psalm abundantly illustrate the God who "richly furnishes us with everything" (I Tim. 6:17). Complementing this epistolary reading especially well is the Gospel story of the rich man and Lazarus, which provides a narrative depiction of the Lukan saying: "Blessed are you poor"; "woe to you that are rich" (Luke 6:20, 24).

Joel 2:23-30

It is a long step from Hosea, the source of the readings for the past two Sundays, to Joel, both chronologically and theologically. While there is no superscription which dates the Book of Joel, the political and religious references fit the Persian period, probably about 400 B.C., more than three centuries after Hosea. While Hosea criticized priests and challenged the validity of rituals, Joel quite likely was a cultic prophet, one who participated directly, and probably in an officially recognized fashion, in the services of worship in the second temple. We hear him giving the call to prayer and fasting, ordering the priests to gather the people, giving instructions for prayer, and then proclaiming, as priests do, the divine response to the people's genuine prayers of confession and contrition.

The Book of Joel is a liturgical work in two parts. In the first part (Joel 1:2–2:17) the prophet directs the community to convene a service of complaint and petition to God, initially because of the threat of a plague of locusts (1:4-20) and then because of the terrifying prospect of the day of the Lord. In the second part (Joel 2:18–3:21) the mood has changed dramatically because the people have repented. God promises salvation and over and over again assures the people that their prayers have been heard. The Day of the Lord has become a day of salvation because the people trusted in their God.

Both in terms of form and content, the passage before us is a series of announcements of salvation. It has been preceded in verses 21-22 by words of assurance to the natural world, spoken by the prophet. The land itself is called to rejoice. Then (verse 23) the prophet issues similar calls to the people to celebrate because God has given the rain. The rain will bring the harvest, so verses 24-25 announce the reversal of the bad fortune described in the first part of the book. The Lord promises that there will be plenty of grain, wine, and oil, and that he will restore the losses caused by the locusts. In a further announcement of salvation (verses 26-27) the bounty of nature is related to the joy of worship and the continuing presence of God among the people. When all these things happen, the people will be assured that there is no other God but Yahweh.

The last verses of our reading (28-30) proclaim the renewal of humankind through the gift of the Lord's spirit. The announcement of salvation has moved beyond the promise of material blessings and looks toward a time when all of the Lord's people will experience divine revelation. The vision is inclusive. There are gifts of the spirit for all, female and male, young and old, free and slave; it will be for "all flesh." Throughout the Old Testament, the "spirit" of the Lord was understood as that which gives life (Gen. 2:7), the difference between a dead body and a living being. It is also the Lord's spirit that grasps prophets and gives them the divine message. The spirit empowers and reveals. Here, when the Lord pours out his spirit the result is prophecy, dreams, and visions. These three are used here almost synonymously for the experience of divine revelation, specifically, the vision of the reign of God. The final verse of our reading (verse 30) actually begins a new unit in the book, but it provides the apocalyptic context in which the vision of the spirit of the Lord should be understood.

Thus the passage moves from celebration of the bounty of nature—the land, animals, pastures, trees, vines, rain—to the promise of the coming kingdom of God. The first may seem too materialistic and worldly and the latter too spiritual for modern tastes—the one too bound to the earth and the present and the other too distant and other worldly. Would we prefer a vision of the reign of God that is neither one nor the other, but a compromise? Remarkably, the Old Testament tradition insists on both. God will reign fully one day, but for the present, God's grace is known in the good gifts of creation.

Psalm 107:1, 33-43

This portion of Psalm 107, excluding the introductory opening verses, is a hymn in praise of Yahweh's providence in the life of the land and its people. The intent of the hymn was to instill faith and confidence in the audience. Verses 33-38 speak of Yahweh's control and use of nature while verses 39-43 affirm his watchfulness over human affairs, especially his special care toward the weak and needy.

God is the transformer of nature. The good and productive perennial streams, gushing springs, and fruitful soil he transforms into thirsty desert and salt flats. The reason offered for such action is the wickedness of its inhabitants (verses 33-34). One could wonder if the composer of this psalm had ever seen or expected his audience ever to see God do such actions. Perhaps the imagery of the old morality tale of the destruction of Sodom and Gomorrah (Gen. 19) lies behind the depiction. On the other hand, the reverse is also true. The desert is watered and the parched land springs into life so that the hungry in it may find sustenance and safety in which to dwell and undertake agricultural pursuits (verses 35-38). Here perhaps we find expressed some of the "ideals" of the ancient Israelites—well-watered land, a place to sow and plant, life for the cattle, and the chance to have children and raise families. The restraints of such expectations are remarkable. Merely the opportunity for normalcy, we might say; no extravagant mansions, pearly gates, or streets of gold, to say nothing of worldwide fame and frothing fans.

The divine providence works to bring the high low and the low high. The oppressors and exploiters, the great men (RSV: princes) are made to lose their way while the needy are raised up and blessed with numerous offspring. One of the stories about the reversal of fate—a motif that runs throughout the Old Testament—is told of the king who lost his mental balance as a result of his exercise of power and was forced to live for a time as an animal. (See Daniel 5 for an example, where the king is Nebuchadnezzar.)

God's patterns of action are intended for a reason and those "wise" will read the lesson. The upright see it and rejoice while the wicked curb their actions and ambitions ("stop its mouth").

I Timothy 6:6-19

What would be our last words to a young, aspiring minister? Today's text provides one possibility. It belongs to the last major section of advice Paul gives to Timothy (6:3-20).

The note on which it begins is to beware of detractors (verses 3-5). They are caricatured here as conceited ignoramuses fixated on stupid, meaningless controversies. Their final flaw is to believe that religion should turn a profit (verse 5). For them, in pursuing the religious life the chief questions are, What is the bottom line? What is the cash value? It is a common type. First there is the sermon, then the request for money. Peddlers of God's word, Paul calls them (II Cor. 2:17).

If this is the standard against which the minister's life will be measured, then what are the dividends? What is the gain? On this note, our text begins.

"Of course religion does yield high dividends, but only to the man whose resources are within him" (verse 6, NEB). This defense of the religious life triggers a set of reflections on riches (verses 7-10), a theme to which our text returns (verses 17-19). Our text sketches life that puts wealth on the periphery rather than at the center of things, that sees money as valuable but not as the ultimate value, as a worthwhile means to an end but not an end in itself. Hold a penny at arm's length, and it will appear as a dot against the sun; hold it next to the eye, it will cover the sun. In our text, life is viewed with the penny held at a distance.

In the first part of our text, riches and wealth are viewed from this radically different perspective. There are four cautions.

First, "godliness with contentment" becomes the aim of our life's pursuit. The word for "godliness" is *eusebeia*. Often translated as "piety," it is better rendered as "religion." It suggests a form of life whose ultimate quest is for God. It is to be preferred over athletic discipline because it enables us to live in the present and face the future (4:8). Coupled with this is "contentment." It is the capacity to be satisfied with what is ours rather than being driven to possess what is not ours. "Be content with what you have" became a proverb in the Hellenistic-Roman world and was wisely appropriated by Christian teaching (Phil. 4:11; Heb. 13:5).

Second, all the trappings of life fade before the double miracles of birth and death. We neither enter nor leave life with assets (verse 7; cf. Job 1:21; Eccles. 5:14; also Gen. 3:19). Riches and possessions are finally to be viewed as decorations along the way. The only real necessities are food and clothing (verse 8), and the ascetic tenor of our text implies that we need little of both (cf. Matt. 6:25-33).

Third, riches are seductive (verse 9). Like the brambles in the parable of the sower (Matt. 13:22), they ensnare through suffocation. What begins as the innocent desire to make a fair profit becomes an obsession to own. Before long, we no longer own but are owned. The desires that were once prudent and constructive become senseless and harmful. What began as modest desire has now become ruin and destruction.

Fourth, the insatiable desire for money is at the root of every form of evil (verse 10; cf. Heb. 13:5). This too became a proverb in the Hellenistic-Roman world, although it circulated in various forms. The love of money is the root, mother, and hometown of all other evils. What the proverb recognized is how avarice establishes a network with other forms of vice. For this reason, it is seen as an enemy of the life of faith (cf. 1:19; Matt. 6:24; Tit. 1:11). Not only this, it leaves a trail of tears (verse 10*b*).

In the second part of our text, we have a positive set of instructions for the rich.

First, the rich are charged not to be haughty (verse 17). Popular proverbs recognized the direct correlation between being rich and being conceited, and a humble spirit is seen as the proper corrective (James 1:10; also Rom. 11:20; 12:16).

Second, we are reminded of the uncertainty of riches and urged to rely on the God who is the source of all we have (verse 17). The story of Job depicts, among other things, how evanescent wealth is, as does the parable of the rich fool (Luke 12:17-21). This alone should caution us against setting our heart on them (Ps. 62:10), instead of on the living God (I Tim. 4:10).

Third, riches can have positive value if they belong to "liberal and generous" persons (verse 18; e.g., Acts 10:1-2). If we make proper disposition of our possessions, we will find ourselves engaged in doing good deeds. And what is the motive for doing so? To lay "a good foundation for the future" (verse 19; cf. Matt. 6:19-21). Perhaps this is not the best of motives, but one the rich well understand.

Bracketed by these instructions on riches is the charge to Timothy as a "man of God" (verses 11-16; cf. II Tim. 3:17; also I Sam. 2:27; I Kings 13:1). In contrast to the opponents (verses 3-5), he is urged to pursue the several Christian virtues (cf. II Tim. 2:22; also Gal. 5:22-23). He is also charged to enter the arena and there pursue "the good fight of the faith" (verse 12; 1:18; II Tim. 4:7; also I Cor. 9:25; Heb. 12:1; Jude 3). The charge that follows (verses 15-16) appears to embody an early Christian confession in which God is praised as the only Sovereign (II Macc. 12:15; Sirach 46:5), King of Kings (Deut. 10:17; Ps. 136:3; Rev. 17:14; 19:16), Lord of Lords (Col. 4:1;

II Macc. 13:4; III Macc. 5:35), immortal and invisible in dazzling, unapproachable light (John 1:18; 5:37; 6:46; 14:9; Rom. 1:20; Col. 1:15; Heb. 11:27; I John 4:12; also Exod. 33:20).

The language here is quite formal and possibly derives from a formal ordination service in which the minister is charged to embark on a life based on the good confession (cf. II Tim. 4:1).

Luke 16:19-31

Before moving to the story of the rich man and Lazarus it may be helpful to review the introductory comments on last week's Gospel lesson in which the general theme and structure of Luke 16 were discussed.

The story of the rich man (called Dives in the Vulgate, "dives" meaning "wealthy" in Latin) and Lazarus offers itself to the preacher as both simple and complex, clear and puzzling. The story is well traveled, existing in several cultures and in many versions. At least seven versions of it appear in rabbinical sources. Many scholars trace it back to Egypt where stories of the dead abounded. In that lore, for example, Osiris offered a cup of cold water to the blessed dead. The version in Luke is a Jewish modification of the story; notice the central place of Father Abraham. If this is properly to be called a parable, it is unusual in that proper names are used. No other parable of Jesus does so. The use of the name Lazarus and the theme of being raised from the dead naturally prompts questions as to the relationship between Luke's story and the account of the raising of Lazarus in John 11. There seems to be more than coincidence here, but questions of sources and influences are still unanswered.

In spite of brevity, the account is rich in detail. The sharp contrast between the rich man and the poor is vivid and evocative. This is true even in death: the rich man died and *was buried;* the poor man died. The contrast continues into the next world. The preacher will want to avoid taking the descriptions of the fates of the two men as providing revealed truths about the hereafter and divine answers to questions about the state of the dead. The popular story simply conveys popular beliefs of the time and is not given by Jesus or by Luke in response to interest in what happens to people immediately after death.

Stating what is *not* the intention of the story does, however, raise the question of what *is* its message. An answer is not easy because the story as we have it here has two parts. The first, verses 19-26, is clearly presenting the reversal of fortunes in this world and the next. The rich man's character is reflected in his refusal of charity to the poor, a violation of the Law of Moses (Deut. 15:4-11), not to mention common human compassion. We know the other man only as poor, but "poor" had come to be in some circles almost a synonym for "righteous" (Luke 4:18; 6:20). That God would reverse the fortunes of such persons was a widely held belief and a strong conviction of Luke's (1:51-53; 6:20-26). Were the story to end at verse 26, therefore, it would be appropriate to the context and to Luke as a whole.

However, the second part of the story, verses 27-31, carries a different theme. Here the reader is told through the conversation between Abraham and the rich man that the Scriptures, that is, Moses and the prophets, are effective and adequate for faith (verse 31). Rejection of the Scriptures means that not even a resurrection from the dead would prove effective. Interestingly enough, this, too, is a strong emphasis in Luke. Not only is Luke careful throughout the Gospel to show that what Jesus does and teaches is according to Scripture but the risen Christ enables his disciples to understand what Moses, the prophets, and the writings taught about the Messiah's passion and resurrection (24:25-27, 44-47). The preaching of the early church, says Luke, continued to establish their message about Jesus from the Jewish Scripture (Acts 2:16-36).

The preacher may, therefore, use Luke 16:19-31 to deal with knotty problems of possessions or to deal with the role of Scripture, the record of what God *has* done, to generate faith in what God *is* doing. Either would be quite Lukan. But why a story with two thrusts? Ready answers are unavailable. Some scholars have suggested that Luke has employed this version of the story to develop two themes introduced earlier in verses 14-17. Those two themes address a love of money which distances one from God (verses 14-15) and the tendency of some enthusiasts to set aside Moses and the prophets as no longer valid (verses 16-17). With some reflection the two themes may really become one: the embrace of material goods as the primary interest of one's life is a base and flagrant dismissal of scriptural command and precedent. The end of such a life is fairly predictable.

Proper 22

Sunday Between October 2 and 8 Inclusive

Amos 5:6-7, 10-15; Psalm 101; II Timothy 1:1-14; Luke 17:5-10

Words of judgment are delivered against Israel in today's Old Testament reading, but as always they are bracketed with a gracious invitation to "seek the Lord and live," to "hate evil, and love good." If the Old Testament reading is a call to fidelity, we have a response in Psalm 101, a coronation psalm in which the king pledges to rule righteously. The reading from the Epistle is an exhortation to moral courage in the form of advice from Paul the veteran apostle to the youthful minister Timothy. In the Gospel reading we hear the Lord urging the disciples to be bold in their faith and dutiful in their service.

Amos 5:6-7, 10-15

Amos is the earliest of the prophets whose words were saved in a book by his name. He was active not long before 745 B.C., in the last peaceful era for the Northern kingdom. It is important to remember that he was an outsider, a shepherd from Judah (1:1; 7:15) who was called to proclaim the word of Yahweh in the North. He must have been active for only a short time, for he was forced to leave the country (7:10-17). The original power of the words of Amos was in their oral presentation. Those oral words were collected and written down, and later generations, beyond the fall of Israel in 722/21 and even the Babylonian Exile, found that they could speak to their own times as well.

In many respects this selection is not typical of the speeches in the Book of Amos. Most of the prophet's addresses are indictments or announcements of punishment against the neighboring nations (1:3–2:5), Israel, a group (the wealthy women of Samaria, 4:1-3), or an individual (Amaziah the priest of Bethel, 7:16-17). A typical address is 4:1-3, which moves from a call to attention that specifies the addressees and indicts them for their sins (verse 1) to the announcement of a day when the city will be captured and the addressees carried away (verses 2-3). Amos indicts the people for social injustice and religious arrogance and proclaims that Yahweh has determined to bring total destruction upon the nation (9:1-4) in the form of military disaster and exile.

In the passage before us today, however, Amos holds out the possibility that the disaster may be averted. The reading contains admonitions calling for the people to change their behavior and indicates that Yahweh may yet "be gracious" (5:15). Admonitions such as this are limited to a few verses in chapter 5; in addition to our reading they are 5:4-5 and 21-24. How do these speeches relate to the prophet's otherwise uncompromising message of doom? Was this his message when he first began, and he became more and more negative as Israel failed to respond? Or is this his last word, as in Ezekiel 18 and 33, that there is always the possibility that Yahweh will change his plans if the people return? It is impossible to know. However, one should not resolve the problem by denying that Amos originated these words, for otherwise they are consistent with his style and his indictment of Israel for social injustice.

The reading contains three distinct units, verses 6-7, 10-13, and 14-15. Verses 8-9, omitted from the lection, contain one of the three short doxologies or hymnic fragments (the others are 4:13 and 9:5-6) that were likely added to the book as it was used in worship during the exilic or postexilic period. All three of our units are speeches by the prophet in which he does not cite the words of Yahweh directly. Verses 4-5 are similar to 5:6-7 except that in it Yahweh himself issues the call.

The key word in the first and third speeches is "seek" (verses 6, 14). The word, a plural imperative, is addressed to the people as a whole, referring to a corporate rather than an individualistic action. Cultic activity seems to stand in the background. In 5:4-6, seeking Yahweh is contrasted with seeking Bethel, Gilgal, and Beer-sheba, probably meaning centers of worship. Second Chronicles 15:12, in a context that concerns foreign gods and the renewal of the covenant, notes that failure "to seek the Lord" made one liable to the death penalty. "To seek" Yahweh in some cases meant consulting a prophet or priest for the divine will. In our context it is clear that "seeking the Lord" is not simply an internal, spiritual matter, but entails faithfulness in the stipulations of the covenant that established justice.

Amos has a great deal to teach us about justice and righteousness (verses 7, 15), mainly in his accusations concerning injustice. Often he bemoans the absence of the simple procedural justice of the law court. Trials, both criminal and civil, were held "in the gate" (verses 10, 12, 15) of the city. The courts are corrupt. One who presents a case ("reproves"), or tells the truth (verse 10) is rejected, people take bribes, and the needy are turned away (verse 12). Distributive justice, as the equitable division of resources, has failed, and that strikes at the heart of the purpose of law in Israel, to protect the weak from the strong. The rich trample the poor and charge them too much in order to build fine houses and vineyards for themselves (verse 11). Finally, the prophet's concerns about social iniquity rest on ancient Israel's understanding of the substance of justice. The people are expected to treat one another with justice because the Lord is just. Consequently, those who trample the poor are threatened with disaster. To seek the Lord and live and to seek the good is to establish justice in society.

Psalm 101

This composition is a royal psalm written for worship services in which the king took an oath of office iterating his commitment to certain standards of behavior. The most likely occasion for the use of such a psalm was the time of a new king's coronation. Under these conditions, it would be similar to a president's taking the oath of office. Another possible occasion for its usage was the annual celebration of the king's coronation which may have involved the king's ritual "dethronement," humiliation, and reenthronement. Evidence for such an annual humiliation-reenthronement ritual is not found spelled out in the Old Testament. Other cultures had such a ritual celebration. A function of this humiliation-exaltation ritual would have been to hold the king accountable for his deeds in office and to remind the monarch of the obligations of the office. Verse 2*b* implies that the king has been momentarily abandoned by God, perhaps a feature of the cultic enactment of the king's dethronement.

The promises made by the king in his oath are tenfold:

1. I will walk with integrity of heart
   within my house;
2. I will not set before my eyes
   anything that is base.
3. I hate the work of those who fall away;
   it shall not cleave to me.
4. Perverseness of heart shall be far from me;
   I will know nothing of evil.
5. Him who slanders his neighbor secretly
   I will destroy.
6. The man of haughty looks and arrogant heart
   I will not endure.
7. I will look with favor on the faithful in the land,
   that they may dwell with me;
8. he who walks in the way that is blameless
   shall minister to me.
9. No man who practices deceit
   shall dwell in my house;
   no man who utters lies
   shall continue in my presence.
10. Morning by morning I will destroy
    all the wicked in the land,
    cutting off all the evildoers
    from the city of the Lord.

The monarch thus assumes responsibility for his own honesty and integrity, promises to abhor those who are apostate, perverse, slanderous, and arrogant, pledges to support and rely upon those who are faithful and blameless, vows to purge the dishonest from government service, and swears to carry out faithfully his role as arbiter of justice.

II Timothy 1:1-14

As the opening section of Paul's second letter to Timothy, today's epistolary lection exhibits the formal characteristics of a Pauline Letter: greeting (verses 1-2), thanksgiving (verses 3-5), an appeal (verses 6-14).

Greeting (verses 1-2). The tone of endearment is already set in the opening greeting from Paul the apostle (Rom. 1:1; I Cor. 1:1; II Cor. 1:1; Eph. 1:1; Col. 1:1) to Timothy, "dear child of mine" (verse 2, JB). Even though Timothy had not been converted by Paul, he had become Paul's understudy and constant companion (Acts 16:1-3; 17:14-15; 18:5; 19:22; 20:4; Rom. 16:21; I Cor. 4:17; 16:10; Phil. 2:19-22; also Heb. 13:23). Were it not for this father-child relationship, the tone would be patronizing. Instead, we have an epistle in which paternal instructions and advice are given to a youthful child in the faith who is following in his teacher's footsteps.

Thanksgiving (verses 3-5). Like the opening thanksgiving in the Epistle to Philemon, this prayer is addressed to an individual. It is similar to other Pauline thanksgivings in its reference to gratitude to God (Rom. 1:8; I Cor. 1:4; Phil. 1:3; Col. 1:3; I Thess. 1:2; 2:13; 3:9; II Thess. 1:3; Philem. 4), unceasing prayer on behalf of the recipient (Rom. 1:9; Phil. 1:14; Col. 1:9; I Thess. 1:2; Philem. 4), and eagerness to visit in person (Rom. 1:11; Phil. 1:8; Philem. 22; cf. II Tim. 4:9, 21).

What is especially remarkable here, however, is the way in which faith as tradition informs the thanksgiving. First, Paul's own service to God "with a clear conscience" (I Tim. 1:5, 19; 3:9; Acts 23:1; 24:16; II Cor. 1:12) is defined with respect to those who preceded him in the faith, "my forefathers" (verse 3, NEB, NIV) or "my ancestors" (JB). Second, Timothy's own faith is indebted to those who preceded him, his grandmother Lois, and his mother Eunice (Acts 16:1). Faith is what is handed down from mother to daughter to son, but not merely as a package passed from one generation to another, but as "a faith which was alive" in mother and daughter and which now lives in the child of the third generation (verse 5, NEB; cf. 3:14-15).

We should note the different set of concerns voiced in this opening prayer. We are already in the third generation where

191

the concern is for continuity with past tradition and what can be done to transmit faith as a living tradition (cf. II Tim. 2:1-2).

An exhortation to courage and endurance (verses 6-14). The appeal from the veteran apostle has at least three aspects.

First, a call for a rekindled spirit (verses 6-7). Timothy is reminded of his ordination to the ministry when he received God's spirit through the laying on of Paul's hands (verse 6; cf. I Tim. 4:14; 5:22; also Acts 6:6; 8:17-19; 9:12, 17; 13:3; 19:6; 28:8; Heb. 6:2; cf. Num. 27:18, 23; Deut. 34:9). Though confirmed by the laying on of human hands, the prophetic ministry is in every sense a gift which comes from God. But as the distance increases between teacher and disciple, what was originally a flame of fire can become an ember. As initial enthusiasm wanes, it may be necessary to "stir into flame the gift of God" (verse 6, NEB).

Above all, it should be remembered that the minister should not roll over and play dead. The spirit we have from God is not a "spirit of timidity" or a "craven spirit" (NEB; cf. Acts 4:13, 20-21; Rom. 8:15; John 14:27). It is rather a spirit of "power and love and self-control" (verse 7). It may seem odd to juxtapose love with power and self-control, but it is a useful reminder that love need not be spineless and undisciplined.

Second, a call for bold witness (verses 8-12). Timothy is charged not to be ashamed of bearing witness to the faith (verse 8), even as Paul was unashamed (verse 12; Rom. 1:16-17). The charge is in keeping with Jesus' warning that the disciple who recoils in shame before the gospel is undeserving of the name, and is finally excluded (Matt. 10:33; Luke 9:26). There is first the scandal of the gospel itself, which runs against the grain of the world (I Cor. 1:18-25), and the more we think of its oddity the less we are willing to go to the mat for it. There is the additional burden of living with and defending its exponents and proclaimers, especially when they shame themselves and the gospel through imprisonment (verse 8). Our text suggests that we have reached a point in Christian history where it is not necessarily popular to defend the reputation and memory of Paul.

Apart from the general shame of the gospel is the pressure it brings, and the minister finally has to suffer in its behalf, as

Paul did (Phil. 1:7, 12-13; Eph. 3:1; 4:1; Col. 4:18; Philem. 1, 9-13). The call to ministry also becomes a call to suffering (2:3; 4:5).

What to do when our call is threatened by pressure and suffering? Return to the creed, what we believe and confess. In the center of this call to bold witness we have an early Christian confession (verses 9-10, printed strophically in Nestle 26th). We are reminded of the God who saved and called us through grace and not through our own merits (cf. Tit. 2:5; Eph. 1:11), and who was manifested through the "appearance," that is, the coming of Christ into the world (Rom. 16:26; II Thess. 2:8; I Tim. 6:14; II Tim. 4:1, 8; Tit. 2:11-13; I Pet. 1:20). It was God who finally abolished death by raising Christ from the dead (cf. Heb. 2:14-15; I Cor. 15:55; I Tim. 2:7; Rev. 12:10) and brought us life and immortality (Acts 26:23; I Cor. 15:53-54; John 1:4, 9). This is the God by whom Paul was commissioned and in whom he believes and places his ultimate hopes (verse 12).

Fidelity to the apostolic faith (verses 13-14). The final reminder is to follow the "outline of the sound teaching" (verse 13, NEB). Typical of the Pastorals is this importance given to the orthodox faith (I Tim. 1:10; 6:3; II Tim. 4:3; Tit. 1:9; 2:1). The faith is that which must be adhered to, guarded, and protected (I Tim. 6:20). It is the divine treasure entrusted to us by the Holy Spirit who dwells within us (verse 14; Rom. 8:11).

In one sense, this final reminder strikes us as being hollow. Where is the existential immediacy of the preached Word? Where is the moving encounter with the risen Christ? And yet we all know the power of the inherited faith, embodied in words and phrases that have been etched out in the life and struggles of the church. We also know how the shape of this faith, even in its written form, can also shape us, but only if the words bear witness to a living faith. We are being reminded that faith understood as the repository of the apostolic witness may not only inform us, but form us. In the face of threats, the faith we confess may become the most stabilizing force we know, especially as we remember the lives of our predecessors in whom faith was not only something believed but something lived.

Luke 17:5-10

Luke 17 opens with four independent sayings (verses 1-2, 3-4, 5-6, 7-10) addressed by Jesus to his disciples (verse 1; apostles, verse 5). Today's lection consists of the last two of these sayings. Variants of verses 5-6 are to be found in both Mark (11:22-23) and Matthew (17:20; 21:21) but the parable in verses 7-10 is in Luke alone. Since all four of these logia address matters of discipleship it is not difficult for the preacher to find ways to join them with some thematic unity. However, that is not necessary. One may choose to frame the message on verses 5-6 or verses 7-10 as self-standing units of tradition with minimal reference to immediate context. Such would not in this case be a violation of the text. Sayings of Jesus in the Gospels often have a proverb-like integrity, carrying their meaning intrinsically rather than contextually.

Verse 5 functions as a transition from the subject of forgiveness (verses 3-4) to that of faith. If one sees verses 5-6 as having a contextual meaning, then very likely the apostles' request for increased faith is an expression of their sense of inadequacy in the face of the unusual demands of caring for weaker members of the community (verses 1-2) and forgiving repeatedly the offending brother or sister (verses 3-4). In other words, "Lord, make us adequate for discipleship." Jesus' response, "If you had faith . . . ," deserves careful examination. The Greek language has basically two types of "if" or conditional clauses—those that express a condition contrary to fact ("if I were you") and those that express a condition according to fact ("if Christ is our Lord"). The conditional clause of verse 6 is the second type. One could translate it, "If you have faith (and you do)." In other words, Jesus' response is not a judgment on an absence of faith but an indirect affirmation of the faith they have and an invitation to live and act in that faith. The apostles request an increase of faith and Jesus says that even the small faith you have is effective and powerful beyond your present realization. The possibilities opened up by faith cancel out such words as "impossible" (a tree being uprooted) and "absurd" (planting a tree in the sea). The small faith already theirs could put them in touch with the power of God.

Students of the passage have pondered Luke's use of sycamine tree rather than mountain as appears in the Markan and Matthean parallels. Is Luke's a different saying or a variant? We cannot be sure. Some commentators have taken Luke's sycamine tree as entering the tradition in this way: Mark and Matthew speak of a mountain being moved into the sea in the context of the story of Jesus cursing the fig tree. The words "sycamine" and "fig" have the same Greek stem, and in the process of transmitting the tradition, sycamine came into the story when it was told in some circles. Interesting, and perhaps true. However, whether trees or mountains, the act of faith taps the fundamental resource of both Christian and Jewish communities: nothing is impossible with God.

The parable in verses 7-10 opens in a fashion common in Luke: "Will any one of you?" or "Which one of you?" (11:5-7; 14:23, 31; 15:4, 8). This story concerns a slave who does double duty, serving in the fields and in the master's house. The slave-master relationship is without analogy in our employee-employer society, and so the preacher is well advised not to draw social and economic lessons from the parable. The rather simple thrust of the story is that the slave's time and labor belong to the master and, therefore, the slave has no claim on the master, even after a period of obedient service. There is no point of fulfilled duty, beyond which the servant can expect special favors in return. There is no ground for boasting (Rom. 3:27), no work of supererogation, no balance of merit after obligation is paid. Disciples of Jesus live by faith, even if it be as small as a mustard seed, but the life of trust is new each day. Like the manna in the wilderness, there is no surplus for tomorrow, no time in which there is more than enough for today. Disciples of Jesus live in obedience, but that, too, is new each day. One does not ever say, "Now that I have completed all the duties of love, it is my turn to be served." Such calculations are foreign to life in the kingdom of God.

Proper 23

Sunday Between October 9 and 15 Inclusive

Micah 1:2; 2:1-10; Psalm 26; II Timothy 2:8-15; Luke 17:11-19

From today's Old Testament reading we again hear prophetic words of judgment reminiscent of last week's lesson from Amos. The severe critique of the preaching of false prophets serves as an effective counterpoint to the epistolary reading from Second Timothy in which Paul urges Timothy to a responsible form of proclamation. There is some continuity of theme between the Old Testament reading and Psalm 26, a personal lament in which the psalmist distances himself from the company of the wicked. The Gospel reading for today relates the story of ten lepers who were healed, only one of whom (a Samaritan) gave thanks.

Micah 1:2; 2:1-10

Micah was another prophet of the eighth century B.C., somewhat later than Amos and Hosea, and a younger contemporary of Isaiah. Like Isaiah, he was active in the city of Jerusalem, announcing judgment on the city for the sins of the people. He was particularly concerned about corruption in high places, including among the wealthy (2:1-5), the political leadership (3:1-4, 9-12), and even the prophets (3:5-8).

The reading for the day provides Micah 1:2 as a heading for what follows. The verse is a call to hear, similar to others in prophetic speech (Amos 3:1; 4:1; 5:1), but it has distinctive features that recall the tradition of Yahweh's lawsuit for violation of the covenant. These include the address to the earth (Isa. 1:2), and the technical expression, "be a witness against you." Yahweh, the plaintiff who brings the charges, will also be a witness, and, before the trial is over, judge and executioner as well. Micah, like Isaiah, takes the holiness of the temple for granted.

Micah 2:1-10 includes two distinct units of prophetic tradition, verses 1-5 and 6-10 (the second unit actually goes through verse 11). Both sections evoke reflection on justice and judgment, and the second one raises the question of the prophetic role as well.

Like many other prophetic addresses, the first unit begins with the cry of "Woe." What usually follows that exclamation is, as here (verses 1-2), the characterization of the addresses in terms of their sinful activities. The first part of the accusation is very general, planning wickedness (verse 1), but the second specifies a particular sin, taking away the property of others so as to oppress them (verse 2). To covet the property of others is to violate the Decalogue (Exod. 20:17). What makes this such a serious crime is the oppression of another's "inheritance." Land and land ownership were sacred in Israel. The owner of the land, God, had allotted it to Israel by tribes, clans, and families (Josh. 13–19). To lose one's inheritance was to lose full rights as a citizen, but more, those who took away that inheritance—even by lawful means—tampered with the divine economy.

Consequently, when the prophet turns to announce punishment, it is Yahweh who speaks (verses 3-5). Yahweh, as well as those who are greedy, can devise evil, planning a punishment that fits the crime. The haughty ones who work such wickedness will be humbled, for the Lord will take away their "portion" or inheritance, dividing their land among their enemies. No one will be able to help them when land is once again divided up in the divine assembly.

The second unit (verses 6-11) is a disputation between Micah and the people concerning his authority to proclaim bad news. As in Ezekiel 18 (see the commentary for Proper 17 in this volume), the prophet quotes the words of his opponents (verse 6) and responds to their charges. The people have good grounds for their objection to Micah's announcement that "disgrace" will overtake them. In the time of Isaiah and Micah, it was widely believed that Zion and the city of Jerusalem were inviolable, that Yahweh would not allow an enemy to enter the sacred precincts. But from that same God Micah has heard a word of judgment. Not allowing himself to be put on the defensive, he accuses the opponents of being the enemy. They have charged him with blasphemy and treason, and he turns the accusation around. Their injustice has made the land unclean (verses 9-10), but they refuse to face reality. The kind of preacher who would satisfy them is one who speaks "wind and lies," talking about "wine and strong drink" (verse 11).

So in addition to calling our attention to specific forms of injustice, this passage raises again the issue of true and false prophecy (see the commentary on Jer. 28:1-9 for Proper 16 in this volume). Micah speaks in the name of the Lord, and the people attempt to stifle his voice. Both sides in the conflict could appeal to theological tradition. Micah knows, like Jeremiah later, that the word of God in the face of injustice is judgment, even against the chosen people and the sacred place. Elsewhere, in a dispute with other prophets (3:5-7), he introduces the issues of commercialism and integrity, accusing other prophets of preaching peace when they have something to eat but judgment against those who do not feed them. We should not conclude, however, that professional prophets or prophets of salvation are necessarily false ones. Resolving the question—then as well as now—is as difficult as discerning the word of God for any given moment.

Psalm 26

This text is best understood as a composition used to claim and affirm one's innocence when the falsely accused was charged with some crime or breach of sacral obligation. Three elements characterize the psalm: the desire to be judged, the affirmation of innocence, and the certainty of the outcome.

The opening section appeals to God for a legal decision or personal assessment ("Vindicate me . . . Prove me . . . try me . . . test my heart and my mind" [literally, "my kidneys and heart"]). Such terminology may suggest an actual religious court context or it may be used metaphorically ("acknowledge my righteousness . . . see for yourself") although the former seems more likely. The presence of a phrase referring to God in the third person in the context of direct address to God (verse 1c) can probably best be explained as a technical expression, "to trust in Yahweh," which came more easily than "to trust in you."

The statement of innocence in verses 4-8 refers to the types of person whom the worshiper avoids. Verses 6-7 refer to what must have been part of the ritual involved in asserting innocence, washing the hands and walking around the altar, and to the events associated with being cleared of charges—a song (psalm) of thanksgiving and public testimony.

Verse 8 affirms the worshiper's devotion to Yahweh. The rather peculiar expression, "I love the habitation of thy house" (or "the dwelling-place of Your glory," NJPSV), may be a circumlocution for saying, "I love Yahweh." The psalm composers did not have the worshipers frequently refer to loving Yahweh (see Pss. 31:23; 97:10; 116:1; 145:20) but used such expressions as to love God's name (Pss. 5:11; 69:36), his law (Ps. 119:47, 48, 97, 113, 119, 127, 159, 163), or his salvation (Pss. 40:16; 70:5). In Deuteronomy where "to love God" is frequently employed, the expression seems to mean, primarily, to obey God's will.

A further plea occurs in verses 9-10, a plea that the worshiper not be placed in the class of sinners or bloodthirsty persons (murderers) or be among those "who have schemes at their fingertips, and hands full of bribes" (NJPSV).

The final verses affirm the worshiper's innocence and integrity, to God (verse 11) and to other humans (verse 12).

Although it probably reads into the psalm more than was originally structured into it, the person's claims in his protestation of innocence can be seen as tenfold:

1. Walking in integrity (1a)
2. Trusting in the Lord (1b)
3. Remembering divine love (3a)
4. Walking in faithfulness (3b)
5. Not sitting with false men (probably idolaters) (4a)
6. No consorting with dissemblers (probably members of some secret cult) (4b)
7. Hating evildoers (5a)
8. Not associating with the wicked (5b)
9. Proper worshiping of God (6-7)
10. Loving the temple (8)

II Timothy 2:8-15

These words of advice continue the theme of last week's epistolary lection: fidelity to the apostolic tradition. Their force is centripetal, driving Timothy back to the center, to that which motivates, orders, and sustains him in a fruitful ministry. They establish what is peripheral—hairsplitting disputes that go hand-in-glove with teaching that veers away from the apostolic tradition (2:14, 16-19). They are a summons to remember, to engage in *anamnesis* concerning the tradition, not only to recollect but to reenact and reappropriate just as it happens in celebrating the Lord's Supper.

First, Timothy is told to "remember Jesus Christ" (verse 8). Since Timothy was not a contemporary of Jesus, this is obviously a call to remember the gospel message of Jesus Christ, specifically which Paul preaches. Hence the wording of JB: "Remember the Good News that I carry." It is a summons to rehear, reappropriate, even relive the preached Christ.

The content of Paul's gospel is summarized in a two-part formula: "Risen from the dead, descended from David" (verse 8). The formulation is reminiscent of earlier traditional summaries appropriated by Paul, and with which he aligned himself (Rom. 1:3-4; cf. Acts 13:22-23). The order is unusual; we would expect the Davidic descent to precede the Easter faith. Also striking is the absence of the cross in this summary of the Pauline gospel (cf. I Cor. 2:2; Gal. 6:14).

Second, the gospel entails suffering (verses 9-10). For the gospel, Paul is fettered (Phil. 1:7, 12-13; Eph. 3:1; 4:1; Col. 4:18; Philem. 1, 9-13), but the gospel itself is always unfettered: "they cannot chain up God's news" (verse 9, JB). Paul did not allow his own circumstances to serve as an obstacle to the progress of the gospel (Phil. 1:12-14). The irrepressibility of the Word of God becomes a major theme in Luke-Acts, and the story of Paul concludes on this very note (Acts 28:31). In the end, nothing could finally hinder Paul's proclamation of the gospel.

The suffering he endured was vicarious—for the sake of the elect, those who have been called by the gospel (I Thess. 2:2; also Matt. 24:22). His apostleship took the form of service for others, in keeping with the essential message of the Christ-event (II Cor. 5:14-15).

Third, the gospel is remembered and appropriated in worship (verses 11-13). As part of this exhortation to fidelity, a fragment of an early Christian hymn is cited. This form-critical judgment has achieved a broad consensus, seen by the fact that these verses are printed strophically by RSV, NEB, JB, NIV. The hymn is introduced as a "faithful saying" (verse 11; cf. I Tim. 1:15; 3:1; 4:9; Tit. 3:8), something we can rely on.

The sentiments of the hymn are resonant with Pauline theology. Dying and rising with Christ recalls his theology of baptism (Rom. 6:5-11; also Gal. 6:14; Col. 2:12). As is the case in the undisputed letters, sharing the resurrection life is a future reality. This sharply contrasts with the overrealized eschatology of the opponents (2:18). Moreover, our sharing in the reign of God, which comes through endurance, is also a future gift (cf. Matt. 10:22; 24:13; Acts 14:22; Rom. 8:17; cf. Dan. 12:12-13).

We are also warned in words reminiscent of Jesus that denying our confession will eventually mean that we are denied by Christ (cf. Matt. 10:32-33; Mark 8:38-39; Luke 12:9; I John 2:22-23; Jude 4). However, the pattern is broken in the last verse with the reminder that our faithlessness will not nullify God's faithfulness (cf. Rom. 3:3). The one surety we have is God's absolute fidelity (I Cor. 1:9; 10:13; II Cor. 1:13; I Thess. 5:24; II Thess. 3:3; Heb. 10:23; 11:11; I John 1:9; Rev. 1:5; cf. Deut. 7:9; Ps. 145:13). "[God] cannot deny himself" (verse 13); the integrity of God remains in tact (Num. 23:19; Tit. 1:2; Heb. 6:18).

Fourth, the centering force is the word of the gospel (verses 14-15). Timothy is charged to remind his hearers of this "faithful saying" in the hope that they will concentrate on the heart of the confession and not be seduced by useless disputes (cf. I Tim. 1:4; 6:4). The main task is for Timothy to become exemplary in his own conduct (verse 15). He too must endure, as Paul endured, in order to receive divine approval. Like Paul, he must remain undeterred in his proclamation of the gospel, and thereby become an unashamed workman (1:8; I Tim. 4:6-7; also Rom. 1:16-17).

And finally, he must deal straight with the message of truth, refusing steadfastly to play fast and loose with the gospel (cf. II Cor. 6:7; Eph. 1:13; Col. 1:5-6; James 1:18).

Once again, we are challenged by this text to be faithful to the gospel we have received. In one sense, it is a call "back to the basics," and we should remember that this is a move typically made in the Pastorals when the faith is being threatened by false teaching. But there are times when this is a worthwhile call. The church can lose sight of the center, and when it does the preacher's task is to reduce the Christian message to its barest essentials and ask the church to engage in *anamnesis* of the Christ who is proclaimed, known, and received through the gospel.

Luke 17:11-19

Luke's repetition of the phrase "on the way to Jerusalem" (verse 11) reminds the reader that the story to follow occurs in the travel narrative begun at 9:51, and also serves to note a transition in the material between verses 10 and 11. The preacher need not struggle to connect the account of healing ten lepers with what precedes. This story is found in Luke alone. While there is some similarity to Mark's account of Jesus healing a leper (1:40-45), common elements are not sufficient to argue for these as variant tellings of one incident.

One is impressed by the realistic detail of the account. Lepers tended to live in groups (II Kings 7:3), they avoided contact with non-lepers (verse 12; Lev. 13:45-46; Num. 5:2), but they kept close enough to populated areas to receive charity. Jesus' command that they show themselves to the priests (verse 14) was also according to the Law of Moses (Lev. 14:2-32). However, one is also struck by elements in the story that raise questions. For example, the location between Samaria and Galilee (verse 11) seems unusual for one going to Jerusalem, especially in view of Jesus having much earlier gone from Galilee into Samaria (9:52). It is quite possible that Luke here uses the Galilee-Samaria border to introduce a story involving both Jews and a Samaritan (verse 16). Another uncertain element in the text is Jesus' command to show themselves to the priests. Did this apply also to the

Samaritan who was outside the rituals of Judaism? Also, why reproach the nine for not returning (verses 17-18) when they had been told to go and show themselves to the priests? In fact, their healing occurred upon their going; their obedience apparently the expression of faith essential to their healing (verse 14). Some commentators, sensitive to these questions, have taken the account as an idealized story joining faith, obedience, and gratitude.

However, it seems more natural to understand Luke 17: 11-19 as a two-part story: verses 11-14 and 15-19. The first part is a healing story with all the elements of a healing: a case of evident need, a cry to Jesus for help; Jesus treats them as already healed, as indicated in his sending them to the priests; their healing occurs in their act of obedient faith. (In Mark 1:40-45, the leper is sent to the priest *after* the healing.) The second part, verses 15-19, is a story of the salvation of a foreigner. It is the foreigner who praises God and gives thanks to Jesus. It is the foreigner to whom Jesus says, "Your faith has made you well" (verse 19). Clearly the expression "made you well" refers to some blessing other than the cleansing from leprosy which has been given to all, including those who did not give thanks and who did not praise God. That additional blessing we usually term "salvation."

Assuming the other lepers were Jews, the story makes two points vital to Luke: the faith of foreigners (7:9; 10:25-27; Acts 10-11) and the blindness of Israel (Acts 26:16-18). In a sense this story is a foreshadowing of Acts 28:26-27, the turning of the Christian missionaries from Jews to Gentiles. It is very important to notice that Jesus did not reject the nine Jewish lepers. They were blessed with his healing. Neither did Jesus set aside Jewish law; he sent them to the priests as the law required. But by the time Luke was written, such stories probably were told in abundance: the Gentile responds affirmatively, Jesus' own people do not. Very likely this account was inspired by an Old Testament story to which Jesus had earlier referred (4:27): the healing of a leper who was a foreigner (II Kings 5:1-14). That story also had two parts: Naaman was cleansed and Naaman was converted to Israel's faith.

We cannot suppose that Luke told this story simply to

paint a favorable picture of a Gentile and an unfavorable one of the Jews. Quite possibly the church in Luke's day had begun to presume upon God's favor and to take blessings for granted, without gratitude. If so, again it was, and is, the outsider who teaches the people of God what faith is, what praise is, and what thanksgiving is.

Proper 24

Sunday Between October 16 and 22 Inclusive

Habakkuk 1:1-3; 2:1-4; Psalm 119:137-144; II Timothy 3:14–4:5; Luke 18:1-8

In the opening words of today's Old Testament reading we hear echoes of our own protest to God against injustice in the world, while in the closing words we are reassured that the righteous will live by faith. The theme of righteousness also pervades the selection from Psalm 119, although the emphasis falls on the righteousness of God. These words might easily be read as a response to the reading from Habakkuk, for they boldy assert and defend God's justice. The epistolary reading speaks of reliability and fidelity of another sort—that which belongs to the tradition and to the written Word of God. Finally, we have a negative portrait of justice in the parable of the unjust judge, the Gospel reading for today. The real emphasis, however, lies on the importunate widow whose plea for justice is heard by God.

Habakkuk 1:1-3; 2:1-4

Since prophetic words are so historically concrete and specific, it is always important to know as much as we can about the circumstances in which they arose. But the Book of Habakkuk, unlike most prophetic books, gives us no date for the prophet. There are historical allusions, but they are uncertain and ambiguous. The most likely historical framework, based on the references to the rise of the Chaldeans (the Neo-Babylonian empire, 1:6), is during the last decades of the Assyrian Empire, 625–612 B.C. Thus the "wicked" mentioned in the book probably are the Assyrians.

Our texts for the day are best understood in the context of the book's structure. It has two distinct parts, chapters 1-2 and chapter 3. The final section, a hymn or song of praise, celebrates the appearance of God to intervene against the nations and thus bring salvation to the people; God acts in wrath against the wicked. The first two chapters are organized as a visionary dialogue between the prophet and God (1:2–2:4), followed by a series of woes against the wicked (2:5-20).

The superscription to the book (1:1) is similar to the one to the Book of Nahum. There is another superscription or title in 3:1, indicating that the two parts of the book may once have circulated separately. The term translated "oracle" could also be read "burden," appearing frequently as the heading to prophecies against foreign nations (Isa. 13:1; 14:28; 15:1; 17:1; 19:1). The word "saw" (also in Isa. 1:1; Amos 1:1) is used here as a technical term for the reception of divine revelation and indicates that those who passed on the written words of the prophet considered them to be the authoritative word of God. Habakkuk is specifically identified as a "prophet," but the contents of the book strongly suggest that he was a cultic prophet, associated with the temple worship.

Remarkably, the first words that follow the superscription are not an oracle or divine revelation at all, but the words of the prophet *to* Yahweh (1:2-4). These lines give the first move in the dialogue, Habakkuk's complaint to God. The form of expression and the tone are quite familiar, like those of the individual complaint or lament Psalms (e.g., Pss. 5, 6, 17, 22). The prophet complains about the presence of evil and suffering and the fact that the wicked overpower the righteous. Addressed to God, this is a question of divine justice. Seen in national and historical context, it may be an objection to the oppression of Israel by Assyria and a prayer for relief.

Habakkuk 1:5-11 reports Yahweh's answer to this initial complaint, a promise that he will raise up the Chaldeans to put an end to these wicked oppressors. Then in 1:12-17 the prophet speaks again, reiterating the complaint, and basing his plea for help on confidence in the justice of God (2:13). How, he asks, can the suffering of the righteous be reconciled with faith in a just God?

The second part of our reading (2:1-4) gives the Lord's

second response. The prophet vows to take his stand to watch and wait for an answer (2:1), recalling the image of Ezekiel as the Lord's sentry (Ezek. 33; see the commentary for Proper 18 in this volume). There are three parts to the revelation. First, the prophet is to "write the vision" plainly, "so he may run who reads it" (2:2). This last expression probably means that the writing must be so legible that a runner can read it without stopping, but it may be metaphorical, suggesting that those who read it will be enabled to go on, to keep in the way of the Lord. Second, the Lord cautions patience. The vision may seem slow in coming, but come it will (2:3). Finally, there is the promise concerning the life of the one who is righteous (2:4).

These lines in 2:4, some of the most famous and influential in the Old Testament, call for special comment. We cannot expect that their meaning here will have been exactly the same as their force in the New Testament (Rom. 1:17; Gal. 3:11; Heb. 10:37-38). "But the righteous shall live by his faithfulness" (RSV fn) translates three well-known Hebrew words. "The righteous" (*sadiq*; cf. Ps. 1) is the one who is faithful to the law, who is just in all human relationships, and who is pious in religious observances. "Faithfulness" is a more accurate reading of the Hebrew *emunah* and refers to steadfastness, fidelity, trustworthiness, especially in the covenant relationship. We have encountered references to "life" in similar contexts in other readings for this season (Ezek. 33; Amos 5:6-7, 10-15), in which cases it means the full, abundant life before God and in the covenant community. Thus Habakkuk 2:4 means, in fidelity to God the righteous one lives the full life. In effect, the full life is defined by faithfulness. To the prophet's question about the justice of God and the suffering of the righteous, God reminds him that the righteous in their faithfulness have their own reward, life.

Psalm 119:137-144

Five of the psalm lections over the three-year cycle are from Psalm 119, the longest composition in the Psalter (see Epiphany 6 and 8 A; Propers 18 and 26 B). This extended eulogy on the Torah is a complex alphabetic poem, a carefully crafted intellectual accomplishment. Working through the twenty-two letters of the alphabet, each stanza consists of eight lines all beginning with the same letter of the alphabet. This construction means that the final form consists of 176 verses. Such a feat as this is, of course, impossible in English and most other languages.

The alphabetic structure was no doubt chosen in this case to reflect the creative ingenuity of the author. (Both the flexibility of the Hebrew language and the creativity of the poet can be appreciated if one looks at the silliness that characterizes our children's ABC books when they deal with certain letters.) The alphabetic structure also allows the composer to give expression to the fullness of praise for and to the totality of the Torah. The psalm preserves many of the interests which we would associate with instruction or teaching.

As in the other eight-line stanzas, verses 137-144 (the eighteenth stanza) uses eight "synonymous" terms in referring to the will of God: thy judgments, thy testimonies, thy words, thy promise, thy precepts, thy law, thy commandments, and thy testimonies (here testimonies is repeated as the eighth term). Sometimes nuances of meaning can be gained by reading another translation. The NJPSV translates these eight terms as "rulings, righteous decrees, words, word, precepts, teaching, commandments, and righteous decrees."

Several emphases are found in this stanza of the psalm in addition to love of and devotion to the law. First, God's righteousness is affirmed (verses 137, 138, 142). Second, the law is the means of achieving order and well-being in life. Life with the law has meaning even if one is "small and despised" (verse 141). Delighting in the law helps overcome trouble and anguish (verse 143). Third, the sight of others who ignore the law produces anguish of soul (verse 139 which the NJPSV translates: "I am consumed with rage over my foes' neglect of Your words.").

This psalm like much of the Old Testament and Judaism as a whole shows joy, delight, and comfort in the law. In Jewish tradition there are 613 commandments in the Torah. One rabbi (Rabbi Judah) commented on these as follows: "248 are positive commandments, corresponding to the 248 members of the human body, each member saying to a person: please perform thus and such a commandment through me. 365 are negative, corresponding to the 365 days of the solar year. Each day calls to a person: do not do thus and such a transgression on me!"

II Timothy 3:14–4:5

It is one thing to be encouraged to learn new things, probe new vistas, push beyond our present boundaries into uncharted territory. It is quite another to be told to "keep to what you have been taught and know to be true" (verse 14, JB). The one values what is new, untested, and potentially eye-opening and life-changing, while the other values what is tried and true. One eyes the future, the other casts a backward eye to the past.

The outlook of today's text, in keeping with the overall perspective of the Pastorals, is traditional. The past is valued and cherished. It not only provides precedent but stability. We are told to hold on to the tradition, what we have been taught, and to continue in that. Sailing new waters, clearing new paths, forging new vistas—all these are frowned on. The way forward is through the old, not the new. It is an outlook foreign to the spirit of the Enlightenment.

One reason for this cautious conservatism is the threat of false teachers, a constant concern of the Pastorals. New teaching has been given a bad name and is repeatedly dismissed as philosophy, myth, senseless disputing pseudo-knowledge (cf. I Tim. 6:20).

What, then, is valued in this approach?

First, past teaching (verses 14-15). We are urged to "stand by the truths you have learned and are assured of" (verse 14, NEB). The focus here is clearly catechetical. It is the truth of the gospel, and the teaching deriving therefrom, that we have received from faithful witnesses (1:12-14; 2:2; also I Tim. 6:20).

As important as what we were taught is the person who taught us: "remember who your teachers were" (verse 14,

JB). For Timothy, of course, they were his grandmother Lois and his mother Eunice (1:5; Acts 16:1), and Paul as well (2:2). He is reminded of the cumulative effect of Christian nurture—becoming acquainted with Scripture through childhood.

Most of our teachers are forgettable, but a few are unforgettable. We remember those who taught us the faith, but especially those who excited us about the faith. Their faces still form fresh images in our minds, and their words still echo within us. What they said blended with who they were, and now their word and character shape what we say and who we are. To say that our teachers have influenced us and shaped the contours of our thinking and living is to acknowledge the power of the tradition. There can be no real doubt of the norming value of what we were taught and who taught us.

Second, sacred Scripture (verses 16-17). The primary referent here is Jewish Scripture, the Old Testament, since the New Testament writings had not yet been collected. It is this sacred text to which the early Christian community looked for guidance and instruction (Rom. 15:4; I Cor. 10:11). This repository of worthwhile teaching does two things: it has the "power to make [us] wise and lead [us] to salvation through faith in Christ Jesus" (verse 15, NEB). We are told that Scripture is "inspired" (verse 16, RSV, JB, NEB) or "God-breathed" (NIV), meaning not only that it speaks of God but that God speaks through it. As the collected oracles of the community of faith in whom God has acted and through whom God has spoken, Scripture speaks to us uniquely of God. Since God called the community into existence, and Scripture bears witness to this divine-human dialogue, its ultimate origin is God and may be said to come from God (II Pet. 1:9-21).

As the repository of the collected wisdom of Israel and the oracles prompted by God, it is uniquely suited to provide instruction in the life of faith. We should note carefully both the extent of the claim being made here for Scripture and the type of value attributed to it. It is said to be "profitable" or "useful" (verse 16), which in itself is a modest claim. It is said to be useful in four respects:

1. Teaching—as a source for positive instruction
2. Reproof—as a source for refuting error
3. Correction—as a source for "guiding people's lives" (JB)
4. Training in righteousness—as a source to provide "discipline in right living" (NEB).

It is most particularly suited for the "man of God" (verse 17; cf. I Tim. 6:11; also I Sam. 2:27; I Kings 13:1), in this case, the minister, but more generally for the person committed to the quest of God.

With this orientation to what has been received and to Scripture as the richest source of the tradition, Timothy is now given a solemn charge to continue steadfastly in the work of ministry. It is a charge made in the very presence of God (verse 1; cf. I Tim. 5:21; 6:11-12) and Christ, the eschatological judge of "the living and the dead" (verse 1; Acts 10:42; Rom. 2:16; 14:9-10; I Pet. 4:5).

The content of the charge is straightforward: "preach the word" (verse 2). This is to be done season in and season out: "press it home on all occasions" (verse 2, NEB). The proclamation of the gospel is to be done in all of its aspects: convincing—using argument and persuasion in speaking the message forcefully; rebuking—using stern words to censure and correct; exhorting—using words of encouragement in trying to elicit a response. All the gestures should be employed: the pointed finger to highlight the argument, the slap of the hand to censure, the arm around the shoulder to encourage. All of this is to be done with enduring patience (verse 2).

Coupled with the charge is a warning that students, left to themselves, will take the easy road (verses 3-5). They will want a dull message whose edge has been sanded off. Their ears will itch for teaching that soothes. The stern demands of the gospel will be interpreted in watered-down form, and the truth will be exchanged for myths. Faced with this prospect, the minister is urged to pursue a steady course of fidelity, even in the face of suffering; in a word, to "work to spread the Gospel" (verse 5, NEB).

Luke 18:1-8

The parable of the unjust judge, found in this Gospel alone, is typically Lukan in structure. The parable itself (verses 2-5) is prefaced by an introduction stating the purpose for the parable (verse 1) and is followed by interpretive comments (verses 6-8). Like the parable of the dishonest steward (16:1-13), the lesson to be learned is drawn from the behavior of someone who is less than admirable. The parable is structured on an argument from the lesser to the greater: if an insensitive and hardened judge will hear the pleas of a widow, how much more can we trust that God will hear the prayers of those who day and night cry for vindication. It would be an error, therefore, for the preacher to draw a straight analogy between the judge and God.

In fact, the introduction to the parable can be slightly misleading. That disciples ought always to pray and not lose heart is a valid and important lesson in constancy, but the point in our text concerns not prayer in general but a specific prayer. Discerning the specific problem being addressed demands that we look at the context and at the interpretive comments at the conclusion of the parable.

The context for today's lection begins at 17:20 with the question concerning when the kingdom of God is to come. This question prompts a series of teachings on the day of the Son of man (verses 22-37). The closing verse of our text continues to speak of the coming of the Son of man (verse 8), making it clear that the parable of the unjust judge is to be interpreted in that context. With this understanding, verse 1 should be interpreted as a word to disciples who have been taught to pray, "Thy kingdom come," but who now have grown weary and are losing heart. Their discouragement is probably due in part to the passing of time and to what is usually referred to as the delay of the Parousia. By Luke's day several generations had passed, and time alone can erode enthusiasm and faithfulness (Heb. 6:11-12; II Pet. 3:11-14; Rev. 21:7). But verses 7-8 make it clear that the faithful are not only experiencing the passing of time but are also undergoing persecution. They are seeking vindication.

The question, How long will the Lord tarry? was a burden

on the faith of Israel as well as the early church. When shall the cup of God's wrath be full so that vindication will come for the faithful? Most of the answers offered by prophets and apocalyptists spoke of God's desire that all have opportunity to repent, and this included those from whom the faithful prayed for deliverance. In the text before us, the disciples are told to continue in sustained faithfulness in their prayer for the coming of the kingdom. In addition they are assured that the time of waiting and of persecution is near an end. God "will vindicate them speedily" (verse 8).

Verse 8, however, poses a new question for the followers of Jesus. The question, When? posed by the Pharisees is clearly the wrong one (17:20-21). The question, How long shall we continue to pray? is doubly answered in the parable and the comments that follow. But the really crucial question is the one asked by Jesus, The Son of man is coming to vindicate his people but who are his people? Will those apparently so interested in the eschaton and the reversal of the fortunes of the evil and the good be faithfully committed to Christ up until the end? Will the Son of man actually find faith among us? As stated by Christ elsewhere, "He who endures to the end will be saved" (Mark 13:13).

Proper 25

Sunday Between October 23 and 29 Inclusive

Zephaniah 3:1-9; Psalm 3; II Timothy 4:6-8, 16-18; Luke 18:9-14

In today's Old Testament reading from Zephaniah, we hear Jerusalem assailed for harboring corruption at every level and the Lord's promise to bring both judgment and reform. As a psalm of personal lament, Psalm 3 provides another angle of vision. Confronting his enemies, the psalmist looks to Yahweh for strength and deliverance. In the epistolary reading, we have the farewell words of Paul facing death. Casting a glance both backward and forward, he finds reason to be confident and hopeful. In the Gospel reading, we have a well-known instance of Lukan reversal: the parable of the Pharisee and the publican. It is a picture of God who vindicates the humble, and in this respect resonates with Psalm 3.

Zephaniah 3:1-9

Zephaniah, like Nahum, Habakkuk, and Jeremiah, was active in the seventh century B.C., during the last decades of the Assyrian Empire. The book's superscription (1:1) places him in the reign of King Josiah (640–609 B.C.), the king credited with reforming the religious practices in Judah and centralizing worship in Jerusalem (II Kings 22–23). Before this time, and especially under Josiah's predecessors Manasseh and Amon, Judah was a virtual vassal of Assyria and foreign religious practices flourished. The reform under Josiah (621 B.C.) implemented the laws at the center of the book of Deuteronomy. Zephaniah makes no references to these events but attacks the kind of religious syncretism also identified as problems by the reformers. Thus he probably preceded and helped pave the way for the reform.

Our reading for the day, consisting mainly of accusations and judgments against Jerusalem (3:1-13), comes from the third of four distinct parts of the Book of Zephaniah. The others are 1:2–2:3, announcements of judgment against Judah and Jerusalem; 2:4-15, a series of woes against foreign nations; and 3:14-20, announcements concerning and celebrations of salvation to Jerusalem.

According to both form and content, this passage consists of four parts. They are verses 1-5, 6-7, 8, and 9 (actually, 9-13). Interpretation of each of these individually is important, for it is likely that each arose separately, and each should be allowed to have its full force. For example, one should not brush quickly past the indictment at the outset to arrive at the good news at the end. However, finally we must see the section both in the context of the book and as a whole, for those who collected and edited the book, if not the prophet himself, saw continuity and coherence.

The prophet begins (3:1) with a woe cry against a city, which the context reveals to be Jerusalem. As elsewhere in prophetic address, the woe is followed by the indictment of the addressees in terms of their evil deeds. Here the city is personified as rebellious, defiled, and oppressing. The accusation of failure to trust in Yahweh or draw near to God suggests false or corrupt worship, quite possibly the idolatry mentioned in 1:4-6. Then Zephaniah turns to those responsible, cataloguing the sins of the political and religious leadership (verses 3-4). Her "officials" (or "princes") and "judges" are compared to wild animals that eat up the people they are supposed to care for and protect. Prophets are corrupt and unfaithful to Yahweh. Priests fail in their most fundamental duties, maintaining the distinction between sacred and profane and teaching the law to the laity (Lev. 10:10-11; cf. Hos. 4:4-10). And through all of this Yahweh's justice is as constant and predictable as the rising sun (verse 5).

Verses 6-7 recall the past. Up to this point only the prophet has spoken; now Yahweh himself is quoted. The Lord has brought his judgment upon nations and cities, as "correction" (see 3:1), in order to evoke faithfulness, but the people were even more eager to act corruptly. Consequently, he promises that a terrible "day" is in store (verse 8). The tone and scope are almost apocalyptic. It is the day of the Lord (1:7, 10, 14; 2:2), the day of the Lord's wrath, when he will arise in anger to judge nations and kingdoms, indeed, "all the earth." The description of judgment that follows in verses 11-13 is quite different, making a distinction between those in Jerusalem who have been rebellious and those who have not. On the day of the Lord there will be punishment against the former, but a remnant will remain of those who are humble and lowly.

The announcement that comes in verses 9-10 is totally unexpected. Immediately on the heels of the prophecy of the destruction of the earth by the Lord's anger we hear the promise of a miraculous transformation of the speech of the peoples of the earth. All will "call on the name of the Lord" in prayer and worship, serving him "with one accord." Note that the agent of the transformation is not the peoples, but God. As the entire passage has come down to us, then, the purpose of disaster is first pedagogical, to lead to the correction of faithlessness and corruption. Then the goal of the final day is to bring all peoples to worship the God who reigns in Jerusalem.

Psalm 3

The content of this psalm suggests that it was composed for use in worship by someone either falsely accused of some crime or by someone beset by numerous enemies. If the psalm was used by the king, then the enemies would have been foreign nations. Whether the trouble is already brewing (and the psalm is therefore a legitimate lament) or merely anticipated (and the psalm was therefore part of a protective or preventive ritual) cannot be determined.

Characteristic of the psalm is a sense of confidence and trust, the belief that, whatever the conditions are, matters will work out well.

The following is an outline of the psalm noting who is being addressed: (1) a description of the trouble addressed to

God (verses 1-2); (2) a statement of confidence addressed to the Deity (verse 3); (3) a statement of confidence spoken to a human audience (officiating priests? accusers? litigants in the case? friends? verse 4); (4) a confessional proclamation to a human audience (verses 5-6); (5) a plea to God for personal deliverance and destruction of the enemy (verse 7); (6) an oracle or statement spoken to a human audience by the worshiper or a priest (verse 8*a*); and (7) a request for blessing addressed to the Deity as an indirect benediction (verse 8*b*).

Several elements in the psalm are noteworthy. (1) A fair amount of what might be called military imagery permeates the material—foes, shield, set themselves (deployed), smite. If these are taken literally, they might suggest that the king, the state's commander-in-chief, is the user of the psalm. (2) Sleep and rest in the night are taken as good signs of innocence and as foretastes of better times. The ability to pass the night tranquilly and awake refreshed is evidence of divine sustenance. (3) The frankness of the plea in verse 7 may appear alarming to the pious and an embarrassment to the weak-hearted. The psalm, however, allows the worshiper to express true sentiments which at the moment is the hope that the enemy will get its teeth busted and it's face slapped. The minister ought at least to try to see what can be done with that in a sermon!

In the course of exegeting and interpreting the Psalms, the rabbis associated many of them with David. The superscription to Psalm 3 already shows this tendency. In Psalm 2 the rabbis associated the enemies in tumult with Gog and Magog (see Ezek. 38–39). Then they asked why Psalm 3 about David's son Absalom was placed next to a psalm dealing with Gog and Magog. Their answer: a wicked son works greater cruelty upon his father than will the wars of Gog and Magog!

II Timothy 4:6-8, 16-18

Faced with death, we tend to say and do certain things. We soberly reflect on our impending death in view of our immediate circumstances. We look at our life in review, then cast a glance into the future that lies beyond death. We also speak of what—or who—ultimately matters to us. And if we are people of faith, these farewell reflections will inevitably speak of God.

In today's text, we have Paul's farewell words, shorn of the human particulars (verses 9-15, 19-21). In one sense the entire epistle of Second Timothy should be read as a last will and testament of Paul, but the words of today's text represent his concluding sentiments. It is hard to say to what degree they are the words of the historical Paul. To be sure, they *themes* echo themes Paul used to describe his own ministry. These include the metaphors of sacrificial libations (Phil. 2:17), fighting either as an athlete or a soldier (I Cor. 9:25-27; cf. I Tim. 1:18; 6:12; also Jude 3), and running the race (I Cor. 9:24-25; Phil. 3:12-14; cf. Acts 20:24). At the very least, they represent how Paul was remembered by his successors who admired him. They should perhaps be read alongside the Lukan version of Paul's words (Acts 20:17-38), or compared with other testaments (cf. Gen. 49:1-27; Deut. 33:1-29).

The two parts of today's text reflect slightly different concerns and moods. In the first section (verses 6-8), we have Paul's sober reflections on his impending death, his former life, and his view of the future. The mood is not so much resignation but matter-of-fact realism: "the time of my departure has come" (verse 6). Nothing of the morbid or macabre here, nor the sentimentalizing of death. Paul is facing death as a fact of life. In the second section (verses 16-18), the mood shifts slightly. There is the sense of abandonment. The old warrior has been forsaken, and we detect a querulous tone as Paul mentions those who deserted him (verse 16; cf. 1:15; 4:10). For the true soldier, the cardinal sin is desertion. But balancing this sense of irritation with the less loyal is the sense of trust in the Lord who never deserts.

death life reward *Reflections on death, life and reward* (verses 6-8). At other times Paul had stared death in the face (I Cor. 15:30-32; II Cor. 1:8-10), and in more contemplative moments expressed the desire to "depart and be with Christ" (Phil. 1:23). He could envision himself as a libation being poured over a sacrificial offering (Phil. 2:17; cf. Exod 29:40; Num. 28:7). But here there is a note of finality, as if the last drop of the libation is being poured on the altar: "my life is already being poured away as a libation" (verse 6, JB).

218

Oddly enough, nowhere in the New Testament is recorded the death of Paul, although there are hints (cf. Acts. 20:29, 38; cf. II Pet. 3:15). It speaks of the death of principal figures in terms that are either brief or allusive (cf. John 21:18-19, 23; Acts 7:54–8:1; 12:2). The notable exception, of course, is Jesus. According to later Christian tradition, Paul was beheaded in Rome during the reign of Nero (A.D. 54–68).

Looking back, Paul summarizes his life confidently, even triumphantly. He is the fighter who has fought well, the runner who has run well (verse 7). He has "kept the faith," meaning that he has been faithful to the tradition. Accordingly, he views the future expectantly, looking to receive the victor's crown (verse 8; cf. I Cor. 9:25; II Tim. 2:5; James 1:12; Rev. 2:10; 3:11; also Wisd. of Sol. 5:16). His eye is fixed on "that Day," the Day of Yahweh, when the exalted Christ serves as "righteous judge" (4:1; cf. Heb. 12:23; James 4:12; 5:9). Sharing with Paul in the reign of God will be "all who have loved his appearing" (verse 8), that is, all who regard his incarnation as the welcome manifestation of God (1:10; Tit. 2:11) as well as those who welcome his final appearing in the Parousia (cf. I Tim. 6:14; Tit. 2:13; II Thess. 2:8).

Human desertion, divine loyalty (verses 16-18). At his first hearing, Paul stands alone. It is a picture reminiscent of the trial of Jesus (Matt. 26:56; Mark 14:50; John 16:32). Earlier he mentioned those who have left—Demas, Crescens, Titus (verse 10). Only Luke accompanies him. In the face of human desertion, Paul finds the Lord to be ever present and near (cf. Acts. 18:9-10; 23:11, 27:23-24; also Phil. 4:5). He also becomes the source of strength out of which the gospel is proclaimed to the Gentiles (cf. Phil. 4: 13; II Cor. 12:9-10; John 15:5). Being "rescued from the lion's mouth" (verse 17) recalls the language of Psalm 22:21 (cf. Ps. 7:2; 17:12; Dan. 6:16-24; I Macc. 6:20), and suggests deliverance from a violent death. In words reminiscent of the Lord's Prayer, Paul looks to be delivered from every evil (verse 18; cf. Matt. 6:13; John 17:15; II Cor. 1:10; II Thess. 3:3) and hopes to share in the heavenly reign (2:12). The final word is a Pauline doxology (cf. Rom. 16:27; also textual addition to Matt. 6:13).

When preaching from this text, the minister will need to ask whether, and to what degree, these are the words of the historical Paul. But the historical-critical question need not set the agenda entirely. What we have here is a portrait of the farewell words of Paul. As we have seen, there are enough echoes and links to the undisputed letters of Paul for it to ring true. Apart from this, however, the text does present us with one way of confronting death, measuring life, and facing the future. For Paul, none of these could be done seriously apart from the life of faith. For that reason, the mood of our text is confident and the message is one of hope.

Luke 18:9-14

With the parable of the Pharisee and the publican we conclude the special section of Luke that began at 9:51. This will not conclude Luke's travel narrative which continues until the entry into Jerusalem (19:40), but 18:14 ends the material in Luke which is a departure from the Markan framework.

As was true of the parable of the unjust judge (18:1-8) immediately preceding, this story is not only unique to Luke but is told in typically Lukan fashion. The format is: an introduction stating the purpose and thrust of the parable (verse 9); the parable proper (verses 10-13); and comments on the parable (verse 14). In this case the closing comments are two: the statement of the justification of the publican, and the statement of the reversed roles of the humble and the proud. This second comment is in the form of a pronouncement and as such was used in a variety of contexts (Luke 14:11; Matt. 18:4; 23:12). If one wonders why this parable is located here, the answer may simply be in the fact that it, like the one before it, deals with prayer. In addition, both parables deal with justification, the word "vindicate" in the previous story being a form of the word here translated as "justify." It may be, however, that Luke thought it wise to follow a parable about the prayers of saints with one about the prayers of sinners, lest arrogant claims be made by either group.

The parable of the Pharisee and the publican conveys in story form the doctrine of God's justification of sinners and judgment on the efforts of those who try to establish their own righteousness. These twin accents are usually associated with Paul, especially his Roman and Galatian Letters, but they are in fact as old as the Garden of Eden, the tower of Babel, and Jonah's mission to Nineveh. The parable makes its point by means of the reversal of stations so familiar in Luke when dealing with the self-righteous and the humble, the strong and the weak, the haves and the have-nots (1:51; 6:20-26; 16:19-31). It would be difficult for any interpreter of the parable to improve on the clear statement of Luke: it is addressed to those who trust in themselves, thinking they are righteous, and who despise others.

However, few parables have been subjected to more distortion than this one. For example, one common error is painting the Pharisee as a villain and the publican as a hero, and in so doing each gets what he deserves. This is exactly the opposite of the parable's message. The Pharisee is not a villian but rather represents complete dedication to observing the Law of Moses. In fact, his recitation of his performance is that of a person exceeding the law's demands. His prayer is a common rabbinic expression of thanksgiving prefaced by the claim of the psalmist with reference to personal behavior (Ps. 17:3-5). Nor is the publican a hero. In fact, as a publican working for Rome collecting taxes from his own people, he is a reprehensible character, religiously unclean and politically a traitor. While his prayer is according to Psalm 51, his life is offensive. To miss this fact is to rob the parable of its radicality. God justifies the ungodly, a truth blurred by popular caricatures which present the Pharisee as a hollow hypocrite and the publican as generous Joe the bartender or Goldie the good-hearted hooker, both to be admired for their rejection of organized religion. Cheap novels that play on these themes do not understand that God justifies sinners who confess and rely on grace. The Pharisee trusts in himself; the publican trusts in God: that's the difference.

The preacher-interpreter will want to be extremely sensitive to Luke's focus, lest the parable be presented in such a way as to make the publican proud and thankful that he is not as others. Nothing is gained if parishioners leave the sanctuary thankful that they are not as the Pharisee.

221

Proper 26

Sunday Between October 30 and November 5 Inclusive

Haggai 2:1-9; Psalm 65:1-8; II Thessalonians 1:5-12; Luke 19:1-10

In contrast to the rather harsh prophetic words from previous Old Testament readings, this text from Haggai speaks of the abiding Spirit of God and the splendor of the new temple. It is a vision of hope propelling us into the future. Psalm 65 is a psalm of thanksgiving set within the context of a bountiful harvest. Since the temple is the gathering place for this harvest thanksgiving, the psalm is linked thematically with the Old Testament reading. The epistolary reading provides us with a stern eschatological text in which the coming Christ responds to power with power, taking vengeance on those who have opposed the gospel. The notion of terror we find here echoes some of the sentiments of today's psalm. In the Gospel reading, we meet the familiar story of Zacchaeus, whose encounter with the Lord results in his conversion and uncommon generosity.

Haggai 2:1-9

Consider what had happened in Judah between the time of Zephaniah, the prophet whose words provided the Old Testament reading for last week, and Haggai, whose words are before us today. Worship had been centralized in the temple in Jerusalem (621 B.C.), and the Assyrians, who had conquered Northern Israel and threatened Judah for generations, had fallen to the Babylonians in 612–609 B.C. The Babylonians had in turn captured Jerusalem in 597 and destroyed it in 587, including the temple. Many of the Judeans were carried off into exile in Babylon, where they

222

remained in captivity until that empire fell in 538 to Cyrus, who established the Persian Empire. Cyrus not only set the captives free, but also authorized the reconstruction of the temple (Ezra 1:1-4). The captives began returning to their homeland, many of them arriving in Jerusalem by 536. Sixteen years later, when Haggai first addressed the returned exiles, they had not yet begun rebuilding the temple. We can be so precise about these dates because the Book of Haggai is quite specific, placing the prophetic addresses in the sixth through the ninth months of the second year of the Persian monarch Darius, that is, 520 B.C.

Haggai is a bridge between prophetic and priestly institutions and theologies. He is identified as a prophet (1:1) and, like earlier prophets, addresses the people with words from God, announcing the future. But his message mainly concerns a particular problem, the rebuilding of the temple in Jerusalem. One might say that he brings the authority and fervor of prophetic revelation to bear on what was traditionally a priestly matter. Like a priest, he is deeply concerned not only with the holy place, but also with maintaining the distinction between what is clean and what is unclean (2:10-19; cf. Lev. 10:10-11).

The message of Haggai is not without its difficulties in Christian preaching. We look in vain among his words for the passionate concern for justice and righteousness that rings through the message of the earlier prophets. Moreover, his first revelation urging the people to rebuild the temple (1:1-11) seems almost crass and simplistic in attributing the relative poverty of the returned exiles to the fact that that they have not begun work on the temple. Prosperity will follow, he suggests, if the people will give their energy to the construction.

When the passage assigned for today's reading begins, the work on the temple had started under the leadership of Zerubbabel the governor and Joshua the high priest. But when the people saw the foundations and imagined how the completed building would appear, they were discouraged. Haggai asks if anyone remembers the old temple in its former glory (verse 3). Few, if any, could possibly remember the first temple, for it had been torn down for sixty-seven years. The comparison they make is between the present reality and the legend of Solomon's glorious temple. But, to judge from the prophet's response, the problem was deeper than disappointment with the building. The temple, along with the monarchy in the line of David, symbolizes for all of them the kingdom of God. Complaints about the building, then, reflect doubts about the presence and power of God.

Haggai responds with words of encouragement and reassurance, appealing first to the past and then to the future. Addressing Zerubbabel the governor and Joshua the chief priest, he urges them to be courageous and pronounces the Lord's assurance of his presence, reminding them that they can stand on the promises made during the Exodus (verses 4-5). Then, in words that reflect a hope similar to that in Isaiah 2:1-4, he promises even more dramatic signs of the coming kingdom of God. The expression, "in a little while," has eschatological overtones; Yahweh will "shake" both the created order and all nations, who will bring their treasures to the temple, which the people find disappointing. This promise signals the expectation that all peoples of the earth will recognize and acknowledge through their gifts that Yahweh is God and Jerusalem is where he is to be worshiped.

What have bricks and mortar to do with the kingdom of God? Haggai knew that the completion of the temple would not bring in the New Age. God himself will do that. He means to set human work and devotion in the full scheme of God's work, past, present, and future. God acted, acts, and will act, calling for each generation to respond, and thus to participate in God's design. Haggai, the practical visionary, calls for his generation to demonstrate its devotion by building the temple, and the God to whom all silver and gold belongs (2:8) will attend to its splendor. The kingdom is that time and place where God's will is done. The temple will be a symbol of God's graceful presence for all the world.

Psalm 65:1-8

Very few psalms of community thanksgiving are found in the Psalter (see Pss. 67; 92; 107). A hymn may have served as the community's response to specific acts of divine providence, and thus no great need existed for writing special thanksgiving psalms. Psalm 65 is probably one of the exceptional psalms of communal thanksgiving.

All of the psalm is direct address to the Deity, although some scholars see a radical change of tone between verses 1-4 and 5 following. Some even argue for three psalms (1-4, 5-8, 9-13). The composition appears, however, to be a unity and the elements of sin, creation, and divine blessing of the crops/harvests are not so unrelated.

Verses 1-4 focus on the human admission and divine forgiveness of sin. Difficulties in translating verses 1-2 make the exact meaning uncertain. For example, in the Hebrew, the opening line says, "To thee praise is silent" or "is waiting." Note the KJV which reads, "Praise waiteth for thee." Verses 2*b* and 3*a* can be translated, "Unto thee all flesh shall bring the requirements of iniquity." At any rate certain factors seem clear. (1) The occasion for the celebration and the praise of God is the fulfillment of vows. These may have been vows made to be carried out if certain conditions were met by God, such as his providing a good crop year or forgiving sins, probably the latter. Moderns look judgmentally on vows or deals with God or at least we publicly express ourselves that way. Ancient Israel was unashamed of such arrangements. (2) A public, communal acknowledgment of sin is made. A basic feature of Israelite religion was a routine day of national repentance (Yom Kippur). Other days of repentance were held when deemed necessary. The minister who preaches on this psalm should imaginatively think about what such days of national repentance might do in contemporary culture where admitting wrong and guilt is itself considered to be . . . a national sin. (3) Worship in the temple is viewed as an exhilarating source of joy and blessedness. The goodness of the temple (verse 4*c*) probably refers to the sacrificial feasts eaten in the temple in conjunction with thanksgiving. (The covered dish dinner has a long genealogy and a most sumptious ancestry!)

In verses 5-8, the psalm shifts to focus on the divine creation of cosmos and the establishment of order in the world. Chaos is represented by the seas, the waves, the people (and their roaring and tumult). Over against these,

God establishes, stills, and pacifies so that the regularity of the mornings and evenings following each other in succession shouts for joy.

It may seem odd that such apparently diverse issues as the forgiveness of sin and creation are brought together in this psalm. In Old Testament priestly theology, sin and impurity were considered disruptions of the orders of creation and even of creation itself. Sin introduced chaos and the breakdown of order into the cosmos. Forgiveness and sacrifice were means of restoring proper relationships and proper order in the world.

II Thessalonians 1:5-12

This is the first of three semicontinuous readings from the Epistle of Second Thessalonians to be read over the next three weeks. They should perhaps be read along with the closely related set of semicontinuous readings from the Epistle of First Thessalonians that serve as the epistolary readings for Propers 24–28 in Year A. Nevertheless, a few introductory remarks to Second Thessalonians are in order here.

The church at Thessalonica was established by Paul and his co-workers Silas and Timothy during his mission in the Aegean area (I Thess. 1:7-10; 2:1-2, 9-12, 17-20; Acts 17:1-9). Predominantly Gentile in its composition (I Thess. 1:9-10), this fledgling church was born and flourished in a hostile setting (I Thess. 2:14-16; Acts 17:5). As those who had "received the word in much affliction" (I Thess. 1:6), they knew the pressure of religious persecution firsthand. But they had demonstrated remarkable patience and steadfastness in the face of open resistance.

Coming from a Gentile background, they were likely less accustomed to Jewish ways of thinking about the end time and life after death. As a result, eschatology confused them. In the Epistle of First Thessalonians, the primary question they asked was whether one of their members who had died would thereby be excluded from the heavenly reign. Was it necessary for one to be alive when the Lord returned? Paul assures them that both those who are alive at Christ's coming and those Christians who have died previously will share in the Lord's coming (I Thess. 4:13-18). They are also reminded that the date of the Lord's coming is unknown, and the proper response is to be constantly alert (I Thess. 5:1-11).

The situation envisioned in the Epistle of Second Thessalonians is slightly different. There is still eschatological confusion, but this time the worry is not about the future. From some outside source, perhaps in the form of a letter forged in the name of Paul, the Thessalonians had been taught that the Day of the Lord had already come (II Thess. 2:1-2). If this had not already been taught, there was the fear that it would be. Paul's response to this is to underscore the futurity of the Lord's Parousia. As he does so, he sketches a series of events that are to occur in the interim, thus demonstrating that some things are still to occur before they can say that the Lord has already come (II Thess. 2:3-12).

Because of the sharp difference between the types of eschatological misunderstanding addressed in each of the Thessalonian Epistles, some scholars have questioned the authenticity of the second epistle. They find it difficult to believe that the situation could have changed so much so soon. Others have noted a more radical apocalyptic tone in the second epistle, suggesting that the instructions given there have a sharper, more vindictive edge than we normally find in Paul.

If the Epistle of Second Thessalonians does not come directly from Paul's hand, it stands very close to the first epistle, both in time and outlook. More important than the question of authorship, however, is to recognize how the letter addresses a congregation of believers for whom the price of faith is persecution (1:4).

Today's text is prompted by the opening thanksgiving (1:3-4), which concludes by noting the afflictions the church is having to endure. The mention of affliction prompts this rather severe statement concerning God's response to the enemies of the people of God.

The response is framed in the clear expectation of the *future* coming of Christ (cf. 2:3-12). This event is conceived in terms informed by Jewish apocalyptic. The Lord is expected to be "revealed from heaven" (Dan. 7:13-14; Mark 9:1; Luke 17:30; I Cor. 1:7; I Pet. 1:7, 13; 4:13), accompanied by a host of "mighty angels" (Matt. 13:39, 41, 49; 16:27; 24:31; 25:31; Luke 12:8-9). In terms reminiscent of Old Testament depictions of the coming Day of the Lord, this event is also to be accompanied by "flaming fire" (verse 7; Exod. 13:22; 19:16; Isa. 66:15; cf. I Cor. 3:13, 15).

Out of this cosmic upheaval comes the exalted Christ "inflicting vengeance" (verse 8; cf. Rev. 19:11-16). It may be an unsettling image to us, this vengeance-bringing Christ, but the notion of a God who vindicates the people of God against their enemies has a long history (cf. Deut. 32:36). It becomes something of an axiom that God can play this role, whereas human beings cannot (Rom. 12:19; 13:4; I Thess. 2:16; Heb. 10:30; Luke 18:3).

The objects of the Lord's vegeance are twofold: (1) "those who do not know God," that is, Gentiles (verse 8; cf. Jer. 10:25; Ps. 79:6; I Thess. 4:5; Gal. 4:8; I Cor. 15:34), and (2) "those who do not obey the gospel of our Lord Jesus," that is, Jews (verse 8; cf. Isa. 66:4; Rom. 10:16; I Pet. 4:17). Another interpretation is to see only one group of resisters who are described in two respects: in terms of their ignorance as well as their disobedience. Whether one group or two, they suffer a similar fate. First, the Lord actually visits them with affliction (verse 7; Phil. 1:28; Rev. 14:13). Second, they suffer "eternal destruction and exclusion from the presence of the Lord" (verse 9; cf. Isa. 2:10, 19, 21; Ps. 64:34; I Thess. 3:13).

In light of the tribulation which is expected to continue, the threat turns to prayer (verses 11-12). Paul's prayer is that those under pressure will be strengthened in their resolve and enabled to be worthy of their call (verse 11; also verse 5; cf. I Thess. 2:12; Phil. 1:27; Eph. 4:1; Col. 1:10). It is, after all, the kingly reign of God for which they are suffering (verse 5; cf. Acts 14:22; I Thess. 2:14; 3:4; Eph. 3:13).

In preaching from this text, we can scarcely ignore its jolting effect. In the plainest terms, we are told that God inflicts punishment on those who afflict God's people. We might well wonder why Christians are instructed to "repay no one evil for evil" (Rom. 12:17; cf. Matt. 5:38-42), while such behavior becomes God. In trying to account for this form of theological response, we do well to remember that it is a response to persecution. In Revelation, there are times when the church under the threat of annihilation no longer finds meek and gentle images of Jesus appropriate forms of response. In some settings, the only meaningful response to oppression may be aggression, as hard as this is to square with ordinary perceptions of the Christian gospel.

Luke 19:1-10

The episode in Luke 19:1-10 is a Lukan story. This is to say it is without parallels in the other Gospels. All three Synoptics have Jesus approaching Jerusalem by way of Jericho, and all three record the healing of a blind man (two blind men in Matt.) near Jericho (Matt. 20:29-34; Mark 10:46-52; Luke 18:35-43). However, only Luke tells of Jesus' encounter with Zacchaeus in Jericho. The story does remind the reader of an earlier story in Luke 5:27-32 (Mark 2:13-17; Matt. 9:9-13) concerning Jesus and Levi. Levi was a tax collector; Jesus was a guest in Levi's house; critics murmured against Jesus for this association; Jesus responded with a pronouncement ("I have not come to call the righteous, but sinners to repentance," verse 32). The structure of 19:1-10 is much the same, including a very similar closing pronouncement (verse 10).

The episode in Luke 19:1-10 is a human interest story. Luke is well known for his parables that have a narrative plot and include more than the usual amount of interesting detail: the good Samaritan, the rich fool, the rich man and Lazarus, the dishonest steward, the unjust judge, the Pharisee and the publican, the prodigal son. It is also the case that Luke evidences conscious literary artistry in narrating non-parabolic stories. The appearance of Jesus to the two disciples on the road to Emmaus (24:13-35) is a classic example of the storyteller's art. The story before us, though briefer, is not without some of the same qualities. In addition to being interesting, Luke 19:1-10 generated some discussion in the early church on the issue of Jesus' stature. The Greek text as well as most English translations permit "because he was small of stature" to refer back to Jesus. An early Jewish critic of Christianity commented on Jesus' short stature as contrary to what one would expect in a son of God.

The episode in Luke 19:1-10 is a conflict story. "And when they saw it they all murmured, 'He has gone in to be the guest of a man who is a sinner'" (verse 7). In that day as well as today, the common wisdom was "birds of a feather flock together" and "you can judge a person by the company he keeps." That Jesus rejected wisdom in his seeking and searching love is a vivid and repeated truth of the Gospels. Loving and forgiving are not condoning, and the behavior of Jesus fulfills rather than abrogates righteousness.

The episode in Luke 19:1-10 is a radical story. Zacchaeus is not only a publican; he is a chief tax collector. All the criticism that could be hurled against a publican (ceremonially unclean, socially ostracized, politically treasonous) could be compounded against Zacchaeus. In a corrupt system the loftier the position the greater the complicity in that corruption. No one need defend Zacchaeus on the grounds that his private conduct is not revealed. The fact is, one is not privately righteous while participating in a corrupt system that robs and crushes other persons. And Zacchaeus is rich. Given Luke's already stated comments on wealth (1:53; 6:24; 16:19-31), the reader is alerted in verse 2 to the radicality of the act of grace that follows.

Finally, the episode in Luke 19:1-10 is a salvation story. Terms important to Luke tell the story. "Saving the lost," a rare expression, is found here in verse 10 and in 15:6, 24, 32. Zacchaeus *and his house* (verse 9) receive salvation, a concept important to Luke (Acts 10:2; 11:14; 16:15-31; 18:8). Most scholars agree that verse 8, which softens the radicality of the act of grace and which may lead some to think Zacchaeus acted so as to merit forgiveness, was probably a post-Easter church reflection inserted to instruct Christians as to what the fruits of repentance would mean. In the Old Testament, voluntary restitution involved the original amount plus 20 percent (Lev. 6:5; Num. 5:7); compulsory restitution called for doubling the original and in some cases repaying four- or fivefold (Exod. 22:1, 3-4; II Sam. 12:6). In Luke's church forgiveness was not solely a transaction of the heart. Genuine repentance bore fruit. This was made clear as early as the preaching of John the Baptist when crowds and tax collectors and soldiers came asking, "What shall we do?" (3:10-14).

Proper 27

Sunday Between November 6 and 12 Inclusive

Zechariah 7:1-10; Psalm 9:11-20; II Thessalonians 2:13–3:5;
Luke 20:27-38

According to ancient tradition, each liturgical year is brought to a close with the use of texts having an eschatological orientation. Therefore, even though today's readings are semicontinuous with no intent of thematic unity, the eschatological flavor does pervade all the texts, even if only by implication. Zechariah answers the question about the role of mourning and fasting with a call for mercy, justice, and the cessation of injustice. The psalmist prays not only for deliverance from, but for the end of, injustice. Today's epistle is a benediction, a word of thanks, and a request for continued prayer. Luke 20 is more directly eschatological in posing the question of resurrection in the concrete terms of marriage and the hereafter.

Zechariah 7:1-10

Zechariah shared many concerns with his contemporary Haggai. His perspective was both prophetic and priestly. He had received in word and vision God's message for his contemporaries. One major section of the book, Zechariah 1:7–6:15, presents reports of his eight night visions in which he announced various aspects of the coming age of salvation. He was convinced that God was working to bring in a religious kingdom, with its center in Jerusalem. Like Haggai (see the comments on Haggai 2:1-9 for Proper 26 in this volume), he encouraged the people to rebuild the temple.

Zechariah and his contemporaries in Judah lived under the relatively benevolent rule of the Persian Empire. Judah was no longer an independent state, but part of the Persian province of Samaria. But the ancient promises of land and self-determination for the people of God continued to live. Among these was the promise (II Samuel 7) that a descendant of David would always sit on the throne in Jerusalem. There is evidence in Zechariah 6:9-15 and Haggai 2:20-23 of an attempt to crown Zerubbabel as the legitimate heir to the throne of David. If so, that would have been revolution against the Persians. Increasingly, however, the hope for a royal messiah was applied to the life of religious practice. Zechariah, with his priestly concerns, was instrumental in that transition.

Our reading is part of a section of the book that contains a collection of various prophecies. The lection consists of two parts, verses 1-7 concerning fasts, and verses 8-10 which begin a sermon (verses 8-14) on obedience to the law.

The first unit begins (verse 1) with a precise date, two years after Zechariah's initial call for the people to repent (1:1-6), or 518 B.C. A delegation from the town of Bethel came to make formal inquiry concerning a matter of ritual practice. Should they continue to "mourn and fast" in the fifth month, as they have done for so long (verse 3)? Since the temple was destroyed in the fifth month (II Kings 25:8-9), the mourning would have been for that loss. Now that the temple was being reconstructed—it was dedicated in 515—should the fasts continue?

It was a good question, and appropriately presented to "the priests . . . and the prophets" (verse 3) for an oracular response. Should mourning for the destruction remain a regular part of the liturgical year? Zechariah indeed responds with the word of Yahweh, but he does not answer the question. Instead, he speaks about the purpose and meaning of fasts. His questions about their motives (verses 5-6) are rhetorical, suggesting that their fasts—like their eating and drinking—are out of concern for themselves, and do not represent devotion to the Lord.

Verse 8 begins a new unit, a sermon on morality based on the message of the preexilic prophets such as Amos, Hosea, Isaiah, and Jeremiah. The prophet instructs and admonishes the people in their duties, the list amounting to a virtual catechism. In Zechariah's call for justice in court, kindness, and mercy (verse 9), the most powerful words of the prophetic tradition parade before us. Then these expectations become specific and concrete in the prohibitions against oppressing the widow, the orphan, the resident alien, or the poor (verse 10). All these are the most vulnerable members of the society. The prophet goes on to remind his hearers that their ancestors failed to attend to the earlier prophets' calls for such behavior, and for that reason they were carried into exile (verses 11-14). Thus, the later prophets such as Zechariah used the ancient traditions, turning what had been announcements of judgment into warnings for their contemporaries.

The reading evokes reflection on questions of piety and worship on the one hand, and concern for social justice on the other. Those alternatives will be familiar to most contemporary Christian congregations, for they represent what are frequently two sides in controversies about the implications of the biblical faith. But obviously Zechariah—and most of the Old Testament—would resist any effort to drive a wedge between piety and social concern, between personal devotion and justice for the neighbor. Both are equally essential responses to the God of the covenant.

Psalm 9:11-20

Psalms 9 and 10 apparently were once a single, unified composition. Since Psalm 10:12-18 was discussed earlier in this volume, the reader may wish to consult the comments made there (see Proper 15).

The following are the components of verses 11-20; (1) a call to the people to praise God (verses 11-12); (2) a plea addressed to God for help combined with a description of an individual's trouble (verse 13); (3) a statement of a promise or vow formulated as a consequence clause (verse 14); (4) proclamation or an oracle (spoken by a priest?) addressed to the congregation (verses 15-18); and (5) a final appeal for God to act (verses 19-20).

Let us now examine each of these elements. In the call to praise four things are noted about God.

1. The Deity is described as the one who dwells or sits

enthroned in Zion. Since the main Judean temple was in Jerusalem (Zion), then the Deity was associated in a special way with the city. As his dwelling place, Zion was divinely protected (see Pss. 46; 48; 76). In later Judaism, Zion was considered the center, "the navel," of the world, the original point of creation, and the spot joining the earthly world with the upper and lower worlds.

2. Yahweh's reputation among the nations, the foreigners, is based on his deeds, or conversely his deeds, manifest in the status and welfare of his people, are the means of establishing his reputation.

3. Yahweh is the one who holds accountable the shedding of blood. Throughout the Old Testament, God is the defender of life and holds humans accountable for killing (see Gen. 9:2; II Sam. 12:9-14). Even the taking of animal life was considered murder if the slaughterer did not give the blood (the life) back to God (see Lev. 17:1-4).

4. Finally, God is declared to be the helper of the afflicted, those oppressed, or the victims of misfortune. (The NJPSV translates verse 13 as "For He does not ignore the cry of the afflicted; He who requites bloodshed is mindful of them," reversing the two lines.)

The short pleas, "Be gracious . . . Behold . . . ," are followed by the nature of the trouble (suffering from enemies or haters) and an epithet of God; he is the one who lifts up from the gates of death (saves from sickness or from being killed). Perhaps the "I" here speaking was originally the king and the enemies would have been foreign powers.

The promise/vow in verse 14 stipulates what the worshiper will do if redeemed: (1) recount God's praises (offer testimony) and (2) rejoice in thanksgiving/celebration. (See Ps. 118, a thanksgiving psalm in which the king offers thanksgiving for victory in battle; note the reference to opening the gates in 118:19 which suggests that the preceding thanksgiving took place in the gates.)

The oracular proclamation in verses 15-18 functions as a priestly response to the appeal of the worshiper. The plans of the nations are declared as rebounding against themselves: they are caught in their own machination. The point made in the text stresses the close connection of deed/consequence, act/result. The nations are caught in their own devices, consumed by their own appetites, caught in their own traps. Here we have expressed the idea that the world and human actions operate in a sphere of moral equilibrium in which disruptions in life rebound against the offenders. In the four lines of verses 15-16, three have the process operate on its own. Only in 16a is God related to the judgment of the enemy/wrongdoer. In other words, in the action/reaction, deed/consequence relationship, God tends to function as the overseer of the process rather than as the avenging judge. Verses 17-18 are parallel to verses 15-16 although they express matters in different terms: the nations/the wicked shall end in Sheol while the needy/the poor/the Israelites shall be remembered and saved. The NJPSV translates verse 19 as: "Not always shall the needy be ignored, nor the hope of the afflicted forever lost."

The appeal in verses 19-20 is a plea that God will act so that nations/humans would realize that they are but flesh and blood; that in the last analysis God rules. Although knowledge of the divine is not stressed in these verses— there is no plea that God would act so that the nations would know he is God—one might say that self-knowledge is equivalent to divine knowledge. God's actions are to reveal humanity's true humanness; where there is true self-knowledge there is God at work.

II Thessalonians 2:13–3:5

Between these words of warmth, comfort, and pastoral appeal and last week's heavily apocalyptic text occurs the extended discussion of the Day of the Lord (2:1-12). As one of the more controversial passages in the Pauline writings, it is perhaps omitted as a lectionary text, but may profitably be pursued in other contexts of Bible study.

Today's passage, however, represents a clear shift in tenor from last week's text. It divides easily into three parts.

Thanksgiving (verses 13-14). One of the unusual features of the Thessalonian Letters is the way the typically brief Pauline prayer of thanksgiving becomes extended throughout the letter (cf. I Thess. 1:2; 2:13; 3:9; II Thess. 1:3). Given the intimate relationship between Paul and the Thessalonian church (cf. I Thess. 2:1-12), we are not surprised to learn that this church is a constant source of thanksgiving (verse 13). They are in every sense "beloved by the Lord" (I Thess. 1:4-5; cf. Deut. 33:12).

The real source of Paul's thanksgiving is in the divine calling they experienced. They were chosen "from the beginning" (verse 13), which may mean that they were his first converts in Europe. This would be difficult to square with the account in Acts where the church at Philippi is established first as part of Paul's Aegean mission. Earlier, he had reminded them of the unique nature of their calling. They had received the "word of God" not as an ordinary human message, but as "what it really is, the word of God, which is at work in you believers" (I Thess. 2:12-13). The preached Word is to be seen as the mediated power and presence of God. It is no mere human voice that is heard through the preaching. As our text suggests, God is actively at work through the gospel choosing and calling, provoking and evoking (cf. Rom. 8:30).

Through the divine call, the Spirit elicits our response to salvation, purifying us and setting us apart to a life of service (James 1:18; I Thess. 5:9). We experience salvation through the sanctifying work of the Spirit (I Cor. 6:11; I Thess. 4:7; I Pet. 1:2). But it is also our conviction that the gospel is true, rings true, indeed is the truth, that causes us to respond to God's call. Through this experience of salvation, we are directed to the glory of Christ (cf. I Thess. 5:9).

Admonition (verses 15-17). Stemming from the thanksgiving is a solidly based exhortation to stability and fidelity: "Stand firm and hold to the traditions" (verse 15). Being loyal to our vocation is difficult enough even in times of relative calm and placidity, but more so in the face of persecution. It is the gospel in which we stand and there we find our stability (cf. I Cor. 15:1-3; also 16:13; Gal. 5:1; Phil. 1:27; 4:1; I Thess. 3:6, 8). One way this occurs is through holding fast to the traditions we were taught in connection with the gospel: the stories of Jesus and the stories about Jesus with the interpretations and guidelines related to Christian behavior (cf. I Cor. 11:2, 23; II Thess. 3:6). What we have been taught forms the beginning of our fidelity (I Thess. 3:4; 4:2, 6; 5:27; II Thess. 2:2, 5).

Coupled with this exhortation to fidelity is a prayer that Christ himself (cf. I Thess. 3:11), along with God the Father, will extend comfort (cf. I Thess. 3:13; II Cor. 1:3-7) and will establish us on the road to worthwhile words and deeds (cf. II Cor. 9:8; Eph. 2:10; Col. 1:10; II Tim. 3:17; Tit. 2:14).

Final appeal (3:1-5). Having prayed for the church, Paul now enlists their prayers in his behalf (cf. Rom. 15:30; Eph. 6:18-19; Col. 4:3; I Thess. 5:25; Heb. 13:18). His hope is that the Word will work among others as it has among them (cf. I Thess. 1:8; Ps. 147:15). Nor is Paul unaware of his enemies, and prays for protection from them (Rom. 15:31). He is all too aware that "not all have faith" (verse 2; Rom. 10:16). His confidence rests in his unalloyed conviction in the absolute fidelity of God. "The Lord is faithful" becomes almost a cliche in Paul, but only because it was an experience out of which he lived. It was not an empty phrase he uttered (cf. I Cor. 1:9; 10:13; II Cor. 1:18; I Thess. 5:24; II Tim. 2:13; cf. Heb. 10:23; 11:11; I John 1:9; Rev. 1:5; also Deut. 7:9; Ps. 144:13).

Even though their church is young and fledgling, Paul is confident the Thessalonians are willing and able to follow his instructions (verse 4; cf. Rom. 14:14; Gal. 5:14; Phil. 1:14; 2:24).

His final prayer in their behalf is for the Lord to direct them toward the love which God has shown them and the steadfastness which Christ himself exhibited (cf. I Chron. 29:18; John 5:42; Luke 11:42; I John 2:15).

Luke 20:27-38

Since much has transpired in the career of Jesus since our lection for last Sunday (19:1-10), we need first to set the context. Jesus is in Jerusalem, he has already cleansed the temple, and he is now engaged in a series of controversies with Jewish leaders. Two questions have already been put to Jesus: the source of his authority (20:1-8) and the matter of paying tribute to Caesar (20:20-26). The question about the resurrection of the dead, our text for today, in Luke is the third and final question before Jesus puts to his interrogators a question concerning the Christ as David's son (20:41-44). Matthew (22:34-40) and Mark (12:28-34) have a fourth question put to Jesus before Jesus himself becomes the questioner, Which is the first commandment? Luke does not include that question here because he dealt with that subject earlier when a lawyer tested Jesus by asking, "Teacher, what shall I do to inherit eternal life?" (10:25-28). On the question before us now, that of the resurrection of the dead, Matthew (22:23-33) and Mark (12:18-27) have parallels which agree completely with each other. Luke's account is noticeably different, not so much in the question but in a portion of Jesus' answer, especially verses 34-36.

It is important in understanding Luke 20:27-38 to keep in mind that the question posed about the resurrection came not from bereaved persons seeking hope or from believers searching for more clarity on the doctrine. Rather, Jesus is being interrogated by persons who already were fixed in their position that there was no resurrection of the dead (verse 27; Acts 23:8). The Sadducees (the name may have derived from Zadok, high priest under Solomon) were one of the several parties within Judaism. They were of the priestly class, many of them aristocratic and wealthy, they were theologically conservative, and they regarded as normative in their religion only the five books of Moses. What was not to be found in the first five books of the Old Testament was not authoritative. The Pharisees, on the other hand, believed there was an oral as well as written tradition from Moses, and within that oral tradition was the basis for belief in the resurrection. It was a subject of heated debate between the two parties (Acts 23:6-10); the Sadducees sometimes baited their opponents with impossible "what if" questions. Such is the game played here with Jesus. Anyone who has been a target for religious questions raised by persons who had no intention of being influenced by the answers can sense the frustration of a no-win situation.

Jesus, however, does not respond to the attitude but to the question. His answer is twofold. The first part (verses 34-36) simply points to the inappropriateness of the question, given a fundamental difference between life in this age and in the age to come. Marriage is appropriate for this age since the fact of mortality necessitates a means for perpetuating life. However, those who attain to the resurrection from the dead are children of God and are as the angels. Such a condition does not have need of marriage. It is important to notice that Jesus does not respond in terms of the widespread belief that everyone has an immortal soul. Rather, resurrection from the dead is an act and gift of God for "those who are accounted worthy to attain to that age and to the resurrection from the dead" (verse 35). Immortality is based on a doctrine of human nature; resurrection is based on a doctrine of God's nature.

The second part of Jesus' answer is a response in kind. The Sadducees, in keeping with their belief in the Pentateuch as Scripture, based their question on Deuteronomy 25:5-10, the levirate law of marriage which spells out the duty of a man toward a deceased brother. Jesus appeals to the same body of Scripture, Exodus 3:6, to affirm God as a God of the living and not of the dead. The inference is that Abraham, Isaac, and Jacob have or will have continuous life with God. Nothing about intermediate states of the deceased is stated or implied.

It is important for Luke's theology that Jesus' teaching on the resurrection is continuous with Judaism, at least as understood in a major tradition, Pharisaism. It is important for Luke and his church as Christians, and for us, that resurrection from the dead is grounded in both the words and the experience of Jesus.

Proper 28

Sunday Between November 13 and 19 Inclusive

Malachi 4:1-6 (3:19-24 in Hebrew); Psalm 82; II Thessalonians 3:6-13; Luke 21:5-19

The eschatological orientation of these texts for the end of the liturgical year becomes more explicit and pronounced for this last Sunday before the celebration of Christ the King. Malachi predicts the punishment of the wicked, the vindication of the righteous, and the return of Elijah, in that final triumph of God for which the psalmist prays. Second Thessalonians addresses the problem of idleness as an erroneous response to the preaching of an imminent Parousia. The Gospel is Luke's version of Jesus' apocalyptic discourse concerning the end of Jerusalem and the temple, the coming of the Son of man, and the eschaton. In all these texts, God's judgment is a time of both distress and joy.

Malachi 4:1-6 (3:19-24 in Hebrew)

Since "Malachi" probably is not a proper name but the title, "my messenger" (see Mal. 3:1), the Book of Malachi is an anonymous book. The style of the book is quite distinctive, consisting almost entirely of dialogues between God or the prophetic figure and the addressees. This style lends a didactic and argumentative character to the work. The topics of the dialogues include God's love for the people (1:2-5), accusations against the priests and people concerning their poor sacrifices (1:6–2:9), marriage to foreign women (2:10-16), questions about the justice of God (2:17-3:5 and 3:13–4:3), tithes and offerings (3:6-12), and admonitions to be faithful for the day of the Lord is coming soon (4:4-5; see also 3:13–4:3).

No date is given for the unnamed prophet, but he surely would have been active in the postexilic period, probably after the dedication of the temple in 515 B.C., but before the time of Ezra and Nehemiah (around 400 B.C.). Like the other prophets of this era, this one is concerned with priestly and cultic matters, such as proper sacrifices, tithes, and offerings. At the same time, however, Malachi is like his prophetic predecessors in his concern for justice (Mal. 3:5), and in his announcement of the coming day of the Lord.

The reading for today, brief as it is, is not a single unit, but encompasses three distinct parts. The first of these, Malachi 4:1-3, is the concluding paragraph in a dispute that began in 3:13. Its theme is the justice of God, specifically directed to those who assert that evildoers prosper. The dispute is not an actual one, but a rhetorical device to present a case and argue a point. The prophet does not directly deny the allegation, but looks beyond the present to a time when God's justice will be established. Records are being kept, he argues, in a "book of remembrance" (3:16; see also Dan. 7:10; Rev. 20:12; 21:27), so that God will distinguish between the righteous and the wicked.

Then in 4:1-3 the prophet announces the coming of the day of the Lord (see also 3:2-4). The expectation of a day of the Lord was already a traditional matter by the time of Amos in the eighth century B.C. Obviously, his contemporaries anticipated a time of salvation for Israel, but he announced that it would be a time of "darkness, and not light," a time when the Lord would judge Israel (Amos 5:18-20). The expectation seems to be rooted in the ancient tradition of the holy war, as the time of the Lord's victory over his enemies. For Amos, there was no separation between sinners and righteous, and Israel had become the enemy of Yahweh. By the time of Malachi, "the day" had become a time when the Lord would establish justice, rewarding the righteous and punishing those who work evil. Malachi, like Amos, has in mind a day within history and on this earth. In our passage the expectation takes on almost apocalyptic overtones, moving more and more in the direction of the detailed and extensive visions of the end in Daniel and Revelation. Thus, while the unrighteous may prosper in the present age, God will on that day vindicate those who "fear him," that is, those whose piety is genuine.

The second part of this passage is a single verse, 4:4. It is a general admonition, similar to those in the book of Deuteronomy, to obey the Mosaic Law. In the context it appears to be a later addition explaining how to be on the side of the righteous.

Finally, verses 5-6 pick up the theme of a messenger sent to prepare the way for the appearance of the Lord on that great and terrible day. Here the messenger is interpreted to be the prophet Elijah, who became an increasingly important figure in the intertestamental literature and then in the New Testament. Elijah's role here is to effect a change in the hearts of parents and children, in order to avert a curse on the land.

The eschatological dimensions of the text are especially appropriate for the end of this season. God will one day make all things right, establishing his just reign over all. But what does one do in the shadow of that day, at once terrible and glorious? One is faithful to God, obedient to the will of God known through the traditions (the Law), and open to the possibility of changed hearts.

Psalm 82

This psalm, even in its present biblical form, reflects an origin in a polytheistic background when other gods or at least heavenly beings shared the rule with Israel's Yahweh. The psalm does not fit into any clearly definable genre being neither a hymn, a lament, nor a thanksgiving. The opening verse provides a context for the divine speech/oracle in verses 2-7. The final verse is a plea asking the Deity to judge the world.

The opening verse probably originally read something like: "Yahweh has taken his place in the council of El; in the midst of the gods he holds judgment." Several factors are presupposed: (1) the world is governed by a consortium of divine beings, a sort of heavenly council (see I Kings 22: 19-22; Job 1:6-12); (2) the old Canaanite Deity El is noted and the council is said to be his or headed by him; El, note the name IsraEl, was a Palestinian god worshiped by some early

Israelites (see Gen. 33:18-20) who came to be identified and/or assimilated to Yahweh; and (3) Yahweh is here assigned pride of place in the heavenly council as the one who takes charge and holds the other deities accountable. (Although the present Hebrew text reads Elohim [= God] in the opening word, Yahweh was probably the earlier reading since throughout Psalms 42–83 "Yahweh" seems to have been replaced frequently with "Elohim." Later rabbinical exegetes understood Elohim as referring to human judges but this does not square with verse 7.)

In the divine speech in verses 2-7, Yahweh condemns the other divine beings for their failure to judge properly and for their display of partiality to the wicked. In some sense, the psalm deals with the question of why life is like it is and why justice does not seem to prevail. The divine beings show partiality. In Hebrew law, one was not to show favoritism or partiality to either rich or poor, to the powerful or the weak (Exod. 23:3; Lev. 19:15). Justice was ideally to be blind.

Verses 3-4 stipulate the requirements placed upon the divine beings (and by extension one can say placed upon humans as well). The divine beings/rulers of the world/ human beings must see that certain powerless classes are not taken advantage of. The weak/the fatherless/the afflicted/the destitute/the needy must be defended against the encroachment of the wicked/those who would take advantage of them.

The interpretation of verse 5 is uncertain. Is it a continuation of verse 4 and thus a description of either the weak and needy or the wicked? Or is it a description of the heavenly beings who are being condemned? The RSV clearly takes it in the latter sense closing the divine quotation with verse 4. It seems better to see verse 5 as a description of one of the groups, or both groups, mentioned in verses 3-4. The powerless and the powerful both could be said to walk about in darkness without knowledge or understanding, that is, they have not the insight and ability to rectify matters themselves. The concluding line, "all the foundations of the earth are shaken," probably means that the moral order of the world is completely askew—there is a lack of justice and the presence of anarchy in too many places.

243

Verses 6-7 have Yahweh condemn the divine beings, here called "Elohims the sons of Elyon," to die like men, to fall like a displaced prince. That is, they will be removed from power and authority.

Finally, the psalm writer has a plea that Yahweh would judge the earth and rule all nations since they belong to him (verse 8).

In preaching on this psalm, the minister must realize some of the larger issues with which the psalm is concerned: (1) the problem of why life does not measure up to and manifest a just order is still clearly an issue today; (2) the division of humanity into the wealthy/powerful/wicked and the needy/poor/powerless, into classes, is not the way the world should be; at least, one class should not be where it is by taking advantage of the other; (3) a responsibility of the divine world is the establishment of justice and equity, (so frequently we have noticed in the Psalms how God is held accountable for his responsibility for order and justice in the world and is charged with failure to do his task); and (4) finally, the psalm breathes an air of hope and expectation in its plea for God to take charge and judge the world himself, to take responsibility for its operation.

II Thessalonians 3:6-13

One of the side effects of eschatological misunderstanding is that it can upset people's schedules. If the Lord is expected to come soon, one response is to put down the tools, fold the arms, and wait for his return. Perhaps this is the reason both Letters to the Thessalonians address those who are idle (verses 6-7, 10-12; I Thess. 5:14). There appear to be instances of idleness unrelated to fixations on the end-time, what might be called cases of general shiftlessness (cf. I Tim. 5:13). One of the main concerns of today's text is to address this tendency to stop working, for whatever reason.

We should notice first the advice to shun those who are living in idleness. Anytime people form themselves into groups, they eventually formulate rules and guidelines for deciding when persons are no longer members. There also develop procedures for removing members who are no longer full members or who, for some reason, have violated the stated or unstated rules of membership. The Old Testament provides extensive instruction governing membership within Israel and establishes guidelines when persons should be removed from the community. The separatist community at Qumran also developed elaborate rules and guidelines for determining when members should be avoided or excluded.

Thus when the early Christian communities show evidence of policing their own membership, they are acting in concert with ancient precedent as well as reflecting an established sociological reality. Paul warns his churches to take note of troublemakers and keep a watchful eye on them (Rom. 16:17). In cases where members violate moral codes, there are clear instructions not to associate with them (cf. I Cor. 5:5, 9, 11; II Tim. 3:5; Tit. 3:10-11; cf. Matt. 18:17). In today's text, it is the person who has stopped working who is to be avoided, primarily because such behavior is not in keeping with the teachings Paul had transmitted to the church. Part of these teachings must have been his instructions to "admonish the idlers" (I Thess. 5:14), but probably there were teachings connected with his eschatology in which he spelled out his conviction that preparing for the end-time did not mean to stop working (I Thess. 5:6, 11; cf. I Cor. 7:27-31).

As a response to the idlers, Paul adduces his own example (verse 7), a typical method of moral instruction (I Cor. 4:16; 11:1; Phil. 3:17; 4:9; I Thess. 1:6; cf. Heb. 6:12; 13:7; also Eph. 5:1; I Thess. 2:14; Gal. 4:12). In his first epistle he had rehearsed with the church the way he had worked night and day in their behalf (I Thess. 2:9). This seems to have been his normal pattern rather than an isolated instance among the Thessalonians (cf. I Cor. 4:12; Acts 18:3; 20:34).

He also stresses that his actions in this respect were exceptional. As an apostle, he had the full right to expect his churches to support him financially (verse 9; cf. I Cor. 9:6). On his side was established religious precedent, the Law of Moses, and the teaching of Jesus (I Cor. 9:3-14; cf. Matt. 10:10). But he chose not to exercise this right and instead paid his own way as he worked to establish new churches.

Accordingly, his rule among his churches was: the one who does not work cannot eat (verse 10). In the first letter, one reason given to support this rule is that it will enable the church to command the respect of outsiders (I Thess. 4:11-12). For Paul, it was important how the church was viewed by pagans (cf. I Cor. 10:33; 14:24-25). His view was that a church full of thumb-twiddlers little commended itself to the pagan public. Consequently, he advised the church to take a responsible course of action in this respect. Christians are to "do their work in quietness and to earn their own living" (verse 12; cf. I. Thess. 4:11).

As a final word, he urges not to "be weary in well-doing" (verses 13; Gal. 6:9; II Cor. 4:1, 16).

In the wrong hands, this text can easily become a club used to beat those who are out of work, especially the long-term unemployed. Clearly, if we are idle and remain idle, for no good reason, we come under the censure of this text. Paul's example also serves as a worthwhile corrective to the 9-to-5 view of ministry. As we all know, genuine ministry often involves us in round-the-clock work. People in need do not punch a clock. But perhaps one of the most important dimensions of this text is its insistence that we best prepare for the end-time not by being idle but by working and earning our own living.

Luke 21:5-19

It is frequently the case with biblical narratives that descriptions of what is going on are interwoven with descriptions of what is really going on. This is to say, historical events are presented but not with the historian's interest. Rather, these events are set in the larger context of God's purpose being worked out, descriptions of which call not for historical language but for images, symbols, and figures. Such is the nature of today's Gospel.

Luke 21:5-19 joins the prediction of the destruction of the temple (verses 5-7) with an apocalyptic discourse on the coming of the Son of man (verses 8-36), our lection ending at verse 19. In early Christian circles, the destruction of Jerusalem (A.D. 66–72) was understood as an eschatological event, a sign that the end was near. That the two subjects were joined in all three Gospels (Matt 24:1-36; Mark 13:1-37) is no surprise. As we shall note in the discussion below, it was a question about the former that led into the latter.

Both Matthew and Mark identify the comment about the beauty of the temple as coming from the disciples while Luke more vaguely says "some spoke of the temple" (verse 5). After Jesus' comment to the effect that not one stone shall be left on another (verse 6), both Matthew (24:3) and Mark (13:3) shift the scene to the Mount of Olives from which Jesus gave the apocalyptic discourse. Luke does not. All three agree on the two questions that follow even though they disagree on who asked them (Matt. 24:3; Mark 13:4; Luke 21:7), When? and What will be the sign?

That portion of the apocalyptic discourse which constitutes our lesson falls in two parts: the signs of the end (verses 8-11) and the time of testimony to precede the end (verses 12-19). What is said in verses 12-19 chronologically precedes the events of verses 8-11. The signs of the end are threefold: the appearance of false messiahs and false calculators of time and place (verse 8); wars, tumults, and international conflicts (verses 9-10); and natural disasters with cosmic terror (verse 11). Concerning these signs the disciples are advised that the end is not yet, and therefore, they are to be neither led astray nor terrified.

Preceding these signs is the time of testimony (verses 12-19). The chronology is reversed in the service of the writer's point. The principle of end-stress says to state last that which is of primary importance. In this case it is the call to faithful witness under great duress and pain. Because of their faithful witness, the disciples will be delivered up before synagogues (fulfilled in Acts 4-5) and before governors and kings (fulfilled in Acts 24-26). They are assured, however, that in those crises they will be given "a mouth and wisdom" (verse 15) which no opponents can withstand (fulfilled in Acts 4:8-13; 6:10). Matthew (24:20) and Mark (13:11) here promise the Holy Spirit as provider of one's speech; Luke had already stated that earlier (12:11-12). Christians are warned that they will be betrayed by relatives and friends (verse 16), that some of them will suffer death, and that all will be hated because of their devotion to Jesus (verse 17). Verse 18 is obscure in view of verse 16. It may be a misplaced saying (Matt. 10:30; Luke 12:7); it may mean that some will die but you will not; it may mean that although the persecutors can kill in a physical sense, in a far more important sense you will be kept safe. In any case, endurance and faithfulness are the keys to life.

The time of Luke's writing and our time fall within verses 12-19: the time of testimony. The end is not yet. During the time of testimony, disciples will experience suffering. They are not exempt. There is nothing here of the arrogance one sometimes sees and hears in modern apocalypticists, an arrogance born of a doctrine of a rapture in which believers are removed from the scenes of persecution and suffering. There are no scenes here of cars crashing into one another on the highways because their drivers have been blissfully raptured. The word of Jesus in our lesson is still forceful: "This will be a time for you to bear testimony. . . . By your endurance you will gain your lives."

Proper 29 (Christ the King)

Sunday Between November 20 and 26 Inclusive

II Samuel 5:1-5; Psalm 95; Colossians 1:11-20; John 12:9-19

The service of Christ the King traditionally echoes Passion/Palm Sunday and anticipates Advent. All the readings for today accomplish that unmistakably. David is make king of Israel (II Sam. 5) and God is praised as the great king above all gods (Ps. 95). The epistle offers one of the most extraordinary christological hymns in the New Testament, praising Christ as creator and reconciler of the cosmos (Col. 1). The Gospel shifts again to John because this Gospel more explicitly than Luke expresses public praise of Christ as king. No more fitting conclusion could be offered than that of the closing line of the Gospel lection: "Look, the world has gone after him."

II Samuel 5:1-5

The Old Testament reading for the celebration of Christ as king concerns that most revered of ancient Israel's kings, David. The narrative tells how David became king over all Israel and gives the basic chronological facts about his reign. Our passage is not a story with a plot that moves from complication to resolution; there is no suspense at all. Rather, it is a bare account of information with little or no effort to engage the interest of the reader and minimal interpretation. However, like any good story, it begins not at the beginning but in the middle, assuming past events and pointing to a future.

The report assumes the long history of events from the time that Samuel anointed David to be king over all Israel and David's arrival in the court of Saul (I Sam. 16). The text before

249

us reports the fulfillment of that sacred designation. More specifically, the account presupposes the events of the seven and one-half years since Saul and Jonathan had been killed by the Philistines. Who, if anyone, would succeed Saul? David became king over Judah in the South (II Sam. 2:11), and Ishbosheth, a son of Saul, had been set up as king in the North by Abner, one of Saul's generals. When Abner had a falling out with Ishbosheth he transferred his loyalty to David, proposing to the elders of Israel that David should be king of all the tribes (II Sam. 3:17-19). Abner's appearance in the South to propose an alliance with David revived the old family feud between Joab, David's general, and Abner. After Joab murdered Abner, several of his captains killed Ishbosheth and carried his head to David in Hebron, thinking he would be pleased. But David had them executed—the account wants to make it clear that David did not come to the throne by taking the life of Saul's successor. Thus as II Samuel 5 begins, David is well established in Hebron as king of the Southern Kingdom, and the North is without a leader, either king or general.

These five verses contain two distinct paragraphs. The first (verses 1-3) reports how "all the tribes of Israel"—doubtless through representatives—came to Hebron to make David king. Two steps were involved, the designation by the tribes and a covenant ceremony that included anointing by "all the elders of Israel." The representatives cite three reasons for coming to David: (1) he is one of them: "We are your bone and flesh" (verse 1); (2) they affirm that he had in fact been their leader even when Saul was king (verse 2a); and (3), and most important, they cite the divine promise that is hereby fulfilled: "the Lord said to you, 'You shall be shepherd of my people Israel, and you shall be prince over Israel' "(verse 2b). David's authority thus derives from his election by Yahweh and also from the people who acknowledge him and that election. The second step is the solemn covenant, between David and the people, and between all of them and their God. Significantly, David in making the covenant submits himself to its stipulations. These stipulations are not spelled out here, but they would have entailed laws obligating king to God and people. That the king does not stand above the law becomes obvious later in the life of David and is further underscored here by the note that the covenant was made "before the Lord," that is, in the sanctuary.

The second unit (verses 4-5) is a historical note concerning David's age and the length of his reign, looking far beyond the immediate events and opening up the future. There is no serious reason to doubt the historical reliability of the information. The forty years of David's kingship would have been ca. 1000–961 B.C.

Two matters that follow this text in Second Samuel are important for understanding its significance, especially for reading and proclamation on this day in the liturgical year. The first of these is the report in the immediately following verses (II Sam. 5:6-10) that David took the city of Jerusalem and made it his capital. The Davidic kingship and the city of Jerusalem would ever after be linked, not simply as the place where David's successors reigned, but also as symbols for the future kingdom of God. The second important matter comes in II Samuel 7, with the divine promise that a son of David would always sit on the throne in Jerusalem. This promise was a powerful force in the history of Israel and Judah, and became important in the Christian understanding of Jesus as the son of David.

Faith and politics, religious commitment and practical questions of leadership come together here, as they so often do in the Old Testament. David comes to the throne in accordance with the will of God. But the process by which that occurs is recounted with stark realism. It happens in the full light of history. David becomes king because the tribes of Israel recognize and acknowledge his divine election, and at the same time see the practical necessity for such a strong leader. The people of God in the world will have a king—a human government—but its actions are subject to a covenant with the people and with God.

Psalm 95

Two primary components make up this psalm: (1) an extended call to worship with hymnically expressed reasons for worship (verses 1-7a) and (2) a divine oracle with God admonishing the people not to be disobedient like the generation that left Egypt and perished in the wilderness (verses 7b-11).

The call or summons to community worship notes many of the sentiments of worship—thanksgiving, praise—as well as the actions involved—sing, make noise, bow down, kneel. The motivations for worship given here are twofold, both introduced by the word "for" (verses 3 and 7). (1) The first motivation is the greatness of God who is described as a great king above all gods (see the discussion of Ps. 82 in last week's lections). The greatness of God is manifest in his role as lord of creation. By utilizing polar opposites—depths of the earth/heights of the mountains and sea/dry land—the composer affirms that God is the ruler of the totality of creation. This is the case even though there are other gods who are subordinate to Yahweh who reigns as king. (2) The second motivation for worship is the status of the people. They are the people of God, "the people He tends, the flock in His care" (NJPSV). This state of dependence upon God is reason for worship.

In verse 7b, an introductory statement calls on the people to listen to God's voice. This is then followed by an accusatory speech of God that appeals to the audience not to be hard-hearted and stubborn like the Hebrews who left Egypt and rebelled in the wilderness.

The wilderness period was used in biblical folklore and theology as a period about which moral lessons could be drawn. It figured for them like the days of the founding fathers for us. When we think of our past and use it for moral instruction, we frequently say that we should (or should not) act (or be) like the people did (or were) in days gone by. The past can function for us as an example of good times or bad times depending on the point we want to make. "Remember the good old days," or "If you think you have it tough. . . ." In biblical folklore the wilderness period could be described as a good time (see Ps. 105; Deut. 8:2-4; Jer. 2:1-3) when things were idyllic or as a time of rebellion (see Ps. 106). It is the last view that characterizes Psalm 95.

The oracle addressed to the people was probably spoken by some cultic official (priest? prophet? king?), speaking as if he were God or his mouthpiece. The murmuring and lack of faith shown at Meribah and Massah (see Exod. 17:1-7; Num. 20:1-13; Ps. 106:32-33) are taken as prime examples, or paradigms, of poor behavior and faithlessness. There were times when Israel was "testing" God, to see if he would destroy them. Later Jewish rabbis argued that the Hebrews tested God ten times in the wilderness (see Num. 14:22): twice at the Red Sea (Ps. 106:7, repetition of the word sea suggested two rebellions), twice with the quail (Exod. 16:13; Num. 11:31-32), once with the manna (Exod. 16:20), once with the golden calf (Exod. 32), once at Paran (Num. 13:26), and three other times but so provokingly that the events weren't recorded (see Deut. 9:22).

Just as the people were bad so God's judgment was harsh (as it can be again). The generation that left Egypt was condemned to forty years of wandering and to death outside the Promised Land (see Num. 14:33). (In Deut. 8:4, the same generation that left Egypt reached Canaan without their clothing wearing out. The ancient rabbis argued that the clothes of the infants that left Egypt grew along with the children!)

Colossians 1:11-20

It would be difficult to find a text more fitting to celebrate the kingship of Christ than today's epistolary text. There is wide agreement among scholars that this text embodies an early christological hymn, or poem, although its extent and arrangement are still disputed.

As to the structure, it is widely agreed that the hymn is introduced in verse 15 as part of the opening prayer of thanksgiving and intercession (verses 9-14). In the twenty-sixth edition of Nestle-Aland, verses 15-18a are printed strophically, whereas the remaining verses 18b-20 are printed as prose. Neither the RSV, NEB, nor NIV print the text strophically, although the notes in the annotated NEB treat it as a Pauline redaction of an earlier hymn. The most graphic layout is provided by JB, which extends the "poem" through verse 20. It is then arranged and analyzed in two parts: (1) verses 15-17 depicting Christ as the supreme head of the

253

created order and (2) verses 18-20 unfolding Christ as the head of the new creation.

Regardless of where we establish the boundaries of the hymnic section, the form-critical investigation of this passage has generated numerous fascinating possibilities for interpretation and homiletical appropriation.

A few preliminary observations are in order. We should remember that the Epistle to the Colossians is written in response to teaching that threatens the supremacy of Christ. There is some evidence that the syncretistic theology of the opposition regarded Christ as a member of the angelic hierarchy (cf. 2:18), thus compromising his preeminent and unique status. It is in this context that this hymn occurs. Most likely, it does represent a Christianized version of any earlier hymn heavily influenced by Jewish wisdom traditions. In its present form, the praise earlier given to Wisdom as the source of all creation, the reflection of God, and that (One) holding the universe together is now transferred to Christ. Apart from the hymnic form, we should notice the nature of the theological response. To combat a competing Christology, Paul draws from the worship experience of the church. The lesson here is that the living experience of the church, its experience of the exalted Christ in worship, is sometimes the best response to an inadequate theology—that is, as long as our hymns are as profound and theologically rich as this early Christian hymn.

Let us look at some of the prominent motifs of this christological hymn.

1. It opens with Christ presented as "the image of the invisible God" (verse 15). In the Jewish wisdom tradition, Wisdom was praised as "a reflection of eternal light, . . . an image of [God's] goodness" (Wisd. of Sol. 7:26). Capitalizing on this development, Christians came to regard Christ similarly (II Cor. 3:18; 4:4; Heb. 1:3, 6).

2. To speak of Christ as the "first-born of all creation" does not imply that he was the first thing to be created, as some held in early Christian controversies concerning the nature of Christ. This is rather a claim to preeminent rank (cf. Ps. 89:27; also Rom. 8:29; Rev. 3:14).

3. Christ is also God's agent in creation: "in him all things

were created" (verse 16). Here again, in the Jewish wisdom tradition, Wisdom was regarded as a crucial actor in creation (Wisd. of Sol. 9:1-2). For Christians, it was the preexistent Christ who played this role (John 1:3, 18; Heb. 1:12; Rev. 3:14), and this became an element of early Christian confession (I Cor. 8:6). As the hymn later states, "all things were created through him and for him" (verse 16; cf. Rom. 11:36). We should note the cosmic proportions of Christ's creative influence (verse 16). No conceivable part of the universe or reality as we can envision it can be explained or accounted for apart from the creative work of Christ.

4. Christ's preexistence is asserted in the claim that he is "before all things" (verse 17). Again, Wisdom was seen to have preceded the created order (Prov. 8:23-31). It is the incarnate Logos who now occupies this position (John 1:1).

5. Related to this is the claim that "in him all things hold together" (verse 17). Christ becomes the organizing principle of the universe, but more than that he is actually seen as the One in whom all reality coheres (Heb. 1:3).

6. Besides being head of the created order, Christ stands at the head of the "new creation." As the exalted Lord, "he is the head of the body, the church" (verse 18)—not a local congregation, but the universal one that reaches into the heights and depths of the cosmos (cf. Eph. 1:22-23; 4:15; 5:23; also I Cor. 11:3).

7. His status as head of the new creation results from his being "the first-born from the dead" (verse 18). As the first one to experience resurrected life through the power and agency of God, Christ becomes resurrection's first child (cf. I Cor. 15:20; Rev. 3:14; also Rev. 1:5; Rom. 8:29; Heb. 1:6).

8. As the preexistent Christ who stands at the head of the created order, and as the incarnate Christ who is raised from the dead, he becomes the full embodiment of God's own presence: "in him the complete being of God, by God's own choice, came to dwell" (verse 19, NEB; cf. 2:9-10; John 1:16; Eph. 1:23; 3:19; 4:10, 13).

9. Because of his unique status, Christ becomes the one through whom reconciliation occurs (verse 20). In his sacrificial death on the cross and the shedding of his blood, peace is made between God and the world (cf. II Cor. 5:18-19;

also Eph. 1:10; 2:13-16). It is a form of reconciliation that reaches to every conceivable level—personal as well as cosmic (verse 20; cf. Eph. 1:10).

If the Feast of Christ the King is intended to lift our vision of Christ, this hymn can certainly serve to launch our thoughts upward. If our tendency is to impose limits on the work of Christ, today's text forces us to enlarge our horizons. We are taken from creation to new creation, from the beginning of time to the end of time, from microcosm to macrocosm, from alienation to peace, and wherever we are taken, there we find a reflection of God in Christ.

John 12:9-19

Today is the last Sunday before Advent and therefore the day of the worship service that closes a church year. What more appropriate way than the celebration of Christ the King? And what more appropriate text than this: "Hosanna! Blessed is he who comes in the name of the Lord, even the King of Israel!" (John 12:13)? One could use this one verse and build a message strong and fitting for the occasion. However, the verse is not simply "from the Bible" but from the Gospel of John and one needs to hear what John is saying to the church.

First, let us fix in mind the context for John 12:9-19. In chapter 11 Jesus performed his last sign, the raising of Lazarus. It is clear from the outset that the raising of Lazarus will set in motion the events that will affect the death of Jesus. Jesus says as much, "That the Son of God may be glorified by means of it" (11:4). The public interest generated by this sign in Bethany causes the religious leaders to begin plotting the death of Jesus (11:45-53). It is Passover time (11:55), the feast which prompts passion speeches and signs in this Gospel (2:13-22; 6:4, 52-59) and which was the occasion of Jesus' death (18:39–19:42). In John 12:1-8 Jesus is in Bethany where he is anointed for his burial. This again is a passion story. Following our lection, Jesus makes the statement, "The hour has come for the Son of man to be glorified" (verse 23); this is to say in Johannine language that the hour of his death is near. All of this is to point out that the proclamation of Jesus as king is, in this Gospel, couched in a passion context. A proper understanding of Jesus as king must, therefore, comprehend his kingship as related to his death.

The crowd who hailed him king did not, of course, understand this. In fact, Jesus' own disciples did not understand until after he was glorified (verse 16). Crowds had earlier sought to make Jesus king because they had responded favorably to a sign: feeding the multitude (6:15). In that case, Jesus withdrew and when the crowds sought him out again, he called for participation in his own passion, his own flesh and blood (6:51-59). In our text today, the crowds have been excited by a sign: the raising of Lazarus. They do not know what it means or what price Jesus must pay. It is important to observe, then, that in John's account, the crowds are already in Jerusalem wondering if Jesus will come; Jesus arrives from the nearby village of Bethany, not from Galilee as in the Synoptics; and the crowds go out to meet Jesus with palm branches and shouting. It is in response to them that Jesus himself then found a colt and rode it as prophesied in Zechariah 9:9 (verses 14-15). This act, of course, was not understood. And this is quite unlike the Synoptic accounts.

What is central to the Evangelist's telling of the story here is that Jesus in not king by public acclamation. He speaks and acts within his own understanding of who he is and what his acts mean. What his disciples did not at that time grasp must now be understood by Jesus' followers, and that is, Jesus is not made a king by anyone's favor; he is king. Those who acclaim him to be such honor him, if their acclamations are not based on a sign performed or a mighty act which amazed them, but rather upon a belief in him for who he is—the revelation of the God no one has ever seen (1:18) who was sent into the world as an act of divine love (3:16). Because of him we are able to know God, which is life eternal (17:3). He was from God and he returned to God, but his return was by way of the cross. Not that he was murdered or was a victim of plots of fear and jealousy. Just as he found his own donkey to ride into the city, just as he carried his own cross (19:17), so he gave his life as a shepherd gives his life for his sheep (10:7-18), as a man lays down his life for his friends (15:13).

All this is involved in his being glorified, in his being lifted up, in his being at God's right hand, in his being king.

Pilate posted on the cross in three languages, for Jews, Romans, and Greeks to read, the word for today: Jesus is king (19:19-20). He was in that act cynical, sarcastic, and vengeful. He was also right.

Visitation, May 31

I Samuel 2:1-10; Psalm 113; Romans 12:9-16b; Luke 1:39-57

The lections for use in commemorating Mary's visit to Elizabeth (Luke 1) focus on Mary and, through Mary as representative, on all the lowly and humble who serve God. Luke uses the song of Hannah (I Sam. 2) in the song of Mary while both Psalm 113 and Romans 12 speak of God as helper of those who do chores for which they get little attention and less praise. By keeping the attention on Mary as God's servant the preacher will avoid making this a premature Advent service.

I Samuel 2:1-10

Hannah's song is the Old Testament lection for the celebration of Visitation, and for several reasons. As the mother of Samuel, Hannah is understood as a type of Mary, the mother of Jesus. Her song of praise and thanksgiving was a model for the Magnificat, suggesting several of its motifs. Moreover, the final verse of the song in particular expresses messianic themes.

Since Hannah's song sits loosely in its narrative context, there are good reasons for concluding that it was not originally part of the story. Except for the first line, nothing in the poem refers specifically to Hannah and her situation or to her son Samuel. The reference to the king in verse 10 is anachronistic, since the monarchy was not initiated until later. The song is appropriate to the situation, however, because it occurs as part of an act of worship, and because of its references to barrenness and birth (verse 5). It may have been added as a kind of response as the story was read in a liturgical context, or simply to present what the editors of the book knew would have been an expression of Hannah's piety.

In its literary context, the song of Hannah is surrounded by a story. Earlier, Hannah, the barren woman, had gone to the sanctuary to pray for a child, vowing that she would dedicate him to Yahweh (I Sam. 1). Her prayer was answered, so she comes to pay her vow by handing over her young son. The song is part of Hannah's act of worship in the sanctuary at Shiloh when she brings her son Samuel to "loan him" to the Lord (I Sam. 1:28).

The wider context places the actions of a faithful woman within the history of Israel and the destiny of a little boy. Hannah and her son stand between the ages, between the chaos of the period of the judges and the rise of the monarchy. "In those days there was no king in Israel; every man did what was right in his own eyes" (Judg. 21:25). The child whose dedication evokes this song will lead his people through some troubled times and will anoint first Saul and then David as kings. This birth and dedication in retrospect can be seen to herald a new age, and Hannah plays an active role by her dedication of Samuel.

Here we see a woman at prayer. In terms of both form and contents, Hannah's song is a thanksgiving psalm with elements of a hymn of praise. Beginning with a declaration of intent to praise (verse 1), it praises Yahweh as the incomparable and all-knowing God (verses 2-3). There are overtones of polemic against other gods. The main theme of this poetic prayer celebrates Yahweh as the one who establishes justice, caring for the weak and needy (verses 4-5), the poor (verses 7-8), and the faithful (verse 9). The song concludes on a distinctly cosmic and messianic note (verse 10).

Certainly the earliest church recognized the obvious similarities between Hannah and Mary, Samuel and Jesus. But the fundamental contents of the song of Hannah parallel the message of the coming of Jesus as well. God is the one who acts and will act to save the weak, the lowly, the poor, and the needy. The God of creation (verse 8) is the God of justice who chooses to make his will known and effective through the incarnation of that will through humanity at its most vulnerable stages, a baby just weaned from his mother's milk, or even one yet unborn.

Psalm 113

This lection was the psalm reading for Proper 5 (see pages 33-35) and was treated under Visitation in Year B.

Romans 12:9-16*b*

Portions of this text (Rom. 12:1-13) also serve as the epistolary reading for Proper 17 in Year A, and the reader may wish to consult additional remarks made there. Since the same texts are used for Visitation in Years A, B, and C, the reader might also wish to consult our remarks made in connection with Years A and B.

On the occasion celebrating Mary's visit to Elizabeth, it is the Gospel reading from Luke that sets the liturgical agenda. This tradition of Mary's "visitation" is recorded only in Luke, and it is the Magnificat that sets the tone for the observance of this day. One of the primary notes sounded in this passage is the exaltation of the lowly: Mary the humble handmaiden of God is raised to an exalted position as the one through whom the promise of God will be fulfilled. It is the reversal of roles we come to expect in Luke: God dethroning the mighty and enthroning the lowly in their place.

What makes today's epistolary reading appropriate in this setting is its insistence that we "not be haughty, but associate with the lowly" (verse 16). We miss the full force of this injunction if we read it as an ethic of politeness. It is more than a call for us not to be conceited in our attitude toward those of lowly estate. It is a mandate to identify with them, to be with them in their lowliness. In a similar fashion, the Magnificat is quite revolutionary in its social outlook. It calls for the reversal of the normal social order and reminds us that Yahweh's concern is to feed the hungry and send the rich away empty. In its boldest form, it envisions a radical redistribution of resources.

So does today's epistolary text call for radical identification with the earth's lowly. Only in this way can the charge to

261

"love one another with brotherly affection" (verse 10) be carried out seriously. What is being called for here is a level of Christian fellowship that transcends all barriers—social, racial, sexual. It is a form of community that expresses itself concretely in displays of genuine hospitality (verse 13), where financial contributions are made as expressions of Christian love. In view here are the "needs of the saints" (verse 13), and the primary focus of this instruction is internal. Yet this urge to transcend self-interest in reaching out to the needs of others extends beyond the Christian circle (cf. Gal. 6:10).

As it turns out, hating "what is evil, and [holding] fast to what is good" (verse 9) may result in self-exposure. That which is evil may very well be our refusal to "associate with the lowly" in any genuine sense of identification and empathy. What it may expose are those subtle forms of discrimination that are masked by other forms of religiosity, even prayer and worship. We may find ourselves being religious in one sense, but discriminatory in another, much more sinister sense. We want to come to God without fully identifying with all of God's creatures: high and low, exalted and humble, franchised and disfranchised, rich and poor.

"Holding fast to what is good" may mean clinging to those from whom all signs of good are ostensibly absent, in whom good no longer appears to reside, for whom there is no more good, who are indeed regarded by us, by the church, and by society as "no good." Only in this way can all signs and expressions of haughtiness and conceit be removed from the Christian fellowship. Only in this way can "love be genuine" (verse 9).

Luke 1:39-57

"In those days Mary arose and went with haste into the hill country, to a city of Judah, and she entered the house of Zechariah and greeted Elizabeth" (Luke 1:39-40). This is the visitation the church remembers in this service. Even though Christians and Easter dominate the church's worship through the year, each of those celebrations have their own cluster of festivals. Just as Easter is the center for Ash

262

Wednesday, Palm Sunday, Good Friday, and Pentecost, so Christmas is anticipated and remembered in the Annunciation, Visitation, Epiphany, and Presentation.

Mary's visit to Elizabeth provides the occasion for the two women to celebrate the angel's word to Mary, which was also the angel's word to Abraham and Sarah: "For with God nothing will be impossible" (1:37; Gen. 18:14). As Paul was to express it, God gives life to the dead and calls into existence things that do not exist (Rom. 4:17). It does not matter whether it is a case of an old and barren couple or a virgin without a husband. The visitation is, therefore, a double celebration of the power of God to give life.

The visitation is also a beautiful reflection, through the women, of the futures of their unborn sons. As Elizabeth is humbled by the visit of "the mother of my Lord" (verse 43) so John was witness and servant to Jesus. As John leaped in Elizabeth's womb when Mary entered (verses 41, 44), so John's joy was that of a groomsman when the bridegroom arrived (John 3:29-30). As Elizabeth blessed Mary not only for her child but also because Mary believed the word of God (verses 42-45), so John would come calling for faith in Jesus as the means of life in the kingdom. There is never any question for Luke that Jesus and not John is the Messiah, but neither is there any question that both Elizabeth and Mary are servants of God's purpose, both their sons are gifts of God, and both sons have appointed ministries in God's plan for the ingathering of the nations.

The visitation is also a study in contrasts. Elizabeth is old, wife of a priest who was part of an ancient order of things in Israel. Having a child in her old age is a reminder of the past: Abraham and Sarah, Manoah and his wife, Elkanah and Hannah, from whom came Isaac and Samson and Samuel. The promises of God survived and continued through the unlikely births to the old and barren. But Mary was young, a life new, virgin, and all promise. She and her child do not remind one of the past; in fact, in them begins a new history. Mary's child is continuous with the past, to be sure, the fulfillment of promise, but in him God is doing a new thing. So radically new is this act of God that the only appropriate means was a woman young, and a virgin.

The visitation is also a preview of reversals yet to come. The ordinary structures of history, the usual cause and effect sequences of events could not sustain or contain what God would be doing. The empty will be full and the full, empty; the poor will be rich and the rich, poor; the powerless will reign and the powerful will be dethroned. In a close approximation of the song of Hannah (I Sam. 2:1-10), Mary sings of the eschatological reversal of stations and fortunes in the realm where and when God's love and justice rule supreme.

A final word: Elizabeth and Mary are not nameless and faceless women who are no more than the wombs which carry great sons. They are persons with names, addresses, beliefs, hopes, and joy in service. Such is Luke's treatment of women in the Gospel story. Mary will reappear in trust and devotion (Acts 1:14), as will other women who join in the mission (Luke 8:1-3), and to them is entrusted the one sustained hallelujah of the Christian faith: He is risen (Luke 24:1-12).

Holy Cross, September 14

Numbers 21:4b-9; Psalm 98:1-5 or Psalm 78:1-2, 34-38;
I Corinthians 1:18-24; John 3:13-17

As is true throughout the liturgical year, the Gospel lection is the magnet that gathers the other readings. The statement in John 3 about Jesus being lifted up makes use of the brazen serpent story in Numbers 21. The Epistle presents Paul's preaching of the cross as God's weakness and foolishness which is stronger and wiser than all human achievements. Both selections from the Psalms praise God whose victory lies not only in strength but in goodness which spares the guilty.

Numbers 21:4*b*-9

The Old Testament reading for this special day in the liturgical year provides the basis of the typological allusion in the Gospel lection. Close reading of the passage reveals that the parallels between the cross of Jesus and the lifting up of the serpent in the wilderness are more substantial than the similarity of a "pole" (Num. 21:8, 9) to a cross. Both the cross and this story concern God's response to human sinfulness.

Numbers 21:4-9 is but one episode in the story of Israel's wandering in the wilderness, the period between the Exodus from Egypt and the entrance into the land of Canaan. This episode, however, contains the two themes that constantly recur in the traditions about Israel's time in the wilderness. On the one hand, it was a time of God's gracious and miraculous care for the people, especially by providing food when they were hungry and water when they were thirsty. On the other hand, it was a period when Israel rebelled against Yahweh, especially by murmuring against him and his servant Moses. These traditions are not limited to the story that runs from Exodus 13:17 through Numbers 10:10, but are found throughout the Old Testament. Psalm 78 sings of Israel's rebellion and God's forgiveness. Jeremiah 2:2-3 remembers the wilderness wandering as a time of faithfulness, but Ezekiel 20:10-26 emphasizes it as a period of disobedience. Deuteronomy 8:15-16 interprets the need for water and manna, as well as the presence of "fiery serpents and scorpions," as the Lord's means of testing the people in the wilderness.

Beginning with a note about the wilderness itinerary (verse 4a), the verses before us present a complete and self-contained narrative. It is a story with a plot that develops from complication to climax and resolution. The tension is set into motion by the people's impatience along the way (verse 4) and their complaints (verse 5). Since the complaints are against Yahweh and Moses, it becomes clear that the outcome of the story is a matter of life and death. As punishment for their rebellion, God sends death-dealing "fiery serpents" among them (verse 6). Obviously, the people know that the serpents are divine punishment, so they present themselves before Moses to confess their sin and ask him to pray to the Lord on their behalf to remove the dangerous snakes.

The Lord answers the prayer, but does not grant exactly what the people ask. Instead of taking away the snakes, the Lord instructs Moses to make a "fiery serpent, and set it on a pole; and every one who is bitten, when he sees it, shall live" (verse 8). When Moses, following the instructions, makes a "bronze serpent" and sets it on a pole, it has the promised effects (verse 9). The story thus moves by way of sin, divine punishment, confession and repentance, to a means of removing the effects of the punishment. The serpents remain—and snake bites as well!—but their power to bring death is canceled.

The bronze snake must reflect the ancient, and nonbiblical, idea that an image of a dangerous animal could serve as protection against it. The snake in particular has been a symbol for healing in more than one culture. But the construction and use of such an image seems to violate the second commandment (Exod. 20:4). Further complicating the problem of the relationship of this image to prohibitions against them is the fact that the term translated "serpent" here occurs in Isaiah's vision in the temple as the name for the six-winged creatures (Isa. 6). Second Kings 18:2-4 reports that King Hezekiah, as part of a reform of worship, destroyed "the bronze serpent that Moses had made," presumably because it had become the object of idolatrous worship. That interpretation is quite different from the one in the text before us, in which the bronze figure is not an idol, but the means by which God heals the people.

Especially for this particular day in the church year, Numbers 21:4b-9, like the cross of Jesus, evokes our deepest reflection on the relationship between sin and God's response to it. The story begins with rebellion, which then leads to a hostile and dangerous environment, suffering, and death—all of which are interpreted as divine punishment. When the people repent and pray that the danger be removed, God responds, but not by changing the environment. God gives life in the midst of death, holding out the possibility of healing, but only if the people who are stricken look at the figure on the pole. The effects of the rebellion remain with them, but they do not die.

Psalm 98:1-5

One of the enthronement hymns, Psalm 98, praises Yahweh as the sovereign reigning over the world of creation and as the special benefactor of the house of Israel. Thus both the universal and the particular domains of Yahweh are noted.

Much of this psalm consists of calls or summons to praise/worship as well as reasons why God should be worshiped and praised. Those called upon to praise God are the community of Israel (implied; verses 1-3), all the earth (all humanity; verses 4-6), and various elements in the world of nature (sea, world, their inhabitants, floods, and hills; verses 7-9). The ancient rabbis, in commenting on verse 8, noted that there are only three references in Scripture (Old Testament) to the clapping of hands: the peoples clapping hand in hand (Ps. 47:1), the trees of the field clapping branch against branch (Isa. 55:2), and the floods clapping against the banks of the river (Ps. 98:8).

The reasons for praise in the first section (verses 1-3) are all associated with the word "victory." God has won victory for himself (verse 1), he has made known his victory (verse 2), and the ends of the earth have seen his victory (verse 3). The marvelous things God has done, which are not spelled out, are related to his vindication ("His triumph"; NJPSV) in the sight of the nations and to the manifestation of his steadfast love and faithfulness to Israel. The reason for praise in the second section (verses 4-9) is the coming of God to judge the world, not simply to judge but to judge with (establish) righteousness and equity (verse 9).

Psalm 78:1-2, 34-38

This psalm is a long composition offering a recital of the historical epochs of Israel's past. The following epochs are covered: (1) the patriarchal period (verses 5-11), (2) the Exodus and wilderness wanderings (verses 12-53), (3) the settlement in the land of Canaan (verses 54-66), and (4) the election of David and Zion (verses 67-72). These epochs and the events associated with them are used as points of departure for preaching and proclamation. In this psalm, most of the past is interpreted as times of disobedience and is utilized to engender a sense of guilt and shame on those addressed in the psalm.

The two sections selected for this lection are part of the introduction (verses 1-2) and a portion of the psalmist's interpretation and preaching on the wilderness theme (verses 34-38). The opening verses present the historical synopsis and interpretation that follow as a teaching or a parable, that is, not as a pure recital of history but as an interpretative reading of the past intended to speak to the present.

Verses 34-38 are a portion of the homily on Israel's behavior in the wilderness. Although cared for, preserved, and fed in the desert, the Hebrews are described as having constantly sinned. The people are depicted as demurring and demanding, unappreciative and uncooperative. Over and over again, God has to act to reprimand them. Verses 34-38 proclaim two things about the people. (1) They were not repentant until they were punished; they did not turn toward God until God had turned against them. Their repentance was the product of divine coercion. (2) Their devotion was superficial and temporary. Their mouths and their tongues were committed to religious expression, not their hearts. Flattery and lies, not fidelity and loyalty, were their hallmarks.

In spite of the people's behavior and their transient faith, they depicted God as their refuge and redeemer (verse 35). Long-suffering and forbearing, God forgave and did not destroy; he withheld his anger and did not give vent to his wrath (verse 38).

I Corinthians 1:18-24

Portions of this text overlap with the epistolary readings in several other liturgical settings. For the Fourth Sunday After Epiphany in Year A and Tuesday in Holy Week in Years A, B, C the longer form of the text is used (verses 18-31). For the Third Sunday of Lent, Year B, a shorter form is used (verses 22-25). The reader may wish to consult our remarks in these other settings for additional information about this passage.

A special feast day celebrating the cross has origins at least as early as the fourth century, when Constantine's mother, St. Helena, is said (according to one tradition) to have discovered the cross on which Christ was crucified. The date was September 14, 320. Some fifteen years later, in Jerusalem two churches were dedicated: the Church of the Cross and the Church of the Resurrection. In connection with this, the cross discovered by Helena became an object of veneration for the faithful, and out of this arose an annual feast celebrating the cross. An important feature of this celebration was to display a relic of the cross by lifting it up for the faithful to see. Because of this, the feast came to be known as the "Exaltation of the Holy Cross."

Among the epistolary readings used in connection with this feast day are Philippians 2:6-11, I Peter 3:17-22, and today's text from First Corinthians. The central theme, of course, is the cross of Christ and its redemptive power in the world.

One of the major themes of today's epistolary text is the paradoxical nature of the cross. Ostensibly, it is a sign of scandal, utterly incomprehensible to everyone (Jews and Greeks) except those of us who experience it as a unique instance of God's love and power. What the cross signifies is the capacity of God to show love through powerlessness, to bring about our redemption through a display of self-giving. Such action on the part of God upsets our normal expectations and the expectations of the world. We would normally expect God to be manifested in great displays of power and strength, not in a moment of utter weakness and powerlessness. And yet the cross becomes one of the chief focal points through which we see God being manifest to us.

One way in which the cross exercises powerful influence on us is by forcing us to think paradoxically about human existence and divine power. As Barth remarks, "Truth cannot be expected to encounter [us] as a phenomenon which is immediately and directly illuminating, pleasing, acceptable and welcome to [us]. [We] would not be who [we] are if the promise of the Spirit came to [us] easily and smoothly." And so it is that the message of the cross cuts across the grain, repels us before it attracts us, transforms us even as it clutches us. We first encounter it as an act of consummate folly, and even after we have been lured by its curious force we may even still find it nonsensical.

Yet for those "who are being saved" it remains "the power of God" (verse 18). Why is this so? For one thing, it continues to reverse our human values. As Barth suggests, we expect truth to encounter us in ways that conform to who we already are, when in fact it encounters us by challenging who we are and what we know. Otherwise, we would already have and embody truth. Left to ourselves, we develop expectations of God that conform to our own views of deity: exaltation without humiliation, power without suffering, rising without dying. It is the cross that constantly rubs against our human grain, presenting us with a God who astounds us with divine folly. In the end, we discover our own folly in thinking that God would act in human ways, much less that God *must* act in human ways. The lingering echo of the cross is that "the foolishness of God is wiser than [humans], and the weakness of God is stronger than [humans]" (verse 25).

John 3:13-17

If the Gospel for the day seems to the preacher to have an unusual beginning and ending; that is, if it seems an extraction from the heart of a conversation, the reason lies in the focus of the service: the cross of Christ. As a magnet, the subject of the cross has been held over the text, drawing to itself those verses pertaining directly to that event. Fairness to the subject and to the text demands, however, that verses 13-17 be set back more honestly and confidently into the context in order to extract them again.

John 3:1-21 is usually regarded as a conversation between Jesus and Nicodemus. However, where the Evangelist ends the conversation and where his own comments begin is not clear. One has but to look at different red-letter editions to see this uncertainty illustrated: Do Jesus' words end at verse 15, at 16, or at 21? The question is, however, a moot one, because the text reveals clearly that John is doing more than reporting a conversation. Such a shift begins at verse 7 with a change from the singular to the plural "you." The message from Jesus, says the writer, is to all and not to Nicodemus alone. The plural continues in verses 11 and 12. In addition, at verse 11 the "conversation" becomes more openly a debate between the church and the synagogue over the subject of life in the kingdom. Note the "we" versus "you" (plural). Furthermore, at verse 13 the passage becomes even more obviously a post-Easter Christian message by the statement in the past tense, "No one has ascended into heaven but he who descended from heaven, the Son of man." The earthly sojourn of the Savior is viewed as a completed event. It would be unfair, therefore, to treat this text within the confines of a private conversation at the beginning of Jesus' ministry, and it would be grossly unfair to be critical of Nicodemus for not understanding it. The Evangelist, by means of Nicodemus, is addressing the reader.

And what is the Evangelist saying to the reader? Let us confine ourselves to the bearing of the text on our subject, the cross of Christ. Since the cross is not mentioned in verses 13-17, how is it to be discerned here? To be sure, in traditional church art, music, and theology, John 3:16 is associated with Golgotha. It is as though it were to be translated, "For God so loved the world that he gave his only Son *on the cross*." That the cross is a part of the Johannine understanding of salvation is beyond question. Jesus lays down his life for the sheep (10:11); he lays down his life for his friends (15:13); he dies as the Passover lamb providing the freedom of a new exodus for the people of God (19:31-37). But the cross in this Gospel is the means of glorifying the Son (12:23-28); that is, of returning the Son to the presence of God. Hence the double meaning of being "lifted up" (verse 14; 8:28; 12:34)—up on the cross and up into glory. This being lifted up is as surely an act of God's grace and love as was the provision for salvation in the camp of Israel when they suffered God's judgment and punishment for their unbelief and disobedience (verse 14; Num. 21). Jesus' being lifted up was an act of love from God toward the world, and to be understood as this Evangelist presents it, that act needs to be seen in the full movement of the descending and the ascending of the Son of man (verse 13). In other words, John sees salvation as effected by the total act of God giving the Son and does not focus on the cross as sharply as does Paul.

In summary fashion, John's message may be stated this way: the Son came into the world to reveal God (1:18), whom to know is life eternal (17:3). That revelation is not only in signs and discourses but also in the cross. However, the cross refers not only to Jesus' death but to his being lifted up to God. This also is a part of the salvation event in that the glorified Christ sends the Holy Spirit to his church (7:39). "Nevertheless I tell you the truth: it is to your advantage that I go away, for if I do not go away, the Counselor will not come to you; but if I go, I will send him to you" (16:7).

All Saints, November 1 or on First Sunday in November

Daniel 7:1-3, 15-18; Psalm 149; Ephesians 1:11-23; Luke 6:20-36

All the readings for today not only make one appreciatively aware of the saints of God but also remind the reader of the hostile forces with which God's people have always had to contend. Daniel sees not only the saints who possess the kingdom but also the four beasts; the psalmist praises God with enemies round about; the writer of Ephesians praises God who through Christ has formed a cosmic body of the reconciled by subduing the powers of hostility and disobedience; Luke's sermon on the plain offers Christ's blessings on the saints, but follows with woes upon those who resist and oppose the way of the kingdom. The Bible is not blind to the immensity of evil in the world.

Daniel 7:1-3, 15-18

The specific link between All Saints Day and this text is its reference to "the saints of the Most High" (verse 18). But a reading from the Book of Daniel is highly appropriate for other reasons as well: its apocalyptic vision of a final judgment day, of the resurrection of the dead (Dan. 12:1-3), and of a kingdom of God in which the saints take their rightful place.

Our lection comes from the central chapter in the Book of Daniel, which was written during the Hellenistic period in a time when faithful Jews were experiencing persecution. The one responsible for their trouble was the Seleucid ruler Antiochus Epiphanes. Since so much of the symbolism of the book relates directly to historical persons and events, it can be dated with confidence to 167–164 B.C.

Daniel 7 contains the first of four vision reports in the book. Though similar in some ways to earlier prophetic visions, the apocalyptic visions are quite distinctive. Like most prophetic visions, they report what was seen and then give its interpretation. Often the visionary sees himself in the revelation and sometimes in dialogue with God or some intermediary. But apocalyptic visions are much longer, and their symbolism is striking, bizarre, and detailed. The more significant contrast is that prophetic visions, like prophetic speeches, generally concern the immediate future, while apocalyptic visions set the immediate situation of the visionary and his contemporaries into the framework of world history as a whole and its imminent radical transformation. The writer of Daniel was convinced that the wars and persecutions of his time were the last throes of the forces of evil, and that God would soon act to establish his kingdom.

The verses that make up our lection should be read in the context of Daniel 7 as a whole. The first and last verses of the chapter provide a narrative framework. The remainder contains the report of what Daniel saw (verses 2-14) and its interpretation (verses 15-27), which at points reverts to the description of the visionary scene. Everything is recounted in the first person, from the perspective of the visionary. Today's reading thus includes the beginning of the vision and the first part of its interpretation.

Verse 1 is the narrative introduction, indicating the date of Daniel's visionary experience and the fact that he recorded what he saw. As in a great deal of apocalyptic literature, the writer has attributed the vision to a famous figure and located it almost four hundred years before his own time. Verses 2 and 3 set the scene and summarize the vision. The four winds and the great sea in tumult provide the background for the appearance of four beasts. Then follows the detailed description of the four terrible beasts, each one composite in form and vicious in behavior. Everything leads up to the fourth beast, which has ten horns, and then a little horn. Each beast represents a different world empire, successively the Babylonians, the Medes, the Persians, and the Greeks.

The ten horns of the fourth beast are the rulers following Alexander the Great, and the little horn stands for Antiochus Epiphanes. It was common in apocalyptic literature to see the history of the world in terms of four eras, with the last the most terrible one of all. Then (verse 9) the scene shifts to the heavenly throne room, with the Ancient of Days passing judgment on the beasts.

Daniel reports that the visions disturbed him (verse 15), so he approached "one of those who stood there" and asked for and was given the interpretation of what he had seen (verse 16). The first two sentences of the interpretation correspond to the two main scenes. The four beasts are four kings who will arise (verse 17), but the vision of the Ancient of Days contains the promise that "the saints of the Most High" will inherit an eternal kingdom. The "saints" are the Jews who have remained faithful to their God during the time of persecution.

This text was originally written primarily for just those saints, to encourage them to endure difficult times. The writer means to communicate a divine revelation concerning the course and end of history, which will be the reign of God in justice. God will put an end to the worldly enemy and set up a kingdom in which the faithful will take their place. Even suffering under bestial powers has meaning, and it will only last for a short time.

For the writer of the Book of Daniel, and for the early Christians, the new age was already breaking in. They could see themselves living in the light of that age, which was the reign of God. The details of that future—when, where, how?—have not been revealed to us. But the confidence that God would ultimately triumph and vindicate the saints has enabled generations of the faithful not only to endure, but to live the abundant life.

Psalm 149

This psalm which, like Psalms 146–150, begins and ends with a hallelujah ("Praise Yahweh") consists basically of two extended summons. The first is a summons to praise and concludes with a reason for praise (verses 1-4). The second is a summons to a very militant type (verses 5-9) of action.

The opening call is a summons to participate in communal worship ("in the assembly of the faithful"). The call is to diverse forms of action in the context of worship—praise, sing, be glad, rejoice, dance, make melody. The object of the worship is described as Israel's Maker, he who called the nation into being, and as King, he who rules over the community centered in Zion (see Ps. 87:4-6). The reason for the praise is the fact that God takes pleasure (delights) in his people and bestows victory upon the lowly.

In the summons to action, the faithful are called on to exult in their glory (to celebrate their triumph/success) and to sing for joy. A string of other actions are noted in verses 6-9. The reference to couches in verse 5 could refer to the pallets on which people sat to eat the sacrificial meals. A change of two letters in the Hebrew word for "on their couches" would give "by their families" and suggest something like a military organization or rallying. A very militant quality runs through the remainder of the psalm as if the call was to warfare. The people are called upon to subdue nations, chastise people, bind kings, and fetter rulers all to the glory of the faithful.

Ephesians 1:11-23

Portions of this text overlap with the epistolary text (Eph. 1:3-6, 15-18) used for the Second Sunday After Christmas in Years A, B, and C, and the reader may wish to consult our treatment of this passage in the respective volumes of *Advent, Christmas, Epiphany*. These verses are included in the text that serves as the epistolary reading for Ascension in Years A, B, and C, and additional information may be found in the respective volumes of *Lent, Holy Week, Easter*.

Set in the context of All Saints Day, this magisterial text from the opening chapter of the Epistle to the Ephesians will highlight the role of the saints of God's overall purpose (verses 15 and 18). It should be recognized, however, that in the new Testament all Christians are designated as "saints." They are the "holy ones" *(hoi hagioi)* whom God has set apart, or sanctified, in the act of redemption. God's church comes to be identified with "those sanctified in Christ Jesus" (I Cor. 1:2), and there is solidarity between such persons in a given locality and all those everywhere who have been called by God (I Cor. 1:2). To be designated as God's "holy ones" means that we live in response to God's call. Sanctification and election go hand in hand.

It is quite likely that "God's holy ones" became the most common, and perhaps most distinctive, form of designation for early Christians. Informed by such passages as Daniel 7:22, which speaks of the "saints of the Most High," early Christians saw themselves as those in whom God's purpose came to fulfillment, and thus as the embodiment of God's people. In this sense, the designation had a sectarian cast, marking Christians off from other Jewish groups who made similar claims on God's promise. Even with its sectarian focus, the term "saints" nevertheless applied to all Christians, and not to a select few, as the term came to be used in later Christian centuries.

In our text from Ephesians, it is the church as a whole, "all the saints" (verse 15), that represents the culmination of God's eternal purpose (3:8-13). Through this new configuration of humanity, it became possible for Jews and Gentiles alike to share in God's promise, and this is the mystery, "hidden for ages" (3:9), that is finally revealed in Christ.

It is impossible, of course, to separate the destiny of the saints from the destiny of Christ. For, as our text suggests, the divine purpose came to fulfillment in Christ, and through Christ by extension came to fulfillment in Christ's people. Sharing in God's promise occurs as we appropriate Christ within us, and as we live in Christ, but it also projects us toward a future hope, the "glorious inheritance in the saints" (verse 18). This is the promise toward which the Christian gospel looks—sharing in the exaltation of Christ ultimately (verses 19-23).

Luke 6:20-36

In the service of thanksgiving and remembrance, Luke 6:20-36 may be viewed as a description of the way of life of those who have entered into the "joy of the Lord." Indirectly but clearly such a treatment of the text would carry a strong imperative for the listeners who would be reflecting on the lives of the departed faithful with a view to imitating their faith (Heb. 13:7).

Our lection falls naturally in two parts: verses 20-26 and 27-36. It is clear that Luke and Matthew are working with the same tradition even though Matthew by locating Jesus' preaching from the mountain (chapters. 5–7) echoes Moses and Mt. Sinai while Luke has Jesus with the people on a level place (verse 17). This identification with the people was seen earlier in his baptism (3:21). The mountain in Luke is Jesus' place of prayer and critical decisions (verses 12-16). Matthew's sermon is four times as long as Luke's, but Luke's differences involve more than omissions. Luke has the pronouncement of woes, for example, while Matthew does not, and some of the sayings vary in order as well as in wording. The important thing for the preacher is to stay with Luke lest the more familiar Matthean sayings bleed unconsciously into the message.

Luke's four blessings and four woes are reminiscent of the blessings and curses of Deuteronomy 11:26-29. The blessings are on the deprived: the poor, hungry, weeping, rejected (4:18-19; 14:12-24) and the woes are on their opposites: the rich, full, laughing, accepted. The reversal of fortunes is as sharp here as in Mary's song (1:46-55). When Jesus announced in Nazareth that his ministry was to the deprived (4:16-19), he said after reading Isaiah 61:1-2, "Today the scripture has been fulfilled in your hearing" (4:21). We can take that to mean that the favor of God upon these people does not have to wait until the eschaton but is at work now. And to say the blessing of God is "at work" is to be taken literally. Blessings and woes are not suggestions for the good life with a list of problems to be avoided. A blessing or a woe is a divine pronouncement and it is performative; that is, it does what it says. Such a view of God's word which accomplishes what it says is not a familiar one in a society that speaks of words as "only words."

The content of verses 27-36 is tightly packed and treats several important subjects. Matthew has this material in a different arrangement (5:39-42, 44-48; 7:12), indicating that both Evangelists are working with a compilation of sayings of Jesus. Verses 27-31 deal with the disciples' response to victimizing persons, those who hate, curse, abuse, strike, steal, and beg. Followers of Jesus may be victims, but they are not to see themselves as such, they are not to have a victim mentality, being shaped and determined by the hostilities unleashed on them. Rather they are to take the initiative, responding not in kind or simply playing dead, whining or excusing themselves as victims. This initiative means acting not according to principles learned from the oppressor but according to the kingdom principles of love, forgiveness, and generosity. This is not a covert strategy for a soft kill but a living out of the life one learns from God who is kind even to the ungrateful and the selfish (verse 35).

And equally important is the warning regarding our relations to those who are loving and generous toward us (verses 32-36). That can be an even more seductive control on our behavior. But to love those who love us, to give to those who give to us, to be friendly toward those who befriend us is no less a case of being directed by the other and of letting the other determine our behavior. The point is, whether in relation to oppressor or neighbor, disciples are to act not react, and the clue to that action lies in the behavior of God toward us all. Thus we will be children of God who does not react but who acts in kindness and grace toward everyone (verses 35-36).

Thanksgiving Day

Deuteronomy 26:1-11; Psalm 100; Philippians 4:4-9;
John 6:25-35

Thanksgiving Day is not an observance growing out of the events of the liturgical year and, therefore, the readings for the day are unrelated to any of the three cycles of the lectionary. The lections are chosen for their appropriateness to the spirit and purpose of this day: to bring an offering and recall God's mercy (Deut. 26); to reaffirm loyalty to the God of our salvation (Ps. 100); to be grateful in all circumstances (Phil. 4); and to partake of the eucharistic bread of heaven (John 6).

Deuteronomy 26:1-11

There could hardly be a more appropriate Old Testament lesson for Thanksgiving Day than Deuteronomy 26:1-11, for the text contains the liturgical instructions for a thanksgiving ceremony in ancient Israel. The ceremony is the celebration of the festival of the first fruits, or the Feast of Weeks, one of the three great pilgrimage feasts prescribed in the book of Deuteronomy. The other two are Passover—unleavened bread and the Feast of Booths (Deut. 16:16-17).

While the reading reflects some of Israel's most ancient traditions, it is in the characteristic style and from the distinctive theological perspective of the book of Deuteronomy. The book, or at least its central portion, has been rightly identified with "the book of the law" that came to light during the reform of King Josiah in 621 B.C. (II Kings 22–23). A major problem perceived by those who propagated the book in the time of Josiah was the corruption of worship through Canaanite religious practices at the local shrines throughout the country. Consequently, they legislated the destruction of those shrines and the centralization of worship in "the place which the Lord your God will choose out of all your tribes to put his name and make his habitation there" (Deut. 12:5), that is Jerusalem. As a result, regular worship became less frequent for the laity, and the pilgrimage festivals became more important.

Although Deuteronomy ("second law") contains legal materials, it is hardly accurate to call it a law code. In its overall structure, it appears as an account of the last words and deeds of Moses, in the wilderness outside the Promised Land, and just before his death. Most of the book purports to give the direct address of Moses to the assembled people, summarizing the previous history, looking to the future, and, above all, interpreting the law to them. The style is homiletical, hortatory, sermonic. The speaker lays the law upon the hearts of the listeners, encouraging them to be obedient, promising life to those who obey and threatening those who disobey. The preachers are actually those who stand centuries from the time of Moses and, like us, are faced with the challenge of interpreting the ancient traditions in and for a new age.

Our reading is in that same second person, direct address preaching style as most of the book. It begins with a temporal clause (verse 1), specifying that the subsequent instructions are to go into effect once the people are in the Promised Land. But even in setting the time, the preacher chooses his words carefully. In no case is Israel's acquisition of the land considered a "conquest." It is a gift which Israel is to accept.

Then follow the instructions for a particular ceremony, in two parts, verses 2-4 and 5-11. In both parts the people are told what to do and what to say. Verse 2 gives the general stipulation for an offering to be collected from the first fruits and taken to the central sanctuary in Jerusalem. The Deuteronomic preachers know that Yahweh does not "dwell" in the sanctuary, but that his "name" does.

There is some slight disagreement between the instructions in verses 3-4 and those that follow. In the first instance the offering is to be handed over to the priest who sets it before the altar, and in the second the worshipers do that themselves (verse 10). In the first instance the offering is handed over before the main response, but afterward in the second case. Very likely these tensions indicate that the passage reflects both older and younger traditions about the service.

Throughout the emphasis of the ceremony is upon the worshiper's acknowledgment that everything is a gift of the Lord. In verse 3 the solemn declaration that accompanies the offering is said to the Lord, and it is a confession that the Lord gave the land.

The more extensive response in verses 5-9 is an example of what has come to be called the "little historical credo." It summarizes the key events of the Pentateuch: patriarchs, Egyptian sojourn and Exodus, entrance into the land. The "wandering Aramean" (verse 5) was Jacob, the ancestor of the twelve tribes. The most important theme of the patriarchal traditions was the promise that their descendants would become a great nation and inherit the land of Canaan. With the sojourn in Egypt the first part of the promise was fulfilled—they became a great nation (verse 5). When they were oppressed, they cried to God who heard them, and brought them out (verses 7-8), and gave them the "land flowing with milk and honey" (verse 9). With verse 10 the language changes from confession of faith to prayer. The implications of the general history are applied to the circumstances of the individual: Because the Lord brought Israel into the land, I have crops, and thus bring an offering of the first fruits of the land.

The passage concludes (verse 11) with a general admonition to "rejoice in all the good which the Lord your God has given to you," but not alone. The rejoicing is a family matter, but it also should include the Levite and the non-Israelite sojourner. Thus thanksgiving begets hospitality.

Ancient Israel knew that life itself brings many reasons for giving thanks and praise to God. If there is food to sustain life, there is cause for celebration. But the call here is not to look so much to the fruitfulness of nature as to the past. One who looks back even a few years or generations, to say nothing of centuries, knows that countless others have helped make life possible. So the main admonition here is to remember, and especially to remember the acts of God in the past. Living in the land is itself proof that God is faithful to promises. It is hardly possible to command someone to be thankful, but thankfulness—and with it hospitality to others—will be evoked if one meditates on the history of salvation.

Psalm 100

This psalm was discussed in Proper 4. See pages 25-26.

Philippians 4:4-9

This same text occurs earlier in Year C as the epistolary text for the Third Sunday of Advent. The reader may wish to consult our remarks in *Advent, Christmas, Epiphany,* Year C. It also overlaps the epistolary text (Phil. 4:1-9) for Proper 23 in Year A, for which additional treatment is provided in *After Pentecost, Year A.*

What makes this an appropriate text to be read on the occasion of Thanksgiving is Paul's injunction "in everything by prayer and supplication with thanksgiving let your requests be made known to God" (verse 6). This is in concert with his exhortation to "give thanks in all circumstances" (I Thess. 5:18; cf. Col. 3:17). This includes giving thanks for the food we eat (Rom. 14:6; I Tim. 4:3), for being delivered from the snares of death (II Cor. 1:11), for being called into the Body of Christ (Col. 3:15), for all humanity, especially those in positions of rule and authority (I Tim. 2:1-2), for everything God has created (I Tim. 4:4).

One of the sure marks of being pagan is being unable to express thanks to the God we know (Rom. 1:21). One of the realities of Christian existence is that the more we experience the abundant grace of God, the more our thanksgiving to God increases (II Cor. 4:15). There is a similar correlation between our generosity and our thanksgiving to God: giving of our means to others "overflows in many thanksgivings to God" (II Cor. 9:12). Expressing gratitude is seen as the most suitable substitute for inappropriate forms of speech (Eph. 5:4). At the very heart of worship is thanksgiving (Eph. 5:20; Col. 3:17).

Paul's instructions to his churches to be thankful in everything also conforms to his typical practice of opening his letters by offering a prayer of thanksgiving (cf. Rom. 1:8; I Cor. 1:4; Eph. 1:16; Phil. 1:3; Col. 1:3; I Thess. 1:2; 2:13; 3:9; II Thess. 1:3; 2:13; Philem. 4), as well as expressing thanks on other occasions (Rom. 16:4; I Cor. 14:18; II Cor. 9:15).

Our inclination to be thankful is anchored in Christ's own experience of gratitude. Before eating, he gives thanks (Matt. 15:36; Mark 8:6; John 6:11, 23), but especially before instituting the Eucharist he does so (Matt. 26:27; Mark 14:23; Luke 22:17; I Cor. 11:24). It becomes his posture in prayer (John 11:41). Jesus' story of the ten lepers who were cleansed, with only one of them—a foreigner—appreciative enough to return and express thanks, points to its importance in his teaching concerning the kingdom of God (Luke 17:11-20). That thanksgiving can be abused is also illustrated in the parable of the Pharisee and publican (Luke 18:11). Saying a prayer of thanksgiving to God may be nothing more than a hollow cliche, masking inner distortions of the soul (Luke 18:11).

In today's text, thanksgiving is the counterpart to anxiety (verse 6). The anxious heart may very well result from our inability to make requests of God that are proper expressions of thankful hearts. It is one thing to supplicate God, quite another to do so with a thankful heart. Asking God to fill our needs may become nothing more than the uncontrolled urge toward self-fulfillment. Even our prayers may be narcissistic. But they can hardly become so if they are uttered as expressions of thanksgiving to a God who has broken through the self, both the divine self and the human self.

Properly understood, thanksgiving excludes the excesses of the self, those urges we have for God to satisfy our own needs as if they were the only needs. Thanksgiving, as Paul understood it, is uttered as a response to God's "inexpressible gift" (II Cor. 9:15). It begins when we recognize that God's own giving was an act of consummate self-giving. The most appropriate response is an act in which we see ourselves as recipients of grace and not as petitioners of grace. It is that which we experience best if we receive it without asking. To think that we receive it *because* we ask is to misunderstand it.

John 6:25-35

The Gospel lection for this Thanksgiving Service is drawn from one of the most profound, multifaceted, and influential chapters not only in the Fourth Gospel but in the New Testament. Lest the preacher and listeners drown in its complexity, it will be wise to allow the nature and intent of the Thanksgiving Day Service serve as a guide to the one among many perspectives, all justified and supportable, which shall be the governing theme for the message. For example, if the worship is to be a eucharistic service, John 6 certainly yields that language and understanding. If the accent is to be on gratitude for God's daily provision, that, too, is in the text in abundance. Or again, if Christ is to be offered as the Bread beyond bread, there is no lack of that emphasis in this chapter. But one best not try to do in one sermon all that the Evangelist accomplishes in chapter 6.

At the risk of oversimplification, John 6 may be divided into three parts in its presentation of Christ: Jesus the provider of bread to the hungry (verses 1-15); Jesus the bread from heaven, the word of God (verses 22-50); and Jesus the eucharistic bread which we must eat in order to live (verses 51-71). The story of walking on water (verses 16-21) has been omitted even though it was early joined to the feeding of the multitudes (Mark 6:30-52), no doubt based on the Exodus story of God's mastery of the sea and the feeding of Israel. As early as Paul, these two events served as types of baptism and eucharist (I Cor. 10:1-5). Our lection for today falls within the second portion of the threefold presentation of Christ. Again it should be said that these divisions are not sharp and firm. For example, in the first movement of the narrative, the feeding of the multitude, there are many clues to the second and third. This is not simply a compassion story because what Jesus is about to do will be a sign; that is, it will point beyond itself (verse 6). The language describing the feeding is eucharistic (verse 11, 23). The event occurs at Passover, the festival that echoes the death of Jesus from chapters 2 through 19. The reader is alerted, then, to look beyond bread to Bread.

It is, however, in verses 25-35 that the meaning of the sign of feeding the crowds begins to develop. It is not enough that Jesus be seen by the people as a prophet like Moses who fed Israel in the wilderness (verse 14; Deut. 18:18). It is not enough that the people desire to make Jesus king (verse 15). Enthroning those who do things for us has a long and disappointing history. That which Jesus urges is the quest for the Bread that truly satisfies, which does not perish, which gives life eternal (verses 25-29). Here Jesus begins to draw attention away from the previous day's meal; after all, their ancestors had been given food in the wilderness and they died (verses 31, 49). Rather Jesus draws attention to himself as the true bread from God.

Jesus as the bread of life (verse 35) is not yet developed in the eucharistic sense ("unless you eat the flesh of the Son of man and drink his blood," verse 53). Within our lection Jesus is the bread of life in that he is the bread of God "which comes down from heaven, and gives life to the world" (verse 33). Here the manna analogy very likely refers to Jesus as the Logos, the Word of God as presented in the Prologue (1:1-18). Or to put it another way, verses 25-35 are a commentary on Deuteronomy 8:3: "And he humbled you and let you hunger and fed you with manna, which you did not know, nor did your fathers know; that he might make you know that man does not live by bread alone, but that man lives by everything that proceeds out of the mouth of the Lord." Jesus as the true bread from heaven not only speaks but is the word of God, making God known to us (1:18), whom to know is life eternal (17:3).

Scripture Reading Index